FREE-THOUGHT
ON THE
AMERICAN FRONTIER

FREE-THOUGHT

ON THE

Edited by
Fred Whitehead • Verle Muhrer

AMERICAN FRONTIER

Including: Robert Owen • Oliver Wendell Holmes • Robert G. Ingersoll
Etta Semple • Mark Twain • Clarence Darrow • Theodore Dreiser
Robert Service • Carl Sandburg • Edgar Lee Masters • Sinclair Lewis
Emanuel Haldeman-Julius • Langston Hughes

PROMETHEUS BOOKS
BUFFALO, NEW YORK

Published 1992 by Prometheus Books

Freethought on the American Frontier. Copyright © 1991 by Verle Muhrer and Fred Whitehead. All rights reserved. No part of this publication may be reproduced, stored in a retrieval system, or transmitted in any form or by any means, electronic, mechanical, photocopying, recording, or otherwise, without prior written permission of the publisher, except in the case of brief quotations embodied in critical articles and reviews. Inquiries should be addressed to Prometheus Books, 700 E. Amherst Street, Buffalo, New York 14215, 716-837-2475. FAX: 716-835-6901.

96 95 94 93 92   5 4 3 2 1

Library of Congress Cataloging-in-Publication Data

Freethought on the American frontier / edited by Fred Whitehead
and Verle Muhrer.
     p.   cm.
   Includes bibliographical references (p.   cm.   ).
   ISBN 0-87975-698-5 (cloth : acid-free)
   1. Free thought. I. Whitehead, Fred. II. Muhrer, Verle.
BL2780.F74   1992
211'.4'0973—dc20   91-35191
                                                    CIP

Printed in the United States of America on acid-free paper.

This is what you shall do: love the earth and sun
and the animals, despise riches, give alms to everyone
that asks, stand up for the stupid and crazy, devote
your income and labor to others, hate tyrants, argue
not concerning God, have patience and indulgence
toward the people, take off your hat to nothing,
known or unknown or to any man or number of
men . . . re-examine all you have been told at school
or church or in any book, dismiss whatever insults your own
soul, and your very flesh shall be a great poem.

—Walt Whitman, *Leaves of Grass*

Contents

7

10   Contents

Acknowledgments

A great many scholars, teachers, and freethought activists have generously shared their knowledge and their expertise in the making of this book. First, we wish to thank Paul Kurtz, the director of Prometheus Books, who, along with Tim Madigan and Norm Allen, made the long trek to Kansas City more than once; on these expeditions they responded readily and with enthusiasm to our accounts of Freethought's dramatic past here in the heart of the United States. Though Easterners all, they enjoyed the rough vigor of the story of Freethought in this far-flung territory, and they warmly encouraged our efforts to draw these diverse materials together into a single volume.

Our dear friend and comrade Meridel LeSueur supported this project with a contribution that enabled us to travel to Illinois and Indiana in the summer of 1990, to see New Harmony and other Freethought sites, including the homes of several Midwestern poets who are represented in this book. Dr. Gordon Stein, the foremost scholar of Freethought history, not only supplied important information on the life of artist Watson Heston, but over many years has set a high mark indeed for scholarship in this field. His bibliographies, *Encyclopedia of Unbelief*, and anthologies have been essential, and should be consulted by all students of Freethought's heritage.

In St. Louis, Missouri, Walter Hoops and Eldon Scholl of the Rationalist Society of St. Louis contributed their knowledge of the *freie Gemeinde* and other intellectual organizations, as well as important bibliographic materials. They and colleagues have sustained

11

their rationalist group since 1948, making it the oldest in the United States. Gerd Alfred Petermann kindly supplied translations of Heinrich Koch and Friedrich Münch, as well as biographical information on these two authors. V. Wilhelm von der Heydt shared his knowledge of the German "Forty-Eighters," and served as a tour guide for the Great St. Louis Freethought Rendezvous, October 13–14, 1990. Professor Steve Rowan took an afternoon and showed us around the Library of the Catholic Central Union, which has preserved many nineteenth-century newspapers, books, and other printed material on subjects of religious controversy.

In Kansas, the main archive for Freethought history is the Special Collections Library at Pittsburg State University, where Gene DeGruson serves as curator. Several sets of the *Appeal to Reason* are located there, along with nearly complete files of the Little Blue Books, the personal library of E. Haldeman-Julius, rare and often unique manuscript materials from the region's labor history, and photographs. Over many years, Gene has given unsparingly of his time, his energy, and his knowledge, not only as a librarian, but as a poet and cultural activist in that part of Kansas, where he has helped publish the *Little Balkans Review*. Anyone who seriously wants to study Midwestern Freethought will find an expedition to Pittsburg a must. Sheryl Williams, curator of the Kansas Collection of the University of Kansas Libraries, provided volumes of *The Truth Seeker* from the Wilcox Collection, books by C. L. Edson, and other hard-to-find literature. Robert P. Hudson and Susan Case of the Clendening Library of the University of Kansas Medical Center supplied the works of Oliver Wendell Holmes, and were otherwise most supportive. The staff of the Kansas State Historical Society Library in Topeka helped provide Kansas newspapers and, especially, photographs of the Garden of Eden in Lucas.

Robert Day, the novelist, contributed the joke about the rancher's hell which concludes the section of folk humor, and has allowed a number of pheasant hunting expeditions into western Kansas to take on a wild, philosophical quality. Historian Harold Dellinger first located the poet H. H. Lewis, who had been living in obscurity near Cape Girardeau, Missouri, and supplied Lewis's poems from his personal archive. Similarly, Professor Douglas Wixson has preserved and published the books and stories of Jack Conroy; Bob Black of Ottawa, Kansas, bought the home and hospital of Etta Semple in that community, and has brought her story to regional attention. Columnist C. W. Gusewelle gave us his recollections of C. L. Edson, as well as his photograph of that author. From Waco,

Texas, Roger Conger directed us to archival sources on William Cowper Brann. Joseph Svoboda, archivist of the University of Nebraska, steered us to the scholarly work of Bruce Garver, on the Czech freethinkers of that State's past. Garver himself helped illuminate some aspects of that heritage in a long-distance telephone conversation. Similarly, historian Howard S. Miller recommended that we seek out Anthony F. C. Wallace's *Rockdale*; he also suggested some perspectives on how the history of the West worked out rather differently from the East. Miller is gathering the work of Missouri's own Kate Austin, a little known but important feminist radical freethinker who was a friend of the anarchist Emma Goldman.

A number of Midwestern historical societies and libraries have opened their resources to us, including the Illinois State Historical Library; the Missouri Historical Society; the State Historical Society of Missouri; the Texas Collection of Baylor University; the Missouri Valley Special Collections of the Kansas City, Missouri, Public Library; the Peoria, Illinois, Public Library; the Cullen-Davis Library of Bradley University; the St. Louis Public Library; and the Indiana State Library. The entire town of New Harmony, Indiana, is a kind of Freethought shrine, as it has numerous scientific and art museums and exhibits, bookstores, historic sites, and especially the Workingman's Institute, which was founded by William Maclure over one hundred and fifty years ago. This Institute combines a public library, a research library and archive, an art gallery, and scientific collections. Indeed, if every town in America had such a splendid Freethought institution, our national culture would be so improved from its currently sorry state, as to be unrecognizable. If any reader desires to physically *see* and experience how early nineteenth-century freethinkers themselves envisioned the future of America, a pilgrimage to New Harmony is essential.

Other sites in the Midwest important to Freethought's heritage include the Carl Sandburg Birthplace in Galesburg, Illinois; the Vachel Lindsay Home in Springfield, Illinois; the Edgar Lee Masters Memorial Home in Petersburg, Illinois; and the Garden of Eden in Lucas, Kansas. Some of those sites are operated by State agencies, but others remain open only through the collective support of volunteers in the local communities.

A number of other people—activists, scholars, editors, and teachers—have furthered this project through advice, encouragement, and their own example: Elizabeth Gerber, Tom Page, Robert Lewis, David Johnson Cumberland, Jeb Carter, Vincent Ferrini, Olga Cabral, Prairie Miller, Neala Schleuning, John Crawford, Marvin Robinson,

Barrows and Alice Dunham, William J. Leahy, Lyle Daggett, Norma Wilson, Lyman Baker, John Exdell, Kale Baldock, C. Robert Haywood, and the late Truman Nelson. Special thanks go to Mike Caddell, editor and publisher of *Frankfort's Alternative Index,* "the only weekly voice of dissent in Kansas." Jeff Longhofer read a part of the manuscript, providing useful comments, as did colleagues in the da Vinci Society of Kansas City, Wilfred Arnold and Loretta Loftus. Danielle Wesley's diligent secretarial skills were indispensable in the preparation of the manuscript, through several versions and revisions, and she also proved to be a patient teacher of the basics of computer word processing. Eugene O'Connor of Prometheus Books was a careful and hard-working editor. Carol Whitehead, who, as an elder in the Presbyterian Church, is skeptical about skepticism, continued along her particular path of Predestination, making pancakes on many a Saturday morning, thus enabling one of the co-editors to stay alive; she has otherwise exemplified the old virtue of forbearance, over several difficult years while this book was in progress.

In editing this book, we sought out a great range of primary materials, but we have also had to depend on secondary works as well, searching for biographical facts on a number of now obscure authors. So while we acknowledge help from all those listed, we assume sole responsibility for errors, shaky intepretations, hasty generalizations, and other occupational hazards of those who attempt to produce intellectual and cultural history. We would be grateful to know of any errors, and all correspondence should be directed to Dr. Fred Whitehead, Box 5224, Kansas City, Kansas 66119.

Introduction

At the close of the nineteenth century, it appeared to many progressive people in the United States—especially in the East—that the key victories in the cause of Freedom had been attained, or at least were close at hand. Harvard's John Fiske observed in 1895 that the social and intellectual sectors of democracy were related, and indeed had developed together "in the spacious virgin soil of the New World," where "political freedom [was] the strongest power on earth." This eminent philosopher of science admitted that "not in a moment was such a grand result achieved; its complete realization has not yet come, and none of us may live to see it, yet towards that goal the whole impetus of men's civilizing work is tending, and there is no power that can prevent the consummation."

From our vantage point a century later, after passing through an era fraught with the turmoil of widespread irrationalism, dictatorship, and world war, we are forced to be more realistic about the aspects for Reason's inevitable success. Indeed, at the very time Fiske was writing, there was a fierce struggle already under way in the Midwest and West of the United States, between the forces of repression and Puritanism, and those who raised on high the banner of Freethought; the ideas and issues of this conflict continue to be a critical part of our present-day debates on ethics, education, culture, and the very future of the American people.

It is striking that the great majority of historians of American philosophy and intellectual life have concentrated on the prestigious universities and journals of the East, as representative of the whole nation. Yet the West produced its own culture, and its typical personalities that were somehow both unusual and common in the territory. An example is the great abolitionist Captain John Brown (1800–1859), who was thus described by Thoreau:

> He did not go to the college called Harvard, good old Alma Mater as she is. He was not fed on the pap that is there furnished. As he phrased it, "I know no more of grammar than one of your calves." But he went to the great university of the West, where he sedulously pursued the study of Liberty, for which he had early betrayed a fondness, and having taken many degrees, he finally commenced the public practice of Humanity in Kansas, as you all know. Such were *his humanities,* and not any study of grammar. He would have left a Greek accent slanting the wrong way, and righted up a falling man.

Such qualities of hardy independence and love of justice will often be met with in the true history of the West, and in the present collection. John Brown, and those represented in this book, were obliged to live according to Emerson's concept of self-reliance, and as we shall see, the struggle for Freethought was in its own way almost as large, dramatic, and momentous as the struggle to destroy the system of chattel slavery.

DEFINITIONS

A popular dictionary currently defines a freethinker as "one that forms opinions on the basis of reason independently of authority; especially: one who doubts or denies religious dogma." Similarly, Freethought is "unorthodox attitudes or beliefs, specifically eighteenth-century deism." While it is true that the latter term originated with the English deists, who contended that reason alone is sufficient to prove God's existence, Freethought's roots go back to antiquity, and have persisted long after deism passed from the scene, except for certain aspects which survive in Unitarian societies.

Samuel Porter Putnam, the most thorough nineteenth-century American historian of Freethought, wrote in 1894, about the same time as Fiske, that the term meant much more than a critique of religion. "Freethought," he insisted, "is also liberty, equality, and fraternity in the domain of politics. These are not assumptions, but verities. As Freethought recognizes the unity of existence it must also recognize the equality of rights." Like Fiske, Putnam conceived social and intellectual democracy as closely allied. "When, therefore, I use the word Freethought," he continued, "I use it in the most comprehensive sense, as an intellectual, moral, industrial, political, and social power. I mean scientific freedom, not a mere capricious freedom. I mean freedom devoted to high ends. I mean doubt for the truth's sake. I mean facts correlated into a vast and splendid system of noble philosophy. I mean liberty whose expression is law, whose spirit is universal equality and universal brotherhood." Guided by such concepts, the historic heritage of Freethought in the United States has been a rich and complex one, starting, to be sure, with a critique of religion, but also encompassing women's rights, the defense of First Amendment freedoms, a lode of folk humor and music, a considerable body of poetry, political radicalism, spiritualism (in several instances), and scientific controverises such as creationism versus evolutionary theory.

The concept of the Frontier is one of the perpetual "problems" of American historiography. A hundred years ago, Frederick Jackson Turner proposed that the Frontier had largely determined our very concept of ourselves as a people, and as a nation. The "closing" of the Frontier with the admission of a number of western states to the Union around 1890, said Turner, marked the passing of an entire phase of our social and economic life. To this day, the "Turner thesis" continues to be hotly debated. The Frontier has sometimes been taken rather narrowly, to refer only to the section of the continent west of Missouri, during the period between 1860 and 1890. However, it is obvious that at the beginning of our nation's colonization, the Puritans and other European settlers saw America precisely as a frontier wilderness. Clearly, the concept has undergone a number of transformations. Immediately after the Revolution, the present States of Ohio and Michigan were the "Northwest," while today we use that word to designate Oregon and Washington. Hollywood perpetuated cowboy and U.S. cavalry heroes on a Homeric scale, and created a mythic world made solid and real through the skill of directors like John Ford. Even today the public relations effort for "Star Wars" is supported by an organization called "High Frontiers."

Yet another approach was taken by Texas historian Walter P. Webb, who argued in *The Great Frontier* that in the last several hundred years, the world has been dominated by a great transformation, in which a European capitalist "Metropolis" has expanded into an indigenous "Frontier," which was every place else. Thus the

American West shared many features of social and economic expansionism with, say, Brazil, South Africa, and Australia. Webb's thesis attempted to synthesize the vast intercontinental drama of the conflict between the forces led by the industrial revolution, and more "primitive" cultures doomed to defeat and submission. The "Frontier" was the zone where this conflict was worked out and resolved. Naturally, there are several difficulties with Webb's attempt to arrive at such large generalizations, but it is worth noting that the activists and writers of the western Freethought movement themselves believed that they were participants in a great drama of social and ethical conflict, with profound implications not only for themselves, but for posterity.

Today, the West is no longer a Frontier in the pure sense of the term, yet it preserves much of the old society and culture, and aspects of its intellectual life as well. In this book, the Frontier means the changing and developing rural society of America, especially in the Midwest and West. Thus, for us now, as for historians in general, the concept is somewhat flexible, having an evolutionary character.

A recent instructive controversy concerns the blithe assumption of us here in this country that the term "American" refers only to the United States. We recognize this charge, but appeal to common usage. We acknowledge that there have been significant Freethought movements in Central and South America, and to some extent, in Canada. Scholars such as James Cockcroft and Donald Hodges have shown how the Liberal party of Mexico, under the leadership of Ricardo Flores Magon, had friends and supporters in this country. This party, often allied with Masonic lodges in Mexico, had a distinct anti-clerical character. An important phase of the party's work was accomplished in the United States; the Program of 1906, which formed the basis for the subsequent Revolution of 1910–1911, was published in St. Louis, Missouri. Magon himself suffered arrest, imprisonment, and death at the hands of the United States government, as he was found dead in his cell in the federal prison in Leavenworth, Kansas, in 1922; his brother contended that he had been strangled. Magon became a national hero in Mexico, and *magonista* workers in Tampico passed on his heritage to young Cesar Augusto Sandino, who led a successful revolt in Nicaragua against the U.S. Marines during the late 1920s. At any rate, a full-scale anthology of Central and South American Freethought would be of the greatest interest, though beyond the scope of the present collection.

PHASES OF FREETHOUGHT HISTORY

The Early Frontier

From the earliest days of colonization, there has been a struggle between Christianity and freethinkers on this continent. In the so-called Merry Mount affair of 1622–1628 in Massachusetts, in what is now Quincy, one Thomas Morton gathered around him a group of adherents, created a Maypole, and led a heathenish and dissolute life. This prompted the Puritan leader William Bradford to condemn Morton as a "Lord of Misrule," who maintained "a School of Atheism." Finally, Miles Standish attacked this community, burnt Morton's house, and drove him back to England. Similarly, the Antinomian controversy of the 1630s pitted Anne Hutchinson and her supporters against the Puritans around the issue of faith alone being necessary for salvation. The entire colonial period is filled with episodes of struggle between various clerical establishments, and those who were determined to stand on the principle of individual conscience. Similarly, American Indian leaders often objected to the activities of the missionaries, pointing out contradictions in their teachings, such as their promotion of the idea of charity, even while the native peoples were being murdered and driven off their ancestral lands. Red Jacket's response to such a missionary, included in this book, is representative of the Indian attitude toward Christianity and its claims. There are several excellent collections of speeches by American Indian leaders, as well as scholarly studies of their relations with the Christian religion. The most recent is Forrest G. Wood's magisterial *The Arrogance of Faith.*

Christian preachers came in for satirical exposure by white settlers as well. There are numerous amusing incidents in early frontier history of resistance to religion, as the result either of alleged ignorance, or of outright hostility to proselytism. Ross Phares's *Bible in Pocket, Gun in Hand: The Story of Frontier Religion,* is full of such tales. For instance, one itinerant minister approached a man working on his farm, and asked if he might "want to be a laborer for the Lord." The man replied, "No thank you, I have a job." Or another of a Presbyterian missionary arriving at a lonely cabin, where he asked a woman, "Are there any Presbyterians in this country?" Apparently assuming that the visitor must be a hunter like her husband, she responded: "Wal, I just couldn't say for sure about that. These woods is full of most every kind of varmet, but I ain't paid much attention to 'em. You might take a look around on the back side of the cabin where my husband keeps his varmet hides, and see if he's got any Presbyterian hides nailed up. If there's any Presbyterians in this country, he's bound to have caught one by now."

Sometimes it was even worse than that. The *WPA Guide To 1930s Missouri,* produced by the Federal Writers Project, relates that in 1817, the Reverend John Mason Peck found that in St. Louis the "Anglo-American population were infidels of a low and indecent grade. . . . Their nightly orgies were scenes of drunkenness and profane revelry. Among the frantic rites observed were the mock celebration of the Lord's Supper and the burning of Bibles. . . . The boast was often made that the Sabbath never had crossed, and never should cross, the Mississippi." To be sure, such accounts must be taken with a grain of salt, as they were often produced in order to secure funds for missionary efforts among the "heathen." In any case, the farther west one traveled, the rougher it got, not only in terrain, but in conflicts of ideas; it was commonly said that there was no law west of Kansas City, and west of Fort Scott, no God. By their own accounts, preachers often had a real struggle on their hands, trying to "civilize" an unruly populace. "The Harp of a Thousand Strings," included in this collection, is an exemplary satire of frontier preachers' rhetoric, as is Jack Conroy's anecdote about a Bible-thumper.

In an open country, various utopian thinkers were tempted to establish social experiments on a grand scale. One of the most famous was that of Robert Owen, who founded the entire southwestern Indiana town of New Harmony on Freethought principles. Amana in Iowa, Bethel in Missouri, Oneida in New York, and most of the other utopias were based on variants of Christian doctrine, albeit of the most heterodox kinds. However heretical they were, they tended to accept the basic premises of religion as such, and are thus outside the scope of this collection. As an organized socialist experiment, Owen's New Harmony lasted only two years, but his sons remained in the town, along with others of his associates, and they continued to take an active role in the political, scientific, and cultural life of the Frontier. Today, New Harmony is a National Historic Landmark, with many of its remarkable buildings preserved or restored; as in Owen's time, the town is a center for research in American social and scientific history, as well as for the arts.

Other European nationalists settled considerable sections of Wisconsin, Missouri, Nebraska, and Minnesota. As refugees from clerical tyranny in their native lands, substantial numbers arrived in the 1830s and 1840s. Another large group, somewhat more radical in their politics, had been active in the revolutions of 1848, which attempted to overthrow the autocratic aristocracies of such countries as France and Germany. The defeat of these revolutions produced refugees from nearly every country in Europe, but most were from Germany; 20,000 "Forty-Eighters" went to Texas alone. In this book the Missouri Germans have been selected as typical of these migrations. Some, like Friedrich Münch and Henry C. Brokmeyer, arrived in the first wave of immigrants, and rose to prominence in the abolitionist movement. Münch, who seems to have remained a theist, though a staunchly rationalist one, became a state senator. Like other freethinking Germans, Brokmeyer became a colonel of a regiment in the Union Army during the Civil War. According to General Ulysses S. Grant, these immigrant forces played a decisive role in saving Missouri for the Union in early 1861. The St. Louis Movement in philosophy and education arose out of the momentum of that war. *The Journal of Speculative Philosophy,* the first of its kind in the United States, was founded by William Torrey Harris and his associates. Brokmeyer produced the first translation of Hegel's *Logic* into English; because of his powerful and magnetic character, he remained the guiding spirit of the Movement. While Harris represented the conservative wing of the Movement, and rose to prominence and respectability as U.S. Commissioner of Education, others such as Denton J. Snider were more radical and bohemian. Snider's dramatic portrait of Brokmeyer is included in Part One, as well as his account of visits to St. Louis by Emerson and Alcott. Snider even produced an entire volume interpreting the Civil War in the framework of Hegel's thesis-antithesis-synthesis philosophy of history. Thus, Missouri freethinkers played an important role in that State's intellectual history, before, during, and after the Civil War.

The Golden Age of Freethought

The victory of the Union and the defeat of slavery led directly to increased settlement of the West. The key Homestead Act of 1862 owed much to the long agitation of George Henry Evans, a radical and outspoken infidel, in his paper, *The Workingman's Advocate.* However, as Evans died before Congress passed this legislation, the terms of the Act gave large portions of western lands to the railroads. In several waves, the West was filled with ranches, farmers, towns, railroads, telegraph systems, and commerce. The peak of postwar settlement was the 1880s, when numerous towns and counties received their charters. The social and economic outlines of the West were established in this period.

In some ways, the career of Robert G. Ingersoll parallels these developments. Born in Dresden, New York, in a house recently restored and dedicated as an historic site, Ingersoll traveled westward in search of opportunities. In Peoria, Illinois, he became a prominent attorney, then served as the colonel of a Union regiment in the Civil War. After that conflict, he served a term as Illinois's attorney general, rising to influence, if not power, in the councils of the Republican party. Ingersoll was also the most famous "Infidel" in America, traveling across the country delivering eloquent orations on "The Gods," "Mistakes of Moses," and similar freethought topics. Paradoxically, Ingersoll was esteemed for his speeches, but faced continual opposition because of his views on religion. During his own lifetime, many said that if he had not held such "irregular" views, he might have become President.

Throughout the country, there were scores of militant grassroots newspapers, of every brand of progressive thought. The names of these convey their flavor: *The American Nonconformist, Lucifer the Light Bearer, The Freethought Ideal, Appeal to Reason*—all these from Kansas alone. Texas produced Brann's *Iconoclast;* Indiana, the *Ironclad Age. The Truth Seeker,* which began in Paris, Illinois, soon moved to New York City, yet printed large columns of correspondence from every section of the land, and prompted tours of Freethought speakers to small towns and cities.

There were Freethought organizations, such as the Liberal League and the American Secular Union. Major figures in the feminist movement, which gained ground rapidly in this same period, were freethinkers; Elizabeth Cady Stanton and her colleagues published the controversial *Woman's Bible,* which presented an interpretation of the sacred text as a fountainhead of patriarchal chauvinism and women's oppression. Similarly, the labor, populist, and socialist movements attracted freethinkers, though there were also freethinkers who opposed political radicalism.

One of the best descriptions of this ferment is in Meridel Le-Sueur's *North Star Country,* published in 1945:

So the questions flew back and forth over the jug, the harvest, in the corn row; thinking came with hunger and drought; despite the poverty, books were selling like hotcakes: Henry George, Bellamy's *Looking Backward,* Ignatius Donnelly's *Caesar's Column,* and pamphlets on cooperation, socialism. Thoughts sprang up after them like dragon's teeth, and talk arose like a storm— government ownership—abolition of private property—unity with

labor—a thousand desires, a thousand unspoken hopes, contradictions, hotly contested—rumination long and slow, discussion on
winter evenings with the Alliance lecturer around the cleared farm
table, and the children listening from the cold bedrooms. . . . The
Populist movement had become a vast university of the common
people, a debating society. There was a renascence of culture.
Everyone could write to the papers, which were supported by his
own pennies. All could speak out their minds, write speeches; songs
and words came to the silent throat—for the wrong, for the
occasion—from the suffering that flowed like the mighty inland
rivers from each inward self to that of others.

It was in such a social context that some of the most brilliant freethinkers flourished, and made their contributions to civilization. This
is not the place to explicate the interrelations of all these cross currents, but suffice it to say, the extensive development of this cultural and intellectual life has led historians to call the period between
1865 and 1914 the "Golden Age of Freethought."

From Wisconsin to Texas, there were communities of freethinkers, usually of Czech or German origin. In eastern Kansas there was
a remarkable concentration, as the State became known nationally
as a "laboratory of social experiment." The Republicans, however,
called them "calamity howlers." Practically every town and community
in the West had a "village atheist," a type of personality ably defended
by Emanuel Haldeman-Julius.

The early 1890s, a time when Fiske and Putnam believed that
the victory of liberalism was in sight, was also the era of the Populist
uprising, described by LeSueur. Lawrence Goodwyn has called this
huge movement of militant farmers, from the Carolinas to Colorado, "the largest democratic mass movement in American history."
As a political movement, the People's party took no stand on religious questions, but it attracted all kinds of radicals and militant
activists. Goodwyn contends that the "movement culture" of "the
Populist Moment" was probably the best chance the country ever
had to form a truly democratic society and government.

In the critical presidential election of 1896, William McKinley
defeated William Jennings Bryan, in the first modern campaign re-
volving around super-patriotism, respectability, and family values.
Bryan was, of course, no freethinker, as he demonstrated in his support of the anti-evolutionists at the Scopes "monkey" trial in Tennessee in 1925. Goodwyn further argues that the defeat of Populism
established the cultural, intellectual, and even the psychological mind-

set of the United States to this day, with a prevalence of resignation and political apathy among the general population. At the time, observers of Populism contended that the ramshackle, undisciplined, and sometimes rather eccentric nature of the movement all led to its inevitable demise. After the cataclysm of 1896, many citizens became nonpolitical; others rejoined the Republicans or Democrats; some moved toward Socialism.

The Republican victory, while decisive, was not complete. Several freethought publications, such as *The Truth Seeker* and the *Appeal to Reason,* continued into the twentieth century. The Industrial Workers of the World (I.W.W.), founded in Chicago in 1905, was mostly a militant labor organization, but it took on the Salvation Army in hundreds of street corner confrontations, and its poets wrote rambunctious parodies of Christian hymns. Therefore, while the activist radical organizations were not concerned only with religion, they had a definite freethought cast. The subsequent repression of all these forces during World War I, so fierce in the heart of the country, cast a pall over American intellectual and cultural life. There were three large trials of the I.W.W.—in Chicago, Wichita, and Sacramento—and hundreds of cases of police raids on their offices, beatings, and deportations. In clear violation of the freedom of speech provision of the First Amendment, Socialist leaders like Eugene Debs and Kate Richards O'Hare were sent to prison for opposing the war. One historian has aptly called this period a "Reign of Terror."

The Revolt from the Village

In this light, we may understand the next phase of freethought history, which we call "The Revolt from the Village," after Anthony C. Hilfer's book of that title. Even during the war, young intellectuals and writers such as Sherwood Anderson, Carl Sandburg, and Edgar Lee Masters had begun a kind of unofficial movement toward mental freedom. They viewed Theodore Dreiser as something of a forerunner and hero, since his novel *Sister Carrie* had been suppressed by its publisher on moral grounds. There is a considerable scholarly commentary on this generation, including the fine study, *Chicago Renaissance,* by Dale Kramer. It is significant that many of these writers came from the small towns of the Midwest. In part, they wanted to expose the withering of the spirit in these communities, not just because they were small, remote, and provincial (though that was part of it), but because the vision of a democratic utopia had been betrayed and crushed by the Republican party's widespread mossback conservatism. Though many of these writers disagreed with each other on many things, on that point they were in accord.

Meridel LeSueur, who around 1914 began to write down farmers' stories she heard told on the town square in Fort Scott, Kansas, has recalled the effect of this conservative backlash on her contemporaries:

> Our trouble was we didn't have any body. We were all trying to get born or get a body. The puritan had robbed not only the land but had robbed us of our being, of our body. [Edward] Dahlberg to me I associate with Sinclair Lewis and Dreiser—they were wonderful because their bodies showed the terrible agony and drought. They were the most remarkable terrible-looking men. They looked like they had been hung on the cross, as they had, and been taken down and rotted in the sun. I mean, they were wonderful, that their bodies were out of the concentration camp of puritanism. . . .

Though critics have sometimes maligned these authors as mere cynics, the truth is that they viewed the malaise that settled on the once promising, democratic villages as a national tragedy, if not an outright crime against humanist culture. Few of these writers returned home, except perhaps for short visits; Dahlberg said he would have stayed in Kansas City if there had been two people he could have talked about books with. They escaped to big cities such as Chicago and New York, where one could at least find a few like-minded people. This whole trajectory was sometimes terribly destructive: Vachel Lindsay committed suicide by drinking disinfectant; Lewis and Dreiser became alcoholics; and after his earlier bohemian radicalism, Sandburg "committed social suicide," as LeSueur has said, by becoming a respectable member of society. The most original American theorist of political economy, Thorstein Veblen, was another Midwesterner forced, because of his eccentricity and caustic character, to live as an academic nomad. Veblen was openly agnostic, and compared the publicizing of religion to the techniques of "modern" salesmanship. Commager has sagely summarized him thus: "His rebellion went so deep that it confounded even dissenters; his heresies were so profane that they baffled orthodoxy and heterodoxy alike."

The Contemporary Frontier

Some aspects of the "Revolt from the Village" have continued into the contemporary literature of Freethought. Writers like Langston

Hughes and Sterling Brown expressed the hypocrisy and brutality of small towns. Country boys like H. H. Lewis migrated to the cities, only to find themselves on skid row. Coming out of a farm near Sheldon, North Dakota, poet Tom McGrath went to the University of North Dakota and earned a Rhodes scholarship about the same time he joined the Communist party. During the McCarthy period, McGrath found himself under subpoena to appear before the House Committee on Un-American Activities, which he defied in a blistering denunciation. In the depths of the blacklist era, McGrath began the long poem, *Letter to an Imaginary Friend,* a vast chronicle of the century, and surely one of the great monuments to the heritage of Freethought in our culture. Another poet, rancher Wallace McRae, has not had a major preoccupation with religious questions in his work, but he is notable for his rugged independence of mind, his thoughtfulness on ethical issues, and his defense of those who still live in the small communities of the West and make their living from the land.

Recent western writers have forthrightly discarded guilt, sexual repression, and the whole complex of Puritanism which so concerned their predecessors. For example, Robert Day's humorous novel, *The Last Cattle Drive,* first published in 1977, and still widely read among the "plain folk" of Kansas, is notable for its joyously profane heathenism. A recent poll suggests that the West still has the highest percentage of those who would appear to be in the freethought tradition; while the national proportion of those who say they have no religion is 8 percent, in Oregon, it is 17 percent; in Washington and Wyoming, 14 percent; in California, 13 percent; and in Arizona, 12 percent. In the summer of 1991, the old issue of reproductive rights arose in Wichita, Kansas, with violent confrontations between federal marshals and religious fanatics. The so-called right-to-life groups chose Wichita because it is right in the heart of the country, bearing out our thesis that throughout much of our history, the hinterlands are indeed where many of the toughest battles have been fought. Similarly, the editors of this volume have engaged in a running battle with the officials of Penn Valley Community College in Kansas City, where both of us are teachers in the Philosophy Department. This is a complex matter, but in part it has involved the defense of academic freedom, Constitutional rights, and professional standards. It is striking, in fact, how similar many present-day college administrators are to the dour, humorless, and repressive Puritans in the Republican party of old. Thus, the old issues of the 1890s, including women's rights, freedom of speech and press, creationism versus the theory of evolution, and academic freedom are still as "hot" today as then.

Anything like an extended consideration of where Freethought is today in America is outside the scope of this essay, but it is surely apparent that the very term is not now in common or popular usage. As we have noted, its "Golden Age" occurred around a hundred years ago. We have seen, too, that several of the central issues of that period continue to play an important role in our culture. There has clearly been a considerable growth of secularism throughout the society, not so much as a developed philosophy of life, as a set of attitudes arising out of the modern industrial or even post-industrial world. And numerous historians have observed that some of the churches themselves have changed to some extent, insofar as they have accepted the findings of modern biblical scholarship and historical criticism, and have assimilated some of the old Freethought concepts of ethics, progressive culture, and toleration. Thus, for many people, religious questions are either not very important in their lives, or they have moderated their approach to them so far as even to make common grounds with humanism.

Although there is not presently an organized Freethought movement like the one that existed a century ago, a city such as St. Louis, whose story is so prominent in this collection, retains both a vigorous Ethical Culture Society and a Rationalist Society (the oldest in the country); *The American Rationalist* magazine is also published there. Madison, Wisconsin, is the headquarters of the Freedom from Religion Foundation, which has thousands of members scattered throughout the country. Their monthly newspaper, *Freethought Today,* ably edited by Annie Laurie Gaylor, often features freethinkers in these isolated communities, "village atheists" who tend to be active in First Amendment issues. Kansas City has the world's first Eupraxophy Center, established according to the concept introduced by Paul Kurtz, meaning the good life according to wisdom; the editors of the present volume were the founders of this Center. Kurtz's Council for Democratic and Secular Humanism has numerous affiliates, including those in the cities of the Midwest and West. Madalyn Murray O'Hair's American Atheists are headquartered in Austin, Texas, where she publishes a monthly magazine, *The American Atheist.* From time to time, O'Hair also issues reprints of freethought classics, and she maintains an extensive research library on the history of atheism and Freethought.

On the West Coast, Berkeley, California, has the Meiklejohn Institute under the direction of Ann Fagan Ginger; it staunchly defends First Amendment and peace issues, and serves as a center for research and documentation. Los Angeles is the home of the Southern California Library for Social Research, which has extensive archives on the social and progressive movements in that region, and also sponsors cultural programs. Thus in the western half of the United States there remains much local and regional grassroots activity. For example, individuals or groups frequently have successfully objected to some infringement of the separation of church and state, such as prayer in the schools, or the placement of a stone tablet of the Ten Commandments in front of a county courthouse. Many of these people have stayed in the forefront in opposing right-wing fanaticism and intolerance, and more positively, in promoting science, humanism, and culture among our people. The issues for which Freethought struggled a century ago remain on our current agenda. And, as both sides have come to recognize, cultural issues are at the center of it all—the Right wishing to make this a "Christian" country, and the freethinkers standing fast to defend the Enlightenment vision of Jefferson, Paine, and Madison. We hope that this volume will provide historical documentation for this prolonged cultural struggle, so that citizens can become more aware of those who engaged in past battles.

NEW INTERPRETATIONS OF AMERICAN HISTORY

Though the Turner thesis of the American frontier continued to be debated into the 1950s, the main outlines of Western history were widely accepted among historians. This concept, sometimes called the "consensus" view, reflected a linear, heroic panorama in which little had occurred in the "Great American Desert" until the arrival of white Christian civilization. Such a view tended to discount or overlook the fact that there already was an ancient civilization on this continent, or rather, quite a few distinct civilizations. The "Indians" had complex societies with a wide range of social and economic forms, from nomadism on the High Plains, to settled agricultural communities which were sometimes quite extensive. For instance, the Cahokia Mounds area near East St. Louis, Illinois, supported tens of thousands of people and, indeed, while it flourished, was larger than most cities in Europe during the "Middle Ages." After surviving outbreaks of disease, slavery, and armed repression over many centuries, these native peoples have slowly and painfully preserved and recovered their art, their culture, and their very forms of society. This achievement is surely the basis for the current renaissance of American Indian literature and arts.

In his recent influential book, *Indian Givers: How the Indians of the Americas Transformed the World,* Jack Weatherford has shown how these people contributed to the development of the whole modern world, not only in agriculture and the capitalist economic system, but in forming our political ideas. Weatherford demonstrates the considerable impact of Indian concepts of ethics and society on such classic thinkers as Montaigne, and thence to the European Enlightenment. The Indian regard for truth and fair dealing sharply contrasted with the authoritarian, corrupt, and capricious governments of the Old World. Revolutionaries like Franklin and Paine were influenced by the Iroquois Federation in designing a new kind of government on this continent. Thus, instead of civilization transforming a Frontier, as Turner and Webb argued, there are grounds for giving real prominence to the reverse process; that is, we are coming to understand that "primitive" societies have contributed a great deal more to world civilization than white people have previously known or acknowledged.

Similarly, new views of African-American culture and thought are emerging, to demonstrate, for instance, how the crushing of Reconstruction in the South after the Civil War impeded the development of democracy throughout the whole society during the "Gilded Age." Following the classic study of W. E. B. DuBois in *Black Reconstruction,* Eric Foner has emphasized the disastrous consequences of Reconstruction's end. Many of the great free speech and free press battles of the Freethought movement closely parallel the struggles of black editors to protest the mass crimes of lynching. In Memphis, Tennessee, Ida B. Wells waged many tough campaigns simply to print the facts of lynching incidents, and to editorialize against this monstrous practice. Among the freethinkers, Moses Harman's *Lucifer* staunchly defended her. Norm Allen's recent anthology, *African-American Humanism,* documents the freethought aspects of this rich heritage.

Other historians have undertaken careful studies of a particular locale. One of the most remarkable of these is Anthony F. C. Wallace's *Rockdale: The Growth of an American Village in the Early Industrial Revolution.* In this work, Wallace assembles an extraordinary range of documentation for one small community in eastern Pennsylvania. Rockdale was a manufacturing town, not far from Philadelphia, and therefore susceptible to influence from the cultural and intellectual currents of that metropolis. Not only does Wallace explicate the complex emergence of the modern factory system in a village society of the early nineteenth century, but from diaries, letters, books, and records of all kinds, he gives us what ordinary people *thought* of this process. In addition to explaining the formation of a local bourgeoisie or middle class, and a proletariat or working class, Wallace establishes the context of the cultural and intellectual domination of the former at the expense of the latter. What makes this so relevant for the history of Freethought is that on the one hand, there was a socially mixed heritage of progress, freedom, and science inherited from the Enlightenment and the Revolution, and on the other, opposition controlled by the new capitalists with the crucial aid of evangelical Christians. In spite of sporadic class struggle, including strikes, and in spite of obstinate resistance from the "Infidels," Wallace contends that by mid-century in Rockdale, the Christians had essentially prevailed.

As a theoretical framework, Wallace uses the "paradigm" concept which Thomas Kuhn proposed for the history of science. That is, there is a controlling pattern, or what we might colloquially call "The Big Picture," which everyone, or at least most people at a given time and place, accept for their lives. Kuhn suggested, for instance, that the Earth-centered Ptolemaic system of the universe was a paradigm that prevailed for hundreds of years, until finally, the sun-centered Copernican system supplanted it. In physics, the Newtonian mechanical system prevailed for some centuries, and in our own time has been replaced by the system advanced by Einstein, though no one has as yet produced any kind of unified field theory. In the discipline of social theory, the Italian Communist Antonio Gramsci developed a concept similar to that of Kuhn's "paradigm," namely that of "hegemony," to describe how a social class seizes control of a whole culture. In any event, Wallace is convincing with reference to the large cultural paradigms of nineteenth-century American society, as far as he goes. We tend to agree with historian Howard Miller, who has argued that out in the West, the conflict between Christians and Infidels continued well beyond the 1850s, to at least the crucial period of World War I, and in some respects, to the present time.

We have already mentioned the seminal contributions of Lawrence Goodwyn, who has argued for the watershed importance of the 1896 victory of McKinley's Republican party over the Populists and Bryan. Goodwyn emphasizes the "paradigmatic" impact of the strategy masterminded by the Republican chieftain and industrialist Mark Hanna. Under Hanna's direction, McKinley portrayed himself as a super-patriot, and during the campaign, each Republican whistle-stop was decorated with hundreds of American flags. Bryan simply had no strategy against this, any more than did Mondale or Dukakis in the Democratic presidential campaigns of the 1980s. Indeed, it could be argued that the Machiavellian Lee Atwater took his campaign strategy directly from that of Mark Hanna ninety years before. All this becomes a part of the broad history of the Freethought movement because today there is, on the one hand, a very large atavistic and reactionary movement being led by evangelical Christians, with the aid of the Republican party, and on the other hand, a small and determined but poorly organized movement of humanists, feminists, scientists, and progressive cultural activists. As we have indicated, there is still considerable grassroots activity among the ranks of the latter, in the Midwest and West.

Yet other historians have recently brought new light to the cross currents of nineteenth-century culture, particularly as they came to bear upon trends of feminism, science, and spiritualism. In *Independent Spirits: Spiritualism and English Plebeians 1850–1910,* Logie Barrow has shown how deeply rooted spiritualism was among English working-class intellectuals. Anne Braude has explored similar tendencies in the United States at the same time, in *Radical Spirits: Spiritualism and Women's Rights in Nineteenth-Century America.* We have found a definite trend toward spiritualism in Freethought, represented by writers included in our collection, such as George Henry Walser, Etta Semple, Lois Waisbrooker, and several others. In present-day freethought and skeptical culture, the lines between scientific rationalism and spiritualism are much more clearly drawn, if not openly antagonistic. Indeed, even in the nineteenth century, as Braude shows, some freethought feminists such as Ernestine Rose spoke out against the "spirit-rappers." Our point here is not to try to unravel such cross currents, but rather to indicate that they exist and are documented herein.

To establish the context for intellectual history, we must also mention a recent book by Page Smith, *Killing the Spirit: Higher Education in America,* wherein he represents a case for the extensive moral and intellectual corruption of our contemporary colleges and universities. He discusses the establishment and growth of large public universities in the Midwest, following the Morrill Act of 1862. J. B. Angell, the president of the University of Michigan, declared that there was "no more conspicuous feature in the history of America . . . than the rapid and brilliant development of State universities. From Ohio to the Pacific, from North Dakota to Texas, nearly every State has established or is preparing to establish a university on the foundation of the United States land grants." In the view of Angell and others, these universities presented an alternative to the growth of denominational colleges. Yet, as Smith shows, Angell himself argued with some delicacy that "our citizens, with almost no exception, desire that the conditions of college life should be helpful, rather than harmful, to the religious development of their children." In these new academic centers, science was to be important, but should not be pressed too far. Our book shows how the Infidel versus Christian conflict was fought in the colleges of America, in the selections by Brann, Semple, Harman, and McGrath.

Curiously, it is in academia itself that a small group of new Western historians has arisen, sometimes called "The Gang of Four." Led by Donald Worster of Kansas and Patricia Limerick of Colorado, with others at Yale and Washington, this group argues, in Worster's words, that the West did not consist of "lone, heroic individuals who went out and, by their own muscle and ingenuity, carved out home and opportunity for themselves . . . that's a lot of fantasy. We look at the West from a more modern perspective and we're seeing a kind of imperialistic mind that has dominated and controlled the West." This view obviously parallels the general argument we are making in these pages. Worster and others of the "Gang of Four" are environmental historians, concentrating on themes such as the critical importance of water in the West, and documenting the process of desertification which perhaps contributed to the Dust Bowl, and has certainly salinized vast sectors of once fertile land. Our point is that the intellectual and cultural history of the West is as fraught with conflict, turmoil, and damage as the environmental history itself. In other words, what happened to the land also happened to the people. Of course, the West has always been legendary for the centrality to its culture of the theme of violence—in the dispossession of the Indians, range wars, gunfights, whippings, and barroom brawls. We suggest that the intellectual conflicts also took on such a coloration. Indeed, it is remarkable how many of the freethinkers in this book had to contend not only with ever-menacing poverty, but with fistfights, jailings, assassinations, near-assassinations, blacklisting, depression, alcoholism, and suicide. A few, of course, led a "normal" existence and died peacefully in their beds of old age, but others faced terrible obstacles throughout their lives.

In the spring and summer of 1991, a major exhibition at the Smithsonian Institution's Museum of American Art, "The West as America: Reinterpreting Images of the Frontier," provoked an extraordinary controversy. This exhibition assembled a large number of Western paintings by such classic artists as Charles Russell and Frederic Remington; the dispute arose because of captions accompanying the paintings, which tended to explain their "hidden" or otherwise symbolic meanings. For instance, Remington's painting of a band of cowboys fleeing an Indian attack was explicated as a vision of "an Anglo-Saxon race in a world 'overrun' with immigrants." The art historians who contributed the captions and the essays in the exhibition's catalog were obviously developing interpretations parallel to the notorious "Gang of Four" group of new Western historians. The controversy grew so hot that Senator Ted Stevens of Alaska openly attacked the Smithsonian, proclaiming "You're in for a battle. . . . I'm going to get other people to help me make you make sense." Former Librarian of Congress Daniel Boorstin wrote acidly in the exhibition's guest book: ". . . a perverse, historically inaccurate, destructive exhibit. No credit to the Smithsonian." The virulence of such reactions suggests both the importance, for some, of the old heroic "consensus" view of Western American history, and the fact that this view has been advanced on the basis of violence, threats, retaliation, and cultural control. We hope that our book will provide more evidence to support the interpretative concepts of the "Gang of Four," the art historians of "The West as America," and others who are courageously trying to understand the complex and often tragic contradictions that have shaped our cultural history.

Perhaps, in a way, the controversy between "consensus" and "conflict" schools of historical interpretation is a false one, insofar as there *has* been a consensus for much of the twentieth century, under the paradigm of "Christian Civilization," under the hegemony of the Republican party and the capitalist class. Yet there has also been a remarkable amount of conflict on the way to "achieving" that consensus. For ours is a republic supposedly founded on principles of equality, but whose past is shot through with racism and class conflict; which is dedicated to free speech and a free press, but which has often repressed and jailed those who engage in either; which, because of its intimate connections to the Enlightenment and modern science among its Founding Fathers, was in its origins dedicated to Freethought principles, but has seen the emergence of masses who are literally either afraid, or unable, to think for themselves. We hope that this book will provide some evidence of how all this came to be among our people.

HOW WE MADE THESE SELECTIONS

First, we were concerned to convey the flavor of the culture of Freethought in the central expanses of the United States over the course of the last one hundred and fifty years, not only as expressed by professional writers like Twain, or famous spokesmen like Ingersoll, but among the grassroots editors, poets, and activists in the movement. Somewhat arbitrarily, we have begun with the early nineteenth century, concentrating mainly on "The Golden Age of Freethought" after the Civil War through World War I, and also including some writers up to the present. We have found a wealth of materials in the archives and historical societies of the Midwest, especially in Missouri and Kansas. Certain limitations, particularly a lack of funds, made it impossible to collect materials from such promising states as Wisconsin and Minnesota, which had vigorous Freethought movements.

While most of the authors we have chosen were either from rural areas or from small towns, we have selected St. Louis as a city to represent the ties between an urban culture, and its surrounding rural environment, in part because it was the "Gateway to the West" in terms of travel and commerce, but also because with its large German population, it became a considerable center for the Freethought movement. Other Midwestern cities, such as Milwaukee, Chicago, and Omaha had freethinkers in their cultures, along with freethought organizations and publications.

We have had a penchant for autobiographical writings, exemplified by the selections from Ingersoll, Darrow, Dreiser, and others, partly because the writing itself is lively, and also because we found that people tended to become freethinkers because of their own life experiences. Indeed, we would argue that the literature of America is particularly rich and interesting in its memoirs and autobiographies, not only in Freethought, but in feminism, ethnic history, and the labor movement.

Not every writer included here was an agnostic or an atheist. Münch, Brann, and Twain, for instance, almost certainly remained theists, though the latter two were of the most unusual kind. Brann, for instance, disagreed with Ingersoll, but also had a great respect for him. Vachel Lindsay proclaimed that he was a follower of the Reverend Alexander Campbell, but from his poetry it is clearly apparent that he wrestled with belief and unbelief. Our objective has been to document the complex spectrum of Freethought in American culture, rather than to include only those who were certifiably unbelievers, though obviously, most of those included here belong in that category.

We have endeavored to select writing that was typical of a period. In some cases, as in the poetry of George Henry Walser, the Victorian idiom now appears creaky or even quaint, but in his day, his style was very popular. There has been some concentration on literature that was dramatic and forceful in expression—sometimes written for the "moment," such as a newspaper editorial penned in the middle of a hot dispute—but sometimes pensive and lyrical, as the work of Lindsay and Masters. Furthermore, we believe that American literature has had a strange blend of tragedy and humor, sometimes in the same author, or even the same piece of writing. In the midst of controversy, or even defeat, freethinkers have often been able to shrug their shoulders, and laugh at the pretensions of their foes. Thus, we have had an eye for literature that might enable the reader to withstand rough times, and hard traveling.

While our concentration has been on the Midwest and West, we have included a few items from New England, such as the speech of Red Jacket and the memoir by Ingersoll. Most of our authors are rather plebeian in origin, but we have included the archetypal Boston Brahmin, Oliver Wendell Holmes, because his poem about the One-Hoss Shay not only has an obviously rural theme, but remained widely popular as a recitation piece in country schools, almost to the present time. The South is represented only by Sterling Brown's "Slim in Hell," and a poem by Langston Hughes. With its humor and wild violence, Brown's poem bears comparison with the song "Silver Jack." The South has an extraordinary heritage of Freethought, going back to the eighteenth century, and deserves an entire volume of its own.

We located and otherwise found reference to a number of feminist freethinkers, but their texts are now available only at distant historical societies and libraries. This is another subject that deserves an entire volume of its own. Much of the West Coast literature has unfortunately remained outside our range of access. If there is to be a strong and vigorous renewal of the Freethought movement in America, we need to have the publication of comprehensive documentary histories for all these subjects.

THE TEXT

There have been some minor alterations, mostly in spelling or punctuation, to produce a modern text, and there has been some editing for continuity, but in the main, we have preserved the linguistic integrity of the selections, especially as regards slang. Dialect and slang have a certain almost folkloric flavor, which has a value and quality of its own. The editors of *The Truth Seeker* had some orthographic peculiarities, which we have modernized. The version of "Silver Jack" printed here differs in one line, referring to "Burley type tobacco"; earlier versions give this as "nigger head tobacco." For obvious reasons, present-day folk singers prefer some alteration of that line, such as the one we have made. Otherwise, the texts are very close to the originals. Freethought is capitalized, usually, when we refer to a social movement, and is in lower case if it is referred to as a habit of mind.

List of Illustrations

Part One

The Early Frontier

1

Excerpt from a Speech
to a Christian Missionary

Red Jacket

Red Jacket (ca. 1758–1830) was a chief and famed orator of the Seneca tribe in upstate New York. His Indian name Sagoyewatha means "He keeps them awake," and his English name derived from a habit of wearing red jackets first given him by the British. He long opposed the encroachment of whites on Indian lands, and strove to preserve the integrity of Seneca language, culture, and religion. In the 1820s, Red Jacket was welcomed as a speaker at meetings of freethinkers in New York City. In his last years he had to cope both with alcoholism and the conversion of much of his own family to Christianity. At his death, contrary to his wishes, Red Jacket was buried in the Christian cemetery on the reservation.

After the missionary had done speaking, the Indians conferred together about two hours, by themselves, when they gave an answer by Red Jacket, which follows:

"Friend and brother, it was the will of the Great Spirit that we should meet together this day. He orders all things, and he has

From William L. Stone, *The Life and Times of Sa-Go-Y-Wat-Ha (Red Jacket)* (New York: Wiley & Putnam, 1891)

given us a fine day for our council. He has taken his garment from before the sun, and caused it to shine with brightness upon us; our eyes are opened, that we see clearly; our ears are unstopped, that we have been able to hear distinctly the words that you have spoken; for all these favors we thank the Great Spirit, and him only.

"Brother, this council fire was kindled by you; it was at your request that we came together at this time; we have listened with attention to what you have said; you have requested us to speak our minds freely; this gives us great joy, for we now consider that we stand upright before you, and can speak what we think; all have heard your voice, and all speak to you as one man; our minds are agreed.

"Brother, you say you want an answer to your talk before you leave this place. It is right you should have one, as you are a great distance from home, and we do not wish to detain you; but we will first look back a little, and tell you what our fathers have told us, and what we have heard from the white people.

"Brother, listen to what we say. There was a time when our forefathers owned this great island. Their seats extended from the rising to the setting sun. The Great Spirit had made it for the use of Indians. He had created the buffalo, the deer, and other animals for food. He made the bear and the beaver, and their skins served us for clothing. He had scattered them over the country, and taught us how to take them. He had caused the earth to produce corn for bread. All this he had done for his red children because he loved them. If we had any disputes about hunting-grounds they were generally settled without the shedding of much blood: but an evil day came among us; your forefathers crossed the great waters, and landed on this island. Their numbers were small; they found friends, and not enemies; they told us they had fled from their own country for fear of wicked men, and come here to enjoy their religion. They asked for a small seat; we took pity on them, granted their request, and they sat down amongst us; we gave them corn and meat; they gave us poison* in return. The white people had now found our country, tidings were carried back, and more came amongst us; yet we did not fear them,—we took them to be friends; they called us brothers; we believed them, and gave them a larger seat. At length their numbers had greatly increased; they wanted more land; they wanted our country. Our eyes were opened, and our minds became uneasy. Wars took place; Indians were hired to fight against Indians,

---

*Spirituous liquor is alluded to, it is supposed.

and many of our people were destroyed. They also brought strong liquors among us: it was strong and powerful, and has slain thousands.

"Brother, our seats were once large, and yours were very small; you have now become a great people, and we have scarcely a place left to spread our blankets; you have got our country, but are not satisfied; you want to force your religion upon us.

"Brother, continue to listen. You say that you are sent to instruct us how to worship the Great Spirit agreeably to his mind, and if we do not take hold of the religion which you white people preach, we shall be unhappy hereafter; you say you are right, and we are lost; how do we know this to be true? We understand that your religion is written in a book; if it was intended for us as well as you, why has not the Great Spirit given it to us, and not only to us, but why did he not give to our forefathers the knowledge of that book, with the means of understanding it rightly? We only know what you tell us about it; how shall we know when to believe, being so often deceived by the white people?

"Brother, you say there is but one way to worship and serve the Great Spirit; if there is but one religion, why do you white people differ so much about it; why not all agree, as you can all read the book?

"Brother, we do not understand these things; we are told that your religion was given to your forefathers, and has been handed down from father to son. We also have a religion which was given to our forefathers, and has been handed down to us, their children. We worship that way. It teacheth us to be thankful for all the favors we receive; to love each other, and to be united; we never quarrel about religion.

"Brother, the Great Spirit has made us all, but he has made a great difference between his white and red children; he has given us a different complexion, and different customs; to you he has given the arts; to these he has not opened our eyes; we know these things to be true. Since he has made so great a difference between us in other things, why may we not conclude that he has given us a different religion according to our understanding; the Great Spirit does right; he knows what is best for his children; we are satisfied.

"Brother, we do not wish to destroy your religion, or take it from you; we only want to enjoy our own.

"Brother, you say you have not come to get our lands or our money, but to enlighten our minds. I will now tell you that I have been at your meetings, and saw you collecting money from the meeting. I cannot tell what this money was intended for, but suppose it was for your minister; and if we should conform to your way of thinking, perhaps you may want some from us.

"Brother, we are told that you have been preaching to white people in this place; these people are our neighbors; we are acquainted with them; we will wait a little while and see what effect your preaching has upon them. If we find it does them good, makes them honest, and less disposed to cheat Indians, we will then consider again what you have said.

"Brother, you have now heard our answer to your talk, and this is all we have to say at present. As we are going to part, we will come and take you by the hand, and hope the Great Spirit will protect you on your journey, and return you safe to your friends."

The chiefs and others then drew near the missionary to take him by the hand; but he would not receive them, and hastily rising from his seat, said, "that there was no fellowship between the religion of God and the works of the Devil, and, therefore, could not join hands with them." Upon this being interpreted to them, "they smiled, and retired in a peaceable manner."

2

A Declaration of Mental Independence

Robert Owen

Born in in 1771, Robert Owen worked his way up from humble beginnings to become the director of the great cotton spinning mills of New Lanark in Scotland. Horrified by the squalid conditions of the early Industrial Revolution, Owen set about developing a progressive and humanist environment for his workers, including decent nutrition and free public education. The success of these innovations brought Owen considerable fame and approval, even from the ranks of the British ruling elite. Owen later emigrated to America, where, in 1825, he purchased from the religious communitarian society of Father George Rapp, the town of Harmony, located on the banks of the Wabash River in southwestern Indiana. In December of that year, Owen, his sons, and several notable scientists and educators sailed down the Ohio River on the *Philanthropist,* which Owen styled "the boatload of knowledge." For various reasons, Owen's formal socialist experiment in New Harmony lasted only a couple of years, but its impact was considerable. Owen's several sons made significant contributions to American intellectual life, especially in geology and public education. In the 1820s, Owen addressed the United States Congress, explaining his concepts of cooperation, i.e., that society should be based on organized efforts for the common good, as opposed to the destructive effects of untrammeled individualism and greed. On the occasion of the fiftieth anniversary of the Declaration of Independence, Owen made a remarkable address in New Harmony itself, which is one of the most concise and forceful expressions of his socialist and freethought ideas. In his later years, however, Owen turned to spiritualism. Though Owen returned to England, where he died in 1858, the town of New Harmony remains a cultural center, especially its Workingmen's Institute, a library and research center which was founded in 1838.

We meet to commemorate the period, when the inhabitants of this new world attained the power to withdraw from the control of the old world, and to form a government for themselves.

This event is likely to prove, in its consequences, as important as any which has occurred in ancient or modern times. It has been the means of preparing a new era in the history of man, and of producing such a change of circumstances as will admit of the introduction of measures to change, entirely, the character and condition of the human race.

The revolution in America, sanctioned and secured by the Declaration of Independence in 1776, gave to a people advancing towards civilization, the first opportunity of establishing a government, which would, by degrees, permit them to acquire that greatest of blessings— MENTAL LIBERTY.

This was, indeed, a most important point gained: it was the first time such privilege had ever been possessed by mankind.

Its fruits have been visible in the gradual advance towards mental liberty, which has been made during the half century which this day completes from that memorable event. But, I conclude, it will be in the next half century, now about to commence, that the wondering world will learn justly to estimate the value of the high achievement which was then attained.

It was not the mere political liberty then conquered from the old world, that was the real victory gained by the inhabitants of these vast regions; for political power had been often wrested from one party and obtained by another. But it was the right which they thereby acquired and used, to establish the liberty of freely extending thought upon all subjects, secular and religious; and the right to express those thoughts openly, so soon as the existing prejudices, derived from the old world, could be so far removed as to direct

---

From *The New Harmony Gazette* 1, no. 42 (July 12,1826). This article first appeared under the title "Oration Containing a *Declaration of Mental Independence,* delivered in the Public Hall at New Harmony, Indiana, at the Celebration of the Fourth of July, 1826."

the mind of the multitude to investigate facts and reject the mysteries of disordered imaginations: to teach them to discern the value of the former, as they always direct to the development of real knowledge; and instruct them rightly to estimate the evil of the latter, as they lead to those errors which have made man a compound of folly and a recipient for misery.

Yes, my friends, the Declaration of Independence, in 1776, prepared the way to secure to you MENTAL LIBERTY, without which man never can become more than a mere localized being, with power to render him more miserable and degraded than the animals which he has been taught to deem inferior to himself. It is true, the right of mental liberty is inherent in our nature; for, while man exists in mental health, no human power can deprive him of it: but until the Revolution of 1776, no people had acquired the *political power* to permit them to use that right, when their minds should be so far freed from early imbibed prejudices as to allow them to derive benefits from its practice. No nation, except this, even yet possesses the political power to enable the people to use the right of mental freedom.

This right—this invaluable right, you now enjoy by the Constitution obtained for you by Washington, Franklin, Henry, and the other worthies associated with them.

You have indeed abundant reason to rejoice in this victory, obtained over the thick mental darkness which, till then, covered the earth.

The collision of mind which produced that victory, and which was produced by it, elicited a spark of light, which enabled the prominent actors in those scenes to discover a glimpse through the long night of error and misrule, with which the inhabitants of all the earth had been previously afflicted.

Still, however, these men, whose minds were in advance of the age in which they lived, were encircled by the prejudices which they and their fathers brought from Europe, and which had descended to the inhabitants of those regions through many ages of despotism, superstition, and ignorance. And although a few of these highly gifted men of the Revolution saw a stronger and clearer light at the distance, as they supposed, of some ages before them; they were too conscious of the extent of the old errors around them to attempt more than to secure the means in the Constitution which they formed, by which their successors might work their way to the superior distant light, and gain for themselves the innumerable advantages which real mental liberty could bestow upon them.

It is for YOU and YOUR successors now to press onward, with your utmost speed, in the course which, by so many sacrifices, for your benefit, they have opened for you. They discovered some of the innumerable impositions which had been practiced on your predecessors; they saw more of them, than in the temper of those times, they could venture publicly to expose; but they have left such decided proofs of their own feelings and views regarding them, that none, who reflect, can doubt the strong desire they felt to attack and destroy still more of them, and, if possible, to annihilate all the arts and mysteries by which the few had so long held a pernicious, despotic sway and control over the many.

These wise men were withheld from going beyond the line determined upon at the Revolution, apprehending that, by attempting to gain a greater advance upon ignorance and superstition, they might put to hazard the benefits they found they could secure; and herein they evinced their knowledge of the times in which they lived and acted.

These worthies knew that their descendants, starting from the point which they had gained, could, in due time, without such risk, make other and still more important advances toward mental liberty— toward that which will, when fully attained, enable man to remove the cause of all crime, and the misery which arises from the commission of crimes. To attain this mental liberty, in its full extent and highest purity, and to be secure in its permanent possession, will be the greatest victory that man can gain.

My friends, it surely cannot be your wish, that any good and great cause should be effected only by halves—and more especially when that which remains to be done, is, beyond all calculation, the more important? There is a noble object before us, to be won by some party or another in this or in some other country. It is no less than the destruction of the threefold causes which deprive man of mental liberty, which compel him to commit crimes, and to suffer all the miseries which crime can inflict. Could we but gain this object— soon would rational intelligence, real virtue, and substantial happiness, be permanently established among men: ignorance, poverty, dependence, and vice would be forever banished from the earth.

Let me now ask,—

Are you prepared to imitate the example of your ancestors? Are you willing to run the risks they encountered? Are you ready, like them, to meet the prejudices of past times, and determined to overcome them at ALL hazards, for the benefit of our country and for the emancipation of the human race? Are you, indeed, willing to sacrifice

Workingmen's Institute. New Harmony, Indiana. Photo by Fred Whitehead.

your fortunes, lives, and reputations, if such sacrifices would be necessary, to secure for all your fellow beings, the GREATEST GOOD, that, according to our present knowledge, it is possible for them ever to receive?

Are you prepared to achieve a MENTAL REVOLUTION, as superior in benefit and importance to the first revolution, as the mental powers of man exceed his physical powers?

If you are, I am most ready and willing to join you in this deed—the last and most daring that has been left for man in his irrational state to perform.

But, my friends, knowing, as I do, the immeasurable magnitude of the GOOD which this Mental Revolution will effect and permanently secure for human nature through all future ages—I deem the continued existence, a little longer here, of a few individuals to be of no consideration whatever in comparison with its attainment; and, therefore, as I cannot know the present state of *your* minds, and as the continuance of life at my age is very uncertain, I have calmly and deliberately determined, upon this eventful and auspicious occasion, to break asunder the remaining mental bonds which for so many ages have grievously afflicted our nature, and, by so doing, to give forever FULL FREEDOM TO THE HUMAN MIND.

Upon an experience, then, of nearly forty years, which, owing to a very peculiar combination of circumstances, has been more varied, extended, and singular than perhaps has ever fallen to the lot of any one man, and, during which period, my mind was continually occupied in tracing the cause of each human misery that came before me to its true origin;—I now DECLARE, to you and to the world, *that Man, up to this hour, has been, in all parts of the earth, a slave to a TRINITY of the most monstrous evils that could be, combined to inflict mental and physical evil upon his whole race.*

I refer to PRIVATE, OR INDIVIDUAL PROPERTY—ABSURD AND IRRATIONAL SYSTEMS OF RELIGION—and MARRIAGE, FOUNDED ON INDIVIDUAL PROPERTY COMBINED WITH SOME ONE OF THESE IRRATIONAL SYSTEMS OF RELIGION.

It is difficult to say which of these grand sources of all crime ought to be placed first or last; for they are so intimately interlinked and woven together by time, that they cannot be separated without being destroyed:—each one is necessary to the support of the other two. This formidable Trinity, compounded of Ignorance, Superstition, and Hypocrisy, is the only Demon, or Devil, that ever has, or, most likely, ever will torment the human race. It is well calculated, in all its consequences, to produce the utmost misery on the mind and body of man of which his nature is susceptible. The division of property among individuals prepared the seeds, cultivated the growth, and brought to maturity all of the evils of poverty and riches existing among a people at the same time; the industrious experiencing privations and the idle being overwhelmed and injured by wealth.

Religion, or superstition,—for all religions have proved themselves to be superstitions,—by destroying the judgment, irrationalized all the mental faculties of man, and made him the most abject slave, through the fear of nonentities created solely by his own disordered imagination. Superstition forced him to believe, or to say he believed, that a Being existed who possessed all power, wisdom, and goodness— that he could do and that he did, everything—and yet, that evil and misery superabound; and that this Being, who makes and does all things, is not the direct or indirect author of evil or misery. Such is the foundation on which all the mysteries and ravings of superstition are erected in all parts of the world. Its inconsistency and inconceivable folly have been such as to keep the world in continual wars, and massacres, to create private divisions, leading to every imaginable evil; and it is probable that superstition has caused more than its third of the crimes and sufferings of the human race.

The forms and ceremonies of marriage, as they have been hitherto generally performed, and afterward supported, make it almost certain that they were contrived and forced upon the people at the same period that property was first divided among a few leading individuals and superstition was invented: this being the only device that could be introduced to permit them to retain their division of the public spoils, and create to themselves an aristocracy of wealth, of power, and of learning.

To enable them to keep their children apart from the multitude who were to be kept in poverty, in ignorance, and consequently without power,—and to monopolize all wealth and power and learning to themselves,—some such contrivance as marriage, with mysterious forms and ceremonies, to hide their real intentions from the ignorant, was absolutely necessary, that they might, through the influence of their wealth, learning, and power, select the most beautiful and desirable women from among all the people,—and thus enslave and make them, in fact, a part of their private property.

This was the commencement of that system which led to such endless crimes and miseries and degradation of the human faculties, by tempting the inexperienced to barter their feelings and affections for wealth, trappings, and power, when, too late for their happiness, they discover they have been deceived, and that wealth, learning, and power can make no amends for the want of those natural feelings and affections, in the union of which all feel the present happiness of life to consist.

Among the truly intelligent, marriage will be respected only when it shall be formed between those who are equal in wealth, education, and condition; who are well acquainted with each other's habits, minds, and feelings before they enter upon the engagement; and who know also, that by their nature the continuance of affection does not depend upon the will of either, but that it will diminish or increase according as they produce pleasurable or disagreeable sensations in each other. Marriage, to make it a virtuous and happy connection, must be contracted by both parties, solely with a view to their happiness. As, then, it is a law of nature that our affections are not at the control of the will; and as happiness can be enjoyed only when we associate with those for whom we cannot avoid having the most esteem, regard, and affection; it should be as reputable, and equally authorized by law, to dissolve marriage when the esteem and affection cannot be retained for each other, and when the union promises to produce more misery than happiness, as to form the marriage in the first instance. When, however, the parties are on a perfect equality in wealth, condition, and education, and intimately acquainted with each other's thoughts and feelings before marriage; and when no motive whatever exists but genuine affection to induce the parties to unite; it is more likely that marriages so formed would be more permanent than they have ever yet been. But the present and past character of man, formed by the inconsistent and incongruous circumstances around hm, have made him so artificial in his feelings, views, and conduct that a decisive conclusion cannot be drawn upon this most interesting part of the subject. Be this, however, as it may, we may be sure, that as soon as man shall be trained rationally, and surrounded by those circumstances only which are in union with his nature, he will act only rationally; that is, in such a manner as to secure the highest and purest happiness to himself and his fellow creatures.

The revolution, then, to be now effected, is the DESTRUCTION of this HYDRA OF EVILS—in order that the many may be no longer poor, wretched beings—dependent on the wealthy and powerful few; that Man may be no longer a superstitious idiot, continually dying from the futile fear of death; that he may no longer unite himself to the other sex from any mercenary or superstitious motives, nor promise and pretend to do that which it depends not on himself to perform.

Upon the experience of a life devoted to the investigation of these momentous subjects, I fearlessly now declare to you, from a conviction, as strong as conviction can exist in the human mind, that this compound of ignorance and fraud IS THE REAL AND ONLY CAUSE OF ALL THE CRIME, AND MISERY ARISING FROM CRIME, WHICH CAN BE FOUND IN HUMAN SOCIETY.

This threefold, horrid monster has been most speciously gilded and decorated with external trappings, to awe the ignorant multitude and deter them from examining the black venom and corruption within. It was in sundry times and places made death for any mortal, except the initiated, to approach these hidden mysteries; and nothing short of the Inquisition with the aid of that fearful unmeaning term SACRED, could have, for so long a period, kept man,—irrational as these terrors made him,—from discovering the imposition which was practiced upon him for the sole purpose of keeping him in mental slavery and bondage.

For nearly forty years I have been employed, heart and soul, day by day, almost without ceasing, in preparing the means and arranging the circumstances, to enable me to give the death-blow to the tyranny and despotism, which, for unnumbered ages past, have held the human mind spellbound, in chains and fetters, of such mysterious forms and shapes, that no mortal hand dared approach to set the suffering prisoner free. Nor has the fullness of time, for the accomplishment of this great event, been completed until within this hour,—and such has been the extraordinary course of events, that the Declaration of Political Independence, in 1776, has produced its counterpart, the DECLARATION OF MENTAL INDEPEN-DENCE, in 1826—the latter just half a century from the former.

Rejoice with me, my friends, that your mental independence rests now as secure as your political independence; for the over-whelming power of TRUTH OVER ERROR is such, that as soon as arrangements can be formed to admit of the full development of Truth to the world, and it is once publicly promulgated, no art, or falsehood, or force, can ever afterwards return it back into forget-fulness, or unteach the truths which it has taught.

Under the circumstances in which this Mental Revolution has been made, no human power can undo, or render nugatory, that which has now been done.

This Truth has passed from me, beyond the possibility of recall; it has been already received into your minds; speedily it will be heard throughout America, and from thence it will pass north and south, east and west, as far as language is known,—and almost as fast as it shall be conveyed, human nature will recognize and receive it. In countries in which ignorance and despotism hold their sway over the multitude, arts will be used to keep it from being heard among them; but neither armies, nor barriers of any kind, can now prevent a great and important truth from finding its way, by some means or another, into the darkest recesses of terror and deception.

Rejoice, then, with me, my friends, that this light is now set upon a hill; for it will increase daily, more and more, until it shall be seen, felt, and understood by all the nations of the earth.

Rejoice with me, that we now live under a government unconnected with any of the superstitions of the dark ages of ignorance; a government established purposely to give man his natural rights; to give him the full power to obtain mental liberty as soon as he could disburthen himself of the prejudices of his ancestors.

The individuals who compose a great majority of your present general government are happily free from the weakening and deadening influence of superstition; their experience is too extensive, their minds are too enlightened, to be longer held in slavery and bondage by imaginary notions unsupported by a single fact. They will therefore rejoice to see their fellow citizens and their fellow men throwing off the yoke which has hitherto kept their finest faculties in bondage, and they will look forward with increased hope to the advantages which the rising generation, freed from these errors, will acquire and possess.

All who are deeply versant in human nature can readily estimate the difference between a generation whose judgment shall have been carefully cultivated from infancy, and whose best faculties shall have been carefully called into full action, and one in which the judgment has been forced to become subservient to a misguided imagination, and in whose mind all natural facts have been distorted and made to bend and support mysteries only calculated to blind the understanding and call forth the weaker and worse feelings of human nature. Your government, and all the enlightened men of these states and of other countries, now look to the improved education of the faculties of children, to produce a race of rational beings, whose minds will be freed from the superstitions, prejudices, and errors of past times; and I trust that, in this respect, no parties will be disappointed.

In furtherance of this great object we are preparing the means to bring up your children, with industrious and useful habits, with natural and, of course rational ideas and views, with sincerity in all their proceedings; and to give them kind and affectionate feelings for each other, and charity, in the most extensive sense of the term, for all their fellow creatures.

By doing this, by uniting your separate interests into one, by doing away with individual money transactions, by exchanging with each other your articles of produce on the basis of labor, by looking forward to apply your surplus wealth to assist others to obtain similar advantages, and by the abandonment of the use of spirituous liquors, you will in a peculiar manner promote the object of every wise government and of all really enlightened men.

And here we now are, as near, perhaps, as we can be in the center of the United States, even, as it were, like the little grain of mustard seed; but with these GREAT TRUTHS before us, with the practice of the social system, as soon as it shall be well understood among us, our principles will, I trust, spread from community to community, from state to state, and from continent to continent, until this system and these TRUTHS shall overshadow the whole earth,—shedding fragrance and abundance, intelligence and happiness upon all the sons of men.

I would that you, and those who now live in this and other countries, could partake, for many years, of all these enjoyments.

3

The Harp of a Thousand Strings:
A Hard-Shell Baptist Sermon

Anonymous

"The Harp of a Thousand Strings" is of indeterminate authorship and origin, though it has been widely reprinted in anthologies and on broadsides since its first appearance in a Mississippi newspaper in the 1850s. It has been attributed to several writers, including Henry T. Lewis and Van Dyke Browne (William P. Brannan), the latter claiming it in a volume entitled *The Harp of a Thousand Strings; with an Autobiography of the Author, Jabez Flint* (1865). Its metaphorical language and accentuation of the final syllable with an "ah!" is typical of Hard-Shell Baptist preachers of the Mississippi Valley region in an earlier era. It is still a favorite with rural mimics and I have heard it rendered to appreciative audiences in a number of Midwestern communities as late as the summer of 1946 in Moberly, Missouri. [Note by Jack Conroy]*

I may say to you my brethring, that I am not an edicated man, an' I am not one of them as believes that edication is necessary for a Gospel minister, for I believe the Lord edicates his preachers

From *Midland Humor: A Harvest of Fun and Folklore,* Jack Conroy, ed. (New York: Current Books, Inc., A. A. Wyn, Publisher, 1947)
*Reprinted by permission of Douglas Wixson, literary executor Conroy Estate.

jest as he wants 'em to be edicated; an' although I say it that oughtn't to say it, yet in the State of Indianny, whar I live, thar's no man as gets bigger congregations nor what I gits.

Thar may be some here today, my brethring, as don't know what persuasion I am uv. Well, I must say to you, my brethring, that I'm a Hard-Shell Baptist. Thar's some folks as don't like the Hard-Shell Baptist, but I'd rather have a hard shell as no shell at all. You see me here today, my brethring, dressed up in fine clothes; you mout think I was proud, but I am not proud, my brethring, and although I've been a preacher of the gospel for twenty years, an' although I'm capting of the flatboat that lies at your landing, I'm not proud, my brethring.

I am not gwine to tell edzactly whar my tex may be found; suffice to say, it's in the Bible, and you'll find it somewhar between the first chapter of the book of Generations, and the last chapter of the book of Revolutions, and ef you'll go and search the Scriptures, you'll not only find my tex thar, but a great many other texes as will do you good to read, and my tex, when you shall find it, you shill find it to read thus:—

"And he played on a harp uv a thousand strings—sperits uv jest men made perfeck."

My tex, my brethring, leads me to speak of sperits. Now, thar's a great many kinds of sperits in the world—in the fuss place, thar's the sperits as some folks call ghosts, and thar's the sperits uv turpentine, and thar's the sperits as some folks call liquor, an' I've got a good an artikel of them kind of sperits on my flatboat as ever was fotch down the Mississippi River; but thar's a great many other kinds of sperits, for the tex says, "He played on a harp uv a *t-h-o-u-s*-and strings, sperits uv jest men made perfeck."

But I'll tell you the kind uv sperits as is meant in the tex, is FIRE. That's the kind uv sperits as is meant in the tex, my brethring. Now thar's a great many kinds of fire in the world. In the fuss place there's the common sort of fire you light your cigar or pipe with, and then thar's foxfire and campfire, fire before you're ready, and fire and fall back, and many other kind uv fire, for the tex says, "He played on the harp uv a *thous*and strings, sperits of jest men made perfeck."

But I'll tell you the kind of fire as is meant in the tex, my brethring—it's HELL FIRE! an that's the kind uv fire as a great many uv you'll come to, ef you don't do better nor what you have been doin'—for "He played on a harp uv a *thous*and strings, sperits uv jest men made perfeck."

Now, the different sorts of fire in the world may be likened unto the different persuasions of Christians in the world. In the first place we have the Piscapalions, an' they are a high sailin' and high-falutin' set, and they may be likened unto a turkey buzzard, that flies up into the air, and he goes up, and up, and up, till he looks no bigger than your finger nail, and the fust thing you know, he cums down, and down, and down, and is a fillin' himself on the carkiss of a dead hoss by the side of the road, and "He played on a harp uv a *thous*and strings, sperits uv jest men made perfeck."

And then thar's the Methodis, and they may be likened unto the squirril runnin' up into a tree, for the Methodis beleeves in gwine on from one degree of grace to another, and finally on to perfection, and the squirrel goes up and up, and up and up, and he jumps from limb to limb, and branch to branch, and the fust thing you know he falls, and down he cums kerflumix, and that's like the Methodis, for they is allers fallen from grace, ah! and "He played on a harp uv a *thous*and strings, sperits of jest men made perfect."

And then, my brethring, thar's the Baptist, ah! and they have been likened unto a possum on a 'simmon tree, and thunders may roll and the earth may quake, but that possum clings thar still, ah! and you may shake one foot loose, and the other's thar, and you may shake all feet loose, and he laps his tail around the limb, and clings and he clings furever, for "He played on the harp uv a *thous*and strings, sperits uv jest men made perfeck."

4

The Laughing Frontier

Jack Conroy

Born at the Monkey Nest coal camp near Moberly, Missouri, in 1898, Jack Conroy had a long and distinguished life as an industrial worker, novelist, folklorist, and man of letters. He edited little magazines like *The Rebel Poet* and *The Anvil,* which carried into practice his motto: "We prefer crude vigor to polished banality." While editor, Conroy discovered many important American writers from the ranks of the common people, including Richard Wright and Nelson Algren. Best known as the author of the Depression-era novel *The Disinherited,* which has been translated into many languages, Conroy was also popular as a lecturer. In his later years, he became known as "The Sage of Moberly," which central Missouri town he styled "The Athens of the West." In 1984, practically the entire population of Moberly turned out to honor him for "Jack Conroy Day." Conroy died in 1990.

. . . I think, in considering frontier humor, that we ought to take heed of what the West meant in the past, or even what it means to some folks now. In New York last summer a woman told me

From *The Jack Conroy Reader,* ed. and introd. by Jack Salzman and David Hays (New York: Burt Franklin & Co., 1979). Reprinted by permission of Douglas Wixson, literary executor Conroy Estate.

she has a son who lives out West in Ohio. Remember the old poem about where "way down East" was?

. . . Indiana was really away out West . . . when Dan Marble, a Yankee actor, was riding in a stagecoach traveling through Ohio in 1840. There was a Hoosier on board, and he kept bragging about how superior Indiana was to Ohio. An old gentleman with a cane acknowledged that Ohio wasn't much of a stock country any more— the range was too worn out for much grazing.

"Well," said the loyal Hoosier, "I don't see how in the hell they all manage to get along in a country where there ain't no ranges and they don't make no beef. A man ain't worth a cuss in Indiana that hasn't got his brand on a hundred head."

A preacher who was in the coach got tired of hearing the Hoosier boast about Indiana beef, and he was even more distressed at the incessant blackguarding. He thought he'd get his mind off both cattle and swearing by talking about the Scriptures. He went on for some time about various miracles and the fulfillment of prophecies. The Hoosier did stop talking about Indiana beef long enough to listen.

"I've just heard of a gentleman," says the preacher, "that's been to the Holy Land, and went over the Bible country. It's astonishing what wonderful things he has seen. He was at Sodom and Gomorrow and seen the place where Lot's wife fell."

"Ah!" says the old gentleman with the cane.

"Yes," says the preacher, "he went to the very spot. What's the remarkable thing of all he seen the pillar of salt she was turned into."

"It is possible!" says the old gentleman.

"Yes, sir, he seen the salt standing there to this day."

"What!" says the Hoosier. "Real, genuwine, good salt?"

"Yes, sir a pillar of salt, just as it was when that wicked woman was punished for disobedience!"

The Hoosier, with an expression of countenance that plainly told that his mind was powerfully convinced of an important fact, asked, "Right out in the open air?"

"Yes. Standing right in the open field where she fell."

"Well, sir," says the Hoosier, "all I've got to say is, IF SHE'D DROPPED IN INDIANA, THE CATTLE WOULD HAVE LICKED HER UP BEFORE SUNDOWN!"

5

Look for the Creator Where
Only He Can Be Found

Heinrich Koch

In the mid-nineteenth century, Missouri received many who had been forced to emigrate from Germany for their involvement in anti-monarchic activities. Among these was Heinrich Koch (1800–1879), a watchmaker, who became involved with *Der Antipfaff (The Anti-Priestling)*, the first rationalist paper in the West, which became increasingly "anti-Latin." The so-called Latin farmers were the more well-to-do liberal, educated elite who moved to the areas of Illinois and Missouri around St. Louis, whereas Koch represented the radical, proletarian element. Koch edited the first German language "labor"—i.e., artisan-communist—paper in the United States, the *Vorwärts,* in 1845.

The great Creator of heaven and earth shows himself again in his most beautiful spring ornament; he who wants to see him must turn his eye away from the dead God of the Bible and admire the living one.

From *Der Antipfaff,* April 19, 1842

Let him go outside
And see the blossoms' magnificent splendor,
As flowers and grasses
In meadows and fields
On mountains and valleys laugh to him.
He sees in obscureness
The living and sprouting,
The shoving and budding
And feels around him
The great, infinite Spirit's presence.

Arise and wander joyfully outside,
Then your heart exults
Grief flees from you
You drive the demon of sins out of you at once,
Oh flee from the gloomy,
Uncanny whispering
Of churches and priestlings
Into the working and creating
Of the faithful and true mother, Nature.

Wherever she surrounds you with her spell
You find truth,
Darkness turns into clarity,
And what we once hated we love again,
Let go of the doubt
Of hell and the devil,
Relish joy
Then you love the great
Infinite Creator and have grasped him.

6

Two Documents by a German Rationalist in America

Friedrich Münch

Born in Germany in 1799, Friedrich Münch attended the Hessian State University in Giessen as a divinity student. After passing his theological examinations in 1818, Münch served for a time as a minister in his father's parish. He later joined the liberal immigration to the United States, and settled in rural Missouri, where he took up the cause of public education, advocating the rights of the individual to his conscience and religious freedom. As a result, he became involved in several extended controversies with orthodox immigrant churches, especially the Lutherans. Münch was a liberal and progressive Christian in the same vein as Boston's famous Theodore Parker; in fact, it was Parker who published Münch's *Treatise on Religion and Christianity* in 1847. Proposing a set of principles which included no role for miraculous or supernatural phenomena, accepting the "higher criticism" of biblical texts, and urging the primacy of reason in any acceptable religion, Münch served several "congregations" in rural Missouri in the 1840s. He also became involved in the struggle against slavery, and his life was threatened several times. Sternly refusing to alter his principles, Münch was at last elected to the state senate, where he played such a distinguished role that he became known as the "Nestor of Missouri." Some years after Münch's death in 1881, his collected works were published in St. Louis.

In addition to his intellectual and political writings, Münch wrote the first book on American grape varieties. The Mount Pleasant winery in Augusta, Missouri, was established by his brother, George Münch, and still produces award-winning wines.

Friedrich Münch, 001–003623. PORTRAITS M–39. By permission of the Missouri Historical Society.

THE FUNDAMENTAL ARTICLES OF GERMAN RATIONALISM

The fundamental articles of genuine German Rationalism may be thus defined:

1. There is a primitive, or original revelation in man's rational nature; education, instruction, and study. can have no other object than to develop the inborn truth.

2. History, though it shows innumerable errors of human reason, yet on the whole discloses a progress of our race in developing the inborn light.

3. There have been historical events more eminently calculated for the advancement of truth and enlightenment; the Mosaic institution was such a one, yet imperfect and adapted to the state of intellectual culture at that time.

4. The establishment of Christianity is the most consummate and perfect effort recorded by history to develop the eternal truths, and has been followed by greater results than any other known. Its author, the wisest amongst the wise, the purest amongst the good, the most exalted in spiritual vigor, is entitled to lasting gratitude and admiration.

5. Unadulterated Christianity is in strict conformity with the dictates of enlightened reason, is the fullest revelation thereof, can never be supplied by any other doctrine of human invention, and will, even though its name should be forgotten, in all ages to come form the substance of the convictions of the wisest and best of men.

6. The belief of a Supreme Being and a future life, together with the obligation of moral behavior, is the substance of all religion.

7. Religious forms and rites are of a temporal, in part national character, and may change; the truth is eternal.

8. Our holy books are to be interpreted according to the same rules applied to other remnants of antiquity.

"The Fundamental Articles of German Rationalism," from *A Treatise on Religion and Christianity, Orthodoxy and Rationalism: An Appeal to the Common Sense of All Who Like Truth Better than Error* (Boston: B. H. Greene, 1847).

Mount Pleasant winery. Augusta, Missouri.
Photo by Fred Whitehead.

9. All conceptions of *supernatural* events and performances are to be attributed to a deficiency of clearsightedness in the observer, narrator, and believer, in taking the extraordinary for the miraculous.

10. All men have a right, and it is their duty, to think for themselves, and live according to their own candid convictions; there ought to be no compulsion in religious matters, no hatred, no denunciation, not even violent disputes; truth must eventually triumph by its intrinsic superiority and strength.

A LETTER TO A NEWSPAPER

All of you who are able to break loose from the overcrowdedness of European life, come and homestead in our spacious, free, and fertile West. Come and see how contented those of your brothers who live here are, who years ago did just that, and who are now enjoying the fruits of their efforts. We have no statues, paintings, and theater, but nature is being increasingly beautified by the diligent hands of man. Although not all living around us are spiritually free, that is to say, free of prejudices, like-minded individuals are not lacking, and the others do not disturb us much—siblings in the various stages of development live peacefully together in the same house—so why should they who have already attained spiritual adulthood and those who are still children not tolerate one another? Moreover, it can be expected that this nation, which is so sensible and radical in everything else, will be emancipated from religious prejudice even faster than the masses of any other country. One must consider whether this people could, in face of all the colossal achievements of the last 200 years, find the time to engage in the intricate investigations, with which the German (and partially the French) scholars pioneered liberal thought in religious matters. One must consider that only in the most recent years German literature has begun to open up to this people (and this has already proven fruitful), whereas English literature has been unable to shed light in this respect. Even without scientific resources (excepting, e.g., the writings of Thomas Paine, which are not absolutely thorough), the free spirit of the West is gaining influence even in religious matters. At least one half of the Americans around us profess the so-called big church; i.e., they belong

"A Letter to a Newspaper," from the *Deutsche Schnellpost* (New York), K. Heinzen and M. Otto, eds., 9, no. 170 (August 1, 1851):1

to no denomination, do not participate in religious practices, and esteem anyone to the degree of his righteousness and diligence, whereas the most extreme religious stultification is upheld by those educated in Europe.

7

The St. Louis Movement

Denton J. Snider

Emerging from a complex matrix of rationalism, religious controversy, and political activism, the St. Louis Movement came about through the meeting of William Torrey Harris and Henry C. Brokmeyer in that city in 1859, when they began to study intensively the works of Georg Friedrich Hegel. Harris, then a school teacher, supported Brokmeyer, a foundry-worker, through an extended period of translating Hegel's *Logic*—a task which was completed and circulated in manuscript versions, although the text has never been published to this day. This same period was one of dramatic political developments, as the pro-Union German "Wide-Awakes" had been for some time preparing militarily for the inevitable conflict soon to break out in the Civil War. These same armed Germans broke up the last slave auction in St. Louis on New Year's Day of 1861.

Western radicals came to interpret events in Hegelian terms: the South's firing on Fort Sumter was the "thesis," the seizing of Camp Jackson near St. Louis by pro-Union forces was the "antithesis," and the general declaration of war was the "synthesis." Denton J. Snider, the author of the following selections, served as a young officer in the Union Army in Ohio, and years later wrote an entire Hegelian history of the conflict, *The American Ten Years' War 1855–1865.*

After the war, Snider and others gathered in St. Louis, where they met Harris and Brokmeyer, and encountered Ralph Waldo Emerson and Bronson Alcott—the aged gray-headed Transcendentalists of the

East confronting the hard-headed young militants of the West. In 1867, Harris began *The Journal of Speculative Philosophy,* the first such journal in the English language. Emerson subscribed, referring to Harris's band of "German Atheists," though it appears that most remained theists of some kind, if only in an attenuated manner. J. B. Bury observed in his *History of Freedom of Thought* that "anyone who comes under Hegel's spell feels that he is in possession of a theory of the universe which relieves him from the need or desire of any revealed religion." Such was the general viewpoint of the St. Louis Movement, though, as Snider suggests in these selections, Harris himself was more conservative in his beliefs. Subsequently, Harris and others founded the Concord School of Philosophy in Massachusetts, and later Harris became United States Commissioner of Education.

Although Henry C. Brokmeyer himself published little, he was clearly the seminal figure of the Movement, and stands as a free inquiring spirit typical of that entire period of American cultural history. Brokmeyer became prominent in Missouri politics, serving a term as lieutenant governor of the state. He spent several years as a railroad agent among the Indians of Muskogee, Oklahoma, and allegedly tried to start a philosophical movement there, though it appears that Brokmeyer was far more influenced by the Indians' language and ideas. Before his death in 1906, he returned to St. Louis, where many of his manuscripts are in the collections of the Missouri Historical Society. Snider, on the other hand, moved more in the direction of literature, and developed a concept of "Literary Bibles," consisting of the works of Homer, Dante, Shakespeare, and Goethe. He lectured on these texts at Communal Universities in Chicago and St. Louis, where he would hold classes at public libraries for little or no fee, offering his books free to those who could not afford them, if only they would promise to read them. In sum, the St. Louis Movement generated in the neighborhood of one thousand books, and helped bring a Western perspective to the development of modern American philosophy.

Several structures connected with the progressive German culture of St. Louis have survived in that city, including the rectory of the first Free Congregation school, and a larger school built by the same organization after the Civil War. In addition, the "Naked Truth" monument was dedicated in 1914, in honor of the city's German-American editors.

Henry C. Brokmeyer. Photo from the collection of Fred Whitehead.

HENRY C. BROKMEYER

Mr. Brokmeyer was born in northern Germany in 1826 (he was
evidently uncertain about the year of his birth; sometimes he gave
it as 1827, or even as 1828; he seems, however, in later life to have
settled upon 1826). He took delight in calling himself a Prussian
Low-German (*Platt-Deutscher*); still he ran away from home and
country, boarded a steamer at Bremen and came to America, while
a mere stripling. He gave as a reason of his flight that his mother,
who was a pietist, caught up one day and burned his first book—
a volume of Goethe's *Lyrical Poems*—"which I had bought with
my own hard-earned and long-saved pennies." A fugitive from his
mother—that certainly touches an untender chord. But I have heard
him give some other reasons for his secret departure from home;
at any rate, here was his first separation—his flight from the old
world to the new. He, while still a youth, must have tramped a
good deal over the United States in the early 40s; he said in conversation at different times that he had worked in New York City,
Philadelphia, Dayton (Ohio), Fort Wayne (Indiana). At last, however,
he as a young man turned southward, and reached Mississippi, starting
a tannery, which business he knew from his German home, in some
place of that state. Here he remained several years, gaining his experience of slavery, and amassing a little fortune. He next concluded
to go to college, feeling himself ignorant of human culture, and
probably hearing the whispers of his genius. The result was that
he went to Georgetown, Kentucky, where was a well-known institution
of learning, and started to take a classical course. Here a deeper
aspiration seized him; he resolved to go to an Eastern school—Brown
University—since in all Western colleges there was and probably still
is a good deal of talk about the superiority of the salt-water institutions.
Another reason he gave for his departure: he had a disagreement
with the president of Georgetown College about the evidences of
Christianity—which act of his was taken as a defiance of authority,
and even of religion. It is manifest that Brokmeyer did not bring
his education from Germany; what he learned came through American
channels; we shall find that when he went back to German culture
and philosophy he started from this country, yea, remained in this
country during the process. Precise years cannot be given for these
various moves in the career of Mr. Brokmeyer; in my time he did

From Denton J. Snider, *A Writer of Books in his Genesis* (St. Louis, Mo.: Sigma
Publishing Co., 1910)

not accurately remember them himself; he was never good at keeping dates in his head, or in his conduct, even those which most intimately concerned him. In a general way, however, it may be affirmed that he reached Brown University, Rhode Island, then under its famous president, Francis Wayland, some time during the early [18]50s. I recollect that he once spoke of attacking before the whole class Wayland's argument for the Higher Law. Thus, he must have come under the direct instruction of the book-writing president, of whom very few traces ever appeared afterward in the thought or word of the pupil. He evidently shuffled off what he was taught by the professors in the college as so much dead material of the dead Past, while outside of these erudite stores he began to drink of the exhilarating stream of the Present, which transformed his life.

Accordingly, I have to believe, though he never acknowledged it, that the great and lasting fact of Brokmeyer's stay at Brown University was that he greedily appropriated, with a genuine hunger of the soul, the New England transcendental movement. He was just ready for that Oceanic swell, and he plunged in headforemost and overhead. Having gotten the idea into that persistent Low-German brain of his, he carried it out to a completeness, yea, to an extremity which made all the Yankee attempts, such as Brook Farm, or Fruit-lands, or Walden, seem pale and diminutive compared to the one grand Titanic outburst. For Brokmeyer's flight from the social order to the backwoods of Missouri, then the distant West, was a far more colossal stride out of civilization than any of those rather timid tiny steps taken by a few transcendentalists in New England. Still he obtained his primal impact from that movement during this time, but he carried it out to its bitter logical result, and, as far as I am aware, is the only one who did so.

He told me that his first questionings were roused by the perusal of certain written products of that period. He did not say what these were specifically; in fact, he was inclined to be reticent in my days upon this whole subject. . . . Brokmeyer spoke and wrote, when at his best, in sporadic outbursts from the depths of his being; his manner, his eye, his word, his thought, came like a flash from a central fire, which was never quite able to get itself outered (or uttered) as a whole. He could, indeed, be very keen and logical; still his logic, even when aflame, was not so much a chain of glowing links as a succession of Jovian thunderbolts separately hurled. One result was that he could never get himself or his things into shape; he would writhe and surge and roar, breaking over limits into the illimitable. Meanwhile he would give a dazzling display of fireworks, yea, blinding to most people, till they learned how to look at him. So in the main he talked when at the top of his mood; so, too, he wrote, though with much less freedom—the giant would rattle his shackles restlessly when chained to a goose-quill. He began perhaps a dozen tales or romances, which, after sputtering and coruscating for a time (chiefly in his talk, by the way), would rush off toward the boundless and so remain unfinished and unfinishable. It seemed to be a necessity of his nature to break loose generally; he reacted against all form and formality, against all conventions and institutions; he became the incarnate spirit, or, perchance, fiend, of Romanticism, and therewith also of transcendentalism, whose grand shout was enfranchisement. Well, enfranchisement from what? From quite everything, enfranchisement made universal, especially liberation from the transmitted fetters of the moral and social order. This is what Brokmeyer proceeded to do when once the transcendental idea had fully entered his soul; he universalized its battle cry of emancipation; he would be completely emancipated, and so he flees to the primeval forest of pure Nature, where he lives alone in his cabin without family, state, church, school, and almost without the economic order, supporting himself chiefly by his rifle and from the wild berries and fruits and nuts of the environing fields and woods. The far-famed flight of Thoreau to Walden Pond was a very tame, inconsequential affair in comparison, hardly a mile distant from his original home and from a civilized town, out of which he could draw supplies for his potato hole, even if he cooked the potatoes himself. Yet this seems almost to have become the typical deed of New England transcendentalism. But Thoreau could form his rather small act and thought in writ, Brokmeyer could not; the result is that the New Englander has stamped his name and fame upon literature, while the Missourian is quite unknown, since his titanic striving for utterance simply burst his pen and spattered the ink about in blotches, incoherent and illegible. Thus the very style of the man enfranchised itself, becoming, indeed, the symbol of his complete enfranchisement—enfranchisement made universal in the woods of Warren County.

But now for a glimpse of the turn in the spiritual genesis of our Mr. Brokmeyer. He has universalized emancipation, has emancipated himself from all—yet not quite from the All. What if now he gets a far-off gleam that he must emancipate himself just from this emancipation, which therein begins to turn back upon itself and apply itself to itself, becoming thus truly universal? Yes, something of that sort is coming, has to come, if the process be carried to its full circle. Such is verily the new emancipation, namely, from

Former rectory of the First *Freie Gemeinde* school. 1318 Hebert, St. Louis Missouri.
Photo by Fred Whitehead.

Former *Freie Gemeinde* building. Dodier Street and Florissant Avenue, St. Louis, Missouri. By permission of the State Historical Society of Missouri

itself, from its own negative stage into aught positive—the transcension of transcendentalism. In this fresh spiritual deliverance he obtains chief theoretical help from Hegel, especially from the *Logic,* with its keen, double-edged dialectic. . . .

When I became acquainted with Brokmeyer, in 1865, the Romantic, or transcendental, stage had been left behind for several years, and he had made his return to civilization out of the woods. He had become again an institutional man, though he was still unreconciled, both in theory and practice, with morality, which transmitted waif of human development the New Englanders still clung to amid their wildest emancipation, which, in their case, accordingly was not altogether universal, being laden with this prominent exception. But, as already stated, Brokmeyer universalized his emancipation to the last notch, throwing overboard the entire transmitted cargo of the prescribed order, not only institutional, but also moral. Thus he became truly a Titan in his absolute defiance of Zeus and the Olympian rule; or we may mythologize him as a new sort of Polyphemus, solitary in his cabin-cave, a gigantic anarch of the forest. But the Titan possessed the power of recovering institutions, bearing with him in his return many visible scars, yea, bleeding wounds, gotten in his former titanic struggles. Such was his state when I first came to know him, and so he remained essentially, though he had also his own peculiar later evolution. Nevertheless, he sought to conceal, if not to deny, his transcendental period as long as I was acquainted with him; he scoffed at the movement and its leaders, not even sparing gentle Emerson, and ridiculing Alcott and Thoreau, though he had done the same thing as they on a far huger scale. Perchance, however, this was only Brokmeyer's present self laughing comically at his former self, which he had transcended. Still his ironical scoff at Romanticism was itself Romantic, especially when it took anything like a spontaneous literary shape, so that it artfully appeared in its very concealment. He would have us believe, and perchance he tried to make himself believe, that he had always been quite as he stood before us spiritually in 1865 and the following years; and I have to confess that I never distinctly caught the stages of his inner genesis till quite forty years after my first acquaintance with him, when we were both old men chatting together upon old times. This incident, which hit me with all the force of a sudden shock, befell as follows:

According to an entry dated the 10th of August, 1904, Mr. Brokmeyer, as I was talking with him in the back room, broke loose on a new theme, and made an astounding revelation of his early self, which seemed to me like the pouring forth of a long-pent-up confession. "In my German boyhood I was a strict Lutheran, as were my parents, and I grew up nourished by the Bible, which I knew by heart. In Mississippi I became a Baptist and joined [the] church; at Georgetown College I still held to that faith, in spite of my tussle with the president on a religious topic. To Brown I came as a Baptist in good standing, with my letter of transfer, which procured me a membership in the church at Providence. But while there I got to reading on the outside and slowly began to drift away from my former moorings." Here it is at last! Brokmeyer, the defiant, often the profane, and even blasphemous Titan—once a meek and believing church member in good standing! That was the greatest piece of news I ever listened to concerning him. If another person had said that, I would not have believed it. And yet it explains him, it is the hitherto missing link of his evolutionary cycle, which he had never told to anybody else, as far as I am aware, in all the intervening years. Dr. Hall, who knew him at his retreat in Warren County, never spoke of it; Mr. Harris, whose acquaintance with him goes back to 1858, made no mention of it, and doubtless had never heard of it; Judge Woerner, who knew him as legislator in the early 60s, never alluded to any such fact, and was probably not aware of it. All these men were intimates of Brokmeyer before my time and kept up their friendship for him; in their many talks with me about him they never called up the church member Brokmeyer, even as a fable of the past. But this stage clearly antedated his transcendentalism, and was the prescriptive, religious, paradisaical period of his career, out of which he was jerked by his New England experience and whelmed into his negative, damnatory, Mephistophelean Inferno of a time, which was the second, deeply separative stage of his spiritual genesis. This was, indeed, an epoch of separation for him—inner and outer. We have already noted how defiantly, yea, how vengefully he separated from the total social establishment of man and took refuge in a purely individual life with Nature. Still, as he was desperately bent on universalizing himself—such was, indeed, the most coercive elemental trait of his character—he had to react against his reaction, to separate from his separation, which thus begins to turn back upon itself and to undo itself of its own inherent dialectic. Or, to take the favorite metaphor, confounding and self-confounding, which he used to employ for this operation: "The thing swallowed itself, and so disappeared."

Naked Truth Monument. Compton Hill Reservoir, St. Louis, Missouri. Photo by Fred Whitehead.

EMERSON AND ALCOTT IN ST. LOUIS

One day during this same season Emerson came to town for the purpose of giving a lecture. Word was passed around among the philosophers, four or five of whom grouped themselves into a little company, and went to the Old Lindell Hotel, where the distinguished thinker was staying. He came into the parlor and saluted us with that courteous reserve for which he is still so well remembered, and which seemed willing generously to play with us a little while, but always at arm's length. Harris was with us, but for some reason Brokmeyer was absent.

From the start his attitude was urbanely critical. He knew of us as students of Hegel, and after the introductory formalities, he whipped out his rapier and began giving sly but very courtly digs at our Teutonic idol. One of his complaints was very characteristic. "I cannot find," said he in substance, "any striking sentences in Hegel which I can take by themselves and quote. There is no period in him which rounds itself out into a detached thought, or pithy saying or rememberable metaphor." I knew little of Emerson, but I already felt the strong Emersonianism of this point of view. He continued: "I always test an author by the number of single good things which I can catch up from his pages. When I fish in Hegel, I cannot get a bite; in addition, the labor is so hard in reading him, that I get a headache," whereat the philosophers smiled in chorus with the speaker. It was on the end of my tongue to say: "Mr. Emerson, that may be the fault of the head, of the peculiar convolution of the brain"; but I kept silent. Harris took the word, but he rambled; he ran off into things remote and obscure, larded with his Hegelian nomenclature; he became as much of a sphinx to his associates as he was to Mr. Emerson. Even as I write I remember my sigh for a flash of Brokmeyer into that darkness. A lull came, when Mr. Emerson again started the discourse, evidently with a side squint at which he had just heard: "My preference is that the hideous skeleton of philosophy be covered with beautiful living tissue; I do not enjoy for my intellectual repast the dry bones of thought." Thus Mr. Emerson applied to us keenly his own standard of writing, seeking to Emersonize us that afternoon; surely the implication was that we were on the wrong track, that it would be better for us to study Emerson than Hegel, though of course he did not say so. At this point I could not contain myself, though I was the youngest of the set and the greenest at the business. I broke in with youthful rashness: "Mr. Emerson, you seem to deny the right of philosophy as a science to have its own distinctive terminology, as well as mechanics or chemistry. I judge that you regard the sole vehicle of thought as simply literary. But we hold that it must have its own well-defined terms, if it is ever to rise to its true scientific value." The beautiful stylist of New England—for such he is supremely—glanced at me with a condescending smile of courteous contempt, while I with fresh audacity continued: "It would seem impossible to organize philosophy into a system without its special nomenclature. The value of Hegel is his vast organization of thought; this is what we are seeking to appropriate, at least as a discipline. But in order to do so, we must learn to read his language, yea, learn to talk it also. Hegel has fine individual ideas, I think, scattered along on many a page, but these are only little stones which go to make the vast architecture of his philosophic temple. In other words, Hegel's system is what we are working so hard to master—his system of thought as an ideal construction of the universe." I probably did not use these words, but the subject-matter I distinctly remember of enforcing with some degree of ardor. To be sure I did not then know what an awful goblin to Mr. Emerson I had conjured up by that word *system,* horror of horrors, not only to him, but to his kindred transcendentalists, as I had occasion afterwards to find out at the Concord School of Philosophy. Indeed I think I may say that the New England mind as a whole, with its decided individualistic bent, does not take kindly to any systematic formulation of thinking. Certainly its supreme excellence has lain in the other direction, as its great literary lights, headed by Emerson, strikingly indicate. During this little colloquy Harris sat self-occupied, and sphinx-like, he gave no sign of approval or disapproval; he evidently did not wish to repel Mr. Emerson by too strong a statement of our doctrine, especially on points of difference. The rest of our company, if I understood them, rather nodded assent to what I said, as it was only reaffirming what they must have often heard before. Harris was our single New Englander, and had a deeper spiritual kinship with Emerson and with Concord than any of us. I have to think that he was already meditating a return to his native rocks when the circumstances were ripe and his western exile was over. And this is what actually happened years later. It was perceptible that he was then making an unusual effort to win Mr. Emerson, to whom he became next neighbor in Concord not so very long afterwards. But the man I sighed for at that meeting was somebody of a very different order, I repeated to myself internally: "O for just ten minutes of Brokmeyer at his best." Mr. Emerson would have heard some of his much-desired pithy sentences white-hot in their creative glow and enwrapped in a metaphorical tornado which would have whirled him off his feet. He might have appreciated it, but probably would not; for Mr. Emerson had little of the titanic or of the demonic in him, though he seemed once to recognize applaudingly some such quality in Walt Whitman. Mr. Harris invited Mr. Emerson to his home, where the philosophic host read to his distinguished guest some of his productions, notably the one on Raphael's Transfiguration (afterwards published in the *Journal of Speculative Philosophy*), to which the gentlemanly transcendentalist gave some of his courteous applause. So Harris reported to us afterward.

And now it is time to say a little of the visit of the second Concord philosopher in St. Louis during this year of 1866—Mr. A. Bronson Alcott. He arrived early in February, and the organization of the Philosophical Society had been hurried up during the preceding month in order to be ready for his presence. One evening Mr. Harris brought him, somewhat to the surprise of us all, as he was not expected so soon. He appearance was notable: An old, tall, spare man with long gray hair dropping to his shoulders, with pale thin face, in which sat eyes turning their glances often upward—the first impression was that of reverence. There were many gatherings at which he gave his talks. These showed his peculiar art-form, which he called the conversation, and of which he deemed himself if not the founder, at least the best representative. The subjects were manifold, some popular and some recondite; so the sessions might be considered exoteric and esoteric. Before the Philosophic Society he read quite a batch of his more recent Orphic sayings, and let the rest of the philosophers guess what they meant. The first series of these mystic oracles had appeared in the old *Dial,* and had caused in Yankeeland no little head-scratching and some amusement. To this day they have the peculiar power of calling forth flashes of Boston wit, chiefly satirical. The old prophet would read his oracular message in a rather sepulchral voice, as if it were issuing from the sacred cave of Trophonius* himself; then he would throw down the written slip and cry out: "What say you to it, gentlemen?" The Orphic utterance was often dark, tortuous, and riddlesome, yet certainly with a content of some kind. I was interested in seeing how diversely the same thought or perchance the same oracle would mirror itself in those different minds. Some twenty men—only men were present—had gathered

---

*A god of oracles in Boeotia (central Greece) whose shrine was greatly revered in antiquity (Ed.)

into a kind of circle before the new Orpheus, while directly in front of him sat Brokmeyer, with alert, probably mischievous eyes, acting as chief interpreter or perchance as hierophant, though others would add their mite of a word. The conduct of the hierophant that evening had more mystery in it than even the Orphic sayings. To some of them he would give an easy, sober significance, which we all understood; but others he seemed to turn inside out and then to shiver into smithereens. Finally he picked up one which had just been read, and at the fiery touch of his dialectic, set off with his Mephistophelean chuckle, he simply exploded it into mist with a sort of detonation, as if it were a soap bubble filled with explosive gas. Mr. Alcott, who had already begun to suspect that his oracles were made to contradict themselves by some Hegelian process which he did not understand, now grew testy and actually lost his temper, raising his voice to a loud raucous one: "Mr. Brokmeyer, you confound us by the multiplicity of your words and the profusion of your fancy." This was the first wholly intelligible saying of Orpheus that evening, and certainly the most impressive. Mr. Brokmeyer restrained himself and calmly replied, "Perhaps I do." It was evident, however, that if it came to a serious intellectual tussle, the poor old man, thin in thews and in thoughts, would not have a philosophic grease spot left on him. So the prophet and his hierophant had a little clash there in our presence. I must say that Brokmeyer's conduct was teaseful, yea provoking; I do not pretend to have the key of his mood, but he was probably in one of his fantastic Rabelaisian spells during which no mortal could ever quite follow his curvetings. Still the enraged prophet should have remembered that his unruly hierophant was president of the Philosophical Society through whose invitation and support he had come to the city. After this stirring interlude Mr. Harris, always the reconciler in any fight but his own, stepped into the breach and took up the interpretation while the reading went on, though not with its pristine vigor. Still, one of these later sayings caused a good deal of comment as well as surmise: It ran thus, as I recollect: "It requires a Christ to interpret a Christ." Ten o'clock struck, and the discussion had zigzagged about in all sorts of twists and turns above and below the surface. I was quizzing with myself: Has the foxy Yankee prophet just coined this little oracle on Brokmeyer, or on Harris, or on all of us together, with himself visible in the background? I rose to my feet and gave expression to the only remark I made during the evening: "Gentlemen, I may be permitted to state my interpretation of this last saying: its hidden meaning is, in my judgment, that only an Alcott can rightly interpret

an Alcott. That being the case, we all had better now go home."
After this rather un-Orphic deliverance little tidbits of tee-hees fluttered
round the circle as the people sprang up and began to take their
hats, while Orpheus himself looked at me somewhat oracularly, I
thought, and shut impatiently his map of oracles.

As we passed out the door, a legal acquaintance of mine addressed
me laughingly: You turned that whole business into a blooming
reductio ad absurdum. I disclaimed any such purpose, for I had
been not only amused but deeply profited by the session. Indeed,
some of its effects I have borne with me through life. . . .

Mr. Alcott at his best was possessed of an immediate power
of poetic expression, a lyrical brightness which was captivating. But
he lacked all organization of any subject, his talk was a string of
detached observations, often luminous, often rather trivial. He remained nearly four weeks, but this long stay caused a distinct loss
to his reputation, since it became the common remark that he repeated
himself and went backward after the first week. Harris sought to
bolster him in every way, having doubtless the future Concord School
already in view. I shall have to confess that I grew tired of him,
and did not care to hear him any longer, unless Brokmeyer were
present to put pulsing vitality and huge substance into the rather
thin Yankee gruel and always getting thinner. Such a confession may
well reveal my limitation, and it certainly bespeaks my tendency and
perhaps my prejudices. Still we had one important meeting, in which
Mr. Alcott set forth his philosophic message, his esoteric worldview,
to five or six of us who had come together for that special purpose.
He gave quite a full exposition of his doctrine of the lapse of the
soul, from the Primal One, dropping in its descent the various orders
of creation down to matter. It was the Alcottian redaction of the
neoplatonic theory of the universe.

Brokmeyer was present and in his highest vein. He revealed a
wholly different mood from that which possessed him during the
Orphic prelection. His perversely fantastic, secretly upsetting Mephis-
tophelian humor had quit him, or he had quit it, for the most earnest
philosophical discussion of the deepest truth which can engage the
human mind. He was courteous and appreciative, but he showed
the Alcottian lapse to be hardly more than a relapse to Oriental
emanation, which had been long since transcended, while he put
stress upon the opposite movement of philosophy, namely, Occidental
evolution, with its principle of freedom. Mr. Alcott must have felt
that he was in the hands of a giant, certainly the rest of us did.
Still there was no gigantic tyranny which sometimes swayed Mr.

Brokmeyer, much to the injury of his idea and of his manner. I believe that I never saw him afterwards so thought-exalted, and his actions partook of his demonic agitation. I sat next to him, and I still recollect the gleams as well as the clouds which would at times dash over his face at some statement of the talker. A brief record of that meeting I have preserved in a notebook (dated February 1866), from which I shall take an extract: "Mr. Brokmeyer seemed impregnated with thought. He at first rocked in his chair; soon he rose and paced the room; he tore a piece of paper from the window; played with his pencil; so restless a man I never saw before. He was all aglow with enthusiasm. He had a fit of ecstacy if there ever was one. When he spoke it was a pure stream of the brightest thought. His enthusiasm overflowed him like a torrent, overpowered him, carried him away"—and certainly carried me along. When I went home that evening, I was dimly aware of having had in my life an epoch-making experience.

Gradually the conviction kept closing round upon me that I must in some way go to school to Brokmeyer. He had something which I had not, but which satisfied the deepest need of my being. Can I get a drop of it, or perchance, two drops? I must try.

8

Poems

Oliver Wendell Holmes

As one of the most distinguished and versatile figures in the American Renaissance of the 1850s, Oliver Wendell Holmes enjoyed a long career as a Boston Brahmin. Born the son of a Calvinist minister in 1809, Holmes later became a physician, a professor of anatomy, and dean of the Harvard Medical School. Holmes made important contributions to the understanding of puerperal fever, and exposed medical cults in his essay "Homeopathy and its Kindred Delusions." In the late 1850s, Holmes wrote columns for the *Atlantic Monthly*, which brought him fame as the "Autocrat of the Breakfast Table."

"The Deacon's Masterpiece," more commonly known by its subtitle "The Wonderful One-Hoss Shay," was for many decades widely popular as a set piece for memorization and school recitals. It was illustrated by W. T. Smedley and Howard Pyle, and set to music for chorus and orchestra. As a physician, Holmes himself drove such a shay.Though it was probably viewed by contemporaries as a light bit of homespun humor, most scholars now interpret it as a sly and clever satire on Calvinist theology, represented by the shay. The tragic Lisbon earthquake of 1755, alluded to in the poem, provoked considerable commentary and controversy among the *philosophes,* notably Voltaire. The question was, of course, If God is just, why would he permit thousands of innocent people to perish? Just before the earthquake, the great Puritan divine Jonathan Edwards had published his monumental work on *Freedom of the Will,* arguing that God punishes us because of Original Sin, a doctrine Holmes found to be repugnant. In a long, penetrating essay, Holmes declared that "a sermon by Edwards is like a nail driven through a human heart."

Holmes recalled the theological aspects of his own childhood in his "Autobiographical Notes": "The effect of Calvinist training on different natures varies very much. The majority take the creed as a horse takes his collar; it slips by his ears, over his neck, he hardly knows how, but he finds himself in harness, and jogs along as his fathers and fore-fathers had done before him. A certain number become enthusiasts in its behalf, and, believing themselves the subjects of divine illumination, become zealous ministers and devoted missionaries. Here and there a stronger-minded one revolts with the whole strength of his nature from the inherited servitude of his ancestry, and gets rid of his whole harness before he is at peace with himself." In his life and thought, Holmes was clearly in the latter category. There is a striking parallel between the shay and the horse collar, as vivid and homely rustic imagery.

Holmes's detestation of the Puritan is also evident in "The Moral Bully," which has a pungent quality worthy of Pope or Swift. Personally, Holmes retained a belief in God as a benevolent Father, somewhat along Unitarian lines. The last of his literary generation, Holmes died in 1894.

THE DEACON'S MASTERPIECE
OR, THE WONDERFUL "ONE-HOSS SHAY":
A LOGICAL STORY

Have you heard of the wonderful one-hoss shay,
That was built in such a logical way
It ran a hundred years to a day,
And then, of a sudden, it—ah, but stay,
I'll tell you what happened without delay,
Scaring the person into fits,
Frightening people out of their wits,—
Have you ever heard of that, I say?

Seventeen hundred and fifty-five.
*Georgius Secundus** was then alive,—
Snuffy old drone from the German hive.

From vol. 1 of *The Poetical Works of Oliver Wendell Holmes* (Boston and New York: Houghton, Mifflin and Company, 1891)
    *King George II (Ed.)

That was the year when Lisbon-town
Saw the earth open and gulp her down,
And Braddock's* army was done so brown,
Left without a scalp to its crown.
It was on the terrible Earthquake day
That the Deacon finished the one-hoss shay.

Now in building of chaises, I tell you what,
There is always *somewhere* a weakest spot,—
In hub, tire, felloe, in spring or thill,
In panel, or crossbar, or floor, or sill,
In screw, bolt, thoroughbrace,—lurking still,
Find it somewhere you must and will,—
Above or below, or within or without,—
And that's the reason, beyond a doubt,
That a chaise *breaks down*, but doesn't *wear out*.

But the Deacon swore (as Deacons do,
With an "I dew vum," or an "I tell *yeou*")
He would build one shay to beat the taown
'n' the keounty 'n' all the kentry raoun';
It should be so built that it *couldn'* break daown:
"Fur," said the Deacon, "'t's mighty plain
Thut the weakes' place mus' stan' the strain;
'n' the way t' fix it, uz I maintain,
     Is only jest
T' make that place uz strong uz the rest."

So the Deacon inquired of the village folk
Where he could find the strongest oak,
That couldn't be split nor bent nor broke,—
That was for spokes, and floor and sills;
He sent for lancewood to make the thills;
The crossbars were ash, from the straightest trees,
The panels of white-wood, that cuts like cheese,
But lasts like iron for things like these;
The hubs of logs from the "Settler's ellum,"—
Last of its timber,—they couldn't sell 'em,

---

*Major General Edward Braddock (1695–1755) and his forces were overwhelmed by French and Indian forces at Fort Duquesne (1755). Braddock died of wounds received in battle. (Ed.)

Never an axe had seen their chips,
And the wedges flew from between their lips,
Their blunt ends frizzled like celery-tips;
Step and prop-iron, bolt and screw,
Spring, tire, axle, and linchpin too,
Steel of the finest, bright and blue;
Thoroughbrace bison-skin, thick and wide;
Boot, top, dasher, from tough old hide
Found in the pit when the tanner died.
That was the way he "put her through."
"There!" said the Deacon, "naow she'll dew!"

Do! I tell you, I rather guess
She was a wonder, and nothing less!
Colts grew horses, beards turned gray,
Deacon and deaconess dropped away,
Children and grandchildren—where were they?
But there stood the stout old one-hoss shay
As fresh as on Lisbon-earthquake day!

EIGHTEEN HUNDRED;—it came and found
The Deacon's masterpiece strong and sound.
Eighteen hundred increased by ten;—
"Hahnsum kerridge" they called it then.
Eighteen hundred and twenty came;—
Running as usual; much the same.
Thirty and forty at last arrive.
And then come fifty, and FIFTY-FIVE.

Little of all we value here
Wakes on the morn of its hundredth year
Without both feeling and looking queer.
In fact, there's nothing that keeps its youth,
So far as I know, but a tree and truth.
(This is a moral that runs at large;
Take it.—You're welcome.—No extra charge.)

FIRST OF NOVEMBER,—the Earthquake day,—
There are traces of age in the one-hoss shay,
A general flavor of mild decay,
But nothing local, as one may say.
There couldn't be,—for the deacon's art

Had made it so like in every part
That there wasn't a chance for one to start.
For the wheels were just as strong as the thills,
And the floor was just as strong as the sills,
And the panels just as strong as the floor,
And the whipple-tree neither less nor more,
And the back-crossbar as strong as the fore,
And spring and axle and hub *encore.*
And yet, *as a whole*, it is past a doubt
In another hour it will be *worn out!*

First of November, 'Fifty-five!
This morning the parson takes a drive.
Now, small boys, get out of the way!
Here comes the wonderful one-hoss shay,
Drawn by a rat-tailed, ewe-necked bay.
"Huddup!" said the parson.—Off went they.
The parson was working his Sunday's text,—
Had got to *fifthly*, and stopped perplexed
At what the—Moses—was coming next.
All at once the horse stood still,
Close by the meet'n'-house on the hill.
First a shiver, and then a thrill,
Then something decidedly like a spill,—
And the parson was sitting upon a rock,
At half past nine by the meet'n'-house clock,—
Just the hour of the Earthquake shock!
What do you think the parson found,
When he got up and stared around?
The poor old chaise in a heap or mound,
As if it had been to the mill and ground!
You see, of course, if you're not a dunce,
How it went to pieces all at once,—
All at once, and nothing first,—
Just as bubbles do when they burst.

End of the wonderful one-hoss shay.
Logic is logic. That's all I say.

THE MORAL BULLY

Yon whey-faced brother, who delights to wear
A weedy flux of ill-conditioned hair,
Seems of the sort that in a crowded place
One elbows freely into smallest space;
A timid creature, lax of knee and hip,
Whom small disturbance whitens round the lip;
One of those harmless spectacled machines,
The Holy Week of Protestants convenes;
Whom schoolboys question if their walk
    transcends
The last advices of maternal friends;
Whom John, obedient to his master's sign,
Conducts, laborious, up to *ninety-nine*,
While Peter, glistening with luxurious scorn,
Husks his white ivories like an ear of corn;
Dark in the brow and bilious in the cheek,
Whose yellowish linen flowers but once a week,
Conspicuous, annual, in their threadbare suits,
And the laced high-lows which they call their boots,
Well mayst thou *shun* that dingy front severe,
But him, O stranger, him thou canst not *fear*!

Be slow to judge, and slower to despise,
Man of broad shoulders and heroic size!
The tiger, writhing from the boa's rings,
Drops at the fountain where the cobra stings.
In that lean phantom, whose extended glove
Points to the text of universal love,
Behold the master that can tame thee down
To crouch, the vassal of his Sunday frown;
His velvet throat against the corded wrist,
His loosened tongue against thy doubled fist!

The MORAL BULLY, though he never swears,
Nor kicks intruders down his entry stairs,
Though meekness plants his backward-sloping hat,
And nonresistance ties his white cravat,
Though his black broadcloth glories to be seen
In the same plight with Shylock's gabardine,
Hugs the same passion to his narrow breast

That heaves the cuirass on the trooper's chest,
Hears the same hell-hounds yelling in his rear,
That chase from port the maddened buccaneer,
Feels the same comfort while his acrid words
Turn the sweet milk of kindness into curds,
Or with grim logic prove, beyond debate,
That all we love is worthiest of our hate,
As the scarred ruffian of the pirate's deck,
When his long swivel rakes the staggering wreck!

Heaven keep us all! Is every rascal clown
Whose arm is stronger free to knock us down?
Has every scarecrow, whose cachectic soul
Seems fresh from Bedlam, airing on parole,
Who, though he carries but a doubtful trace
Of angel visits on his hungry face,
From lack of marrow or the coins to pay,
Has dodged some vices in a shabby way,
The right to stick us with his cutthroat terms,
And bait his homilies with his brother worms?

Part Two

The Golden Age of Freethought

9

Silver Jack

Anonymous

This anonymous song been has been passed down through the oral tradition of the West. With variations, it is still sung and recited as a poem today. This version is adapted from one performed by Bob Suckiel of Kansas City, Missouri.

I was on the drive in eighty
Working under Silver Jack,
Which the same is now in Denver
And ain't soon expected back,
And there was a fellow 'mongst us
By the name of Robert Waite;
Kind of cute and smart and tonguey—
Guess he was a graduate.

He could talk on any subject
From the Bible down to Hoyle,
And his words flowed out so easy,
Just as smooth and slick as oil.
He was what they call a skeptic,
And he loved to sit and weave
Highfalutin' words together
Tellin' what he didn't believe.

One day we all were sittin' round
Smokin' Burley type tobacco
And hearing Bob expound;
Hell, he said, was all a humbug,
And he made it plain as day
That the Bible was a fable,
And we 'lowed it looked that way.
Miracles and such like
Were too rank for him to stand,
And as for him they called the Savior
He was just a common man.

"You're a liar," someone shouted,
"And you got to take it back!"
Then everybody started,
'Twas the words of Silver Jack.
He cracked his fists together
And he stacked his duds and cried:
" 'Twas in that thar religion
That my mother lived and died;
And though I haven't always
Used the Lord exactly right,
When I hear a chump abuse him
He's got to eat his words or fight."

Now this Bob he weren't no coward
And he answered bold and free:
"Stack your duds and cut your capers,
For there ain't no flies on me."
And they fought for forty minutes
And the crowd would whoop and cheer
When Jack spit up a tooth or two,
Or when Bobby lost an ear.

But at last Jack got him under
And he slugged him once or twict,
And straightway Bob admitted
The divinity of Christ.
But Jack kept reasoning with him
Till the poor cuss gave a yell
And 'lowed he'd been mistaken
In his views concerning hell.

Then the fierce encounter ended
And they riz up from the ground,
And someone brought a bottle out
Which he kindly passed around.
We drank to Bob's religion
In a cheerful sort o' way,
But the spread of Infidelity
Was checked in camp that day.

10

"Mysterious Dave" Mather

Robert M. Wright

Robert M. Wright, born in 1840, was from Maryland, but "took a notion" at age sixteen to go West, where he settled on a farm near St. Louis, Missouri. Subsequently, he went to Dodge City, Kansas, and became a contractor for cutting hay and wood, and hauling grain. Achieving prominence as a merchant, Wright served as postmaster, and then as a four-term state representative from Ford County. Later historians have tended to give "Mysterious Dave" the last name of Mather, instead of Mathews, as Wright has it.

Once upon a time, a long while ago, when Dodge was young and very wicked, there came a man to town, an itinerant preacher. In the present age you would call him an evangelist. Well, anyway, he possessed a wonderful magnetic power, he was marvelously gifted that way; he would cast his spell over the people, and draw crowds that no one ever dreamed of doing before. In fact, he captured some of the toughest of the toughs of wicked Dodge, and from the very first he set his heart on the capture of one Dave Mathews—alias, Mysterious Dave—who was city marshal at the time, said to be a very wicked man, a killer of killers. And it was and is an undoubted

From *Dodge City: The Cowboy Capital* (Wichita, Kans.: Wichita Eagle Press, 1913)

"Mysterious Dave" Mather. By permission of the Kansas State Historical Society.

fact that Dave had more dead men to his credit, at that time, than any other man in the West. Seven by actual count in one night, in one house, and all at one sitting. Indeed he was more remarkable in his way than the preacher was in his.

Well, as I said, he set his heart on Dave, and he went after him regularly every morning, much to the disgust of Dave. Indeed he was so persistent, that Dave began to hate him. In the meantime, the people began to feel the power of the preacher, for he had about him an unexplainable something that they could not resist, and the one little lone church was so crowded they had to get another building, and this soon would not hold half the audience. Finally they got a large hall known as the "Lady Gay Dance Hall" and fitted it up with boards laid across empty boxes for seats. There was a small stage at the rear of the building, and on this was placed a goods box for a pulpit for the preacher. Now whether or not Dave had become infected by the general complaint that seized the people, or whether the earnest persistence of the preacher had captured him I know not. Anyhow, certain it was, he promised the preacher to attend the meeting that night, and certain it was, Dave would not break his word. He was never known to do that. If he promised a man he would kill him, Dave was sure to do it.

It was soon noised around by the old "he pillars" of the church, and the "she pillars" too that Dave was captured at last, and what a crowd turned out that night to see the wonderful work of God brought about through the agency of the preacher—the capture of Mysterious Dave.

Soon the hall was filled to its utmost capacity, and Dave, true to his promise, was seen to enter. He was at once conducted to the front, and given the seat of honor reserved for him in front of the preacher, and Oh! how that preacher preached straight at him. He told how wonderful was the ways of Providence in softening the heart of wicked Dave Mathews, and what rejoicing there would be in heaven over the conversion of such a man. Then he appealed to the faithful ones, the old "he pillars" of the church, and said to them, now he was ready to die. He had accomplished the one grand object of his life. He had converted the wickedest man in the country, and was willing now and at once to die, for he knew he would go right straight to heaven. Then he called upon the faithful ones to arise and give in their experience, which they did, each one singly, and said, they too, like the preacher, were willing to die right now and here, for they knew that they, too, would go right straight to heaven for helping to carry out this great work. In fact, most of them said, like the preacher, that they wanted to die right now so they could all go to heaven rejoicing together. Dave sat there silent with bowed head. He told me afterwards, he never in all his scrapes was in such a hot box in his life. He said he would much rather to have been in a hot all-around fight with a dozen fellows popping at him all at once, than to have been there. He said he would have been more at ease, and felt more at home, and I expect he told the truth.

Finally he raised to his feet and acknowledged he had been hard hit and the bullet had struck a vital spot, and at last religion had been poured into him; that he felt it tingling from his toes through his whole body, even to his fingertips, and he knew he had religion now, sure, and if he died now would surely go to heaven, and pulling both of his six shooters in front of him, he said further, for fear that some of the brothers here tonight might backslide and thereby lose their chance of heaven, he thought they had better all die tonight together as they had so expressed themselves, and the best plan, he said, would be for him to kill them all, and then kill himself. Suddenly jerking out a pistol in each hand, he said to the preacher, "I will send you first," firing over the preacher's head. Wheeling quickly he fired several shots into the air, in the direction of the faithful ones.

The much-frightened preacher fell flat behind the drygoods box, as also did the faithful ones who ducked down as low as they could. Then Dave proceeded to shoot out the lights, remarking as he walked towards the door, "You are all a set of liars and frauds, you don't want to go to heaven with me at all." This broke up the meeting, and destroyed the usefulness of that preacher in this vicinity. His power was gone, and he departed for new fields, and I am sorry to relate, the people went back to their backsliding and wickedness.

11

Why I Am an Agnostic

Robert G. Ingersoll

Undoubtedly the most famous American freethinker of the nineteenth century, Robert G. Ingersoll was born in Dresden, New York, in 1833, the son of a Congregational minister. After working as a teacher, Ingersoll moved in 1854 to Peoria, Illinois, where he opened a law practice with his brother. During the Civil War, he served as the colonel of the 11th Illinois Cavalry of the Union Army, and subsequently was elected state attorney general. It was as an orator that Ingersoll had an enormous impact on American society, not only as a prominent spokesman for the Republican party, but as a popularizer of the concepts of agnosticism in hundreds of small towns and cities. His clear and forthright style was very effective among the common people—workers and farmers—who came by the thousands to hear him. Ingersoll's lectures enjoyed a wide circulation in printed form, and, after his death in 1899, his works were collected and published in twelve volumes. Today, there is a statue of Ingersoll in Peoria, and his home in Dresden is presently being restored as a freethought museum. The following excerpt describes Ingersoll's early years and formative religious experiences.

I

For the most part we inherit our opinions. We are the heirs of habits and mental customs. Our beliefs, like the fashion of our garments, depend on where we were born. We are molded and fashioned by our surroundings.

Environment is a sculptor—a painter.

If we had been born in Constantinople, the most of us would have said: "There is no God but Allah, and Mohammed is his prophet." If our parents had lived on the banks of the Ganges, we would have been worshipers of Siva, longing for the heaven of Nirvana.

As a rule, children love their parents, believe what they teach, and take great pride in saying that the religion of mother is good enough for them.

Most people love peace. They do not like to differ with their neighbors. They like company. They are social. They enjoy traveling on the highway with the multitude. They hate to walk alone.

The Scotch are Calvinists because their fathers were. The Irish are Catholics because their fathers were. The English are Episcopalians because their fathers were, and the Americans are divided in a hundred sects because their fathers were. This is the general rule, to which there are many exceptions. Children sometimes are superior to their parents, modify their ideas, change their customs, and arrive at different conclusions. But this is generally so gradual that the departure is scarcely noticed, and those who change usually insist that they are still following their fathers.

It is claimed by Christian historians that the religion of a nation was sometimes suddenly changed, and that millions of pagans were made into Christians by the command of a king. Philosophers do not agree with these historians. Names have been changed, altars have been overthrown, but opinions, customs, and beliefs remained the same. A pagan, beneath the drawn sword of a Christian, would probably change his religious views, and a Christian, with a scimitar above his head, might suddenly become a Mohammedan, but as a matter of fact both would remain exactly as they were before—except in speech.

Belief is not subject to the will. Men think as they must. Children do not, and cannot, believe exactly as they were taught. They are not exactly like their parents. They differ in temperament, in experi-

From vol. 4 of *The Collected Works of Robert G. Ingersoll* (New York: The Dresden Publishing Co., C. P. Farrell, 1908)

Statue of Robert G. Ingersoll. Glen Oak Park, Peoria, Illinois. Photo by Fred Whitehead.

ence, in capacity, in surroundings. And so there is a continual, though almost imperceptible, change. There is development, conscious and unconscious growth, and by comparing long periods of time we find that the old has been almost abandoned, almost lost in the new. Men cannot remain stationary. The mind cannot be securely anchored. If we do not advance, we go backward. If we do not grow, we decay. If we do not develop, we shrink and shrivel.

Like most of you, I was raised among people who knew—who were certain. They did not reason or investigate. They had no doubts. They knew that they had the truth. In their creed there was no guess— no perhaps. They had a revelation from God. They knew the beginnings of things. They knew that God commenced to create one Monday morning, four thousand and four years before Christ. They knew that in the eternity—back of that morning, he had done nothing. They knew that it took him six days to make the earth—all plants, all animals, all life, and all the globes that wheel in space. They knew exactly what he did each day and when he rested. They knew the origin, the cause of evil, of all crime, of all disease and death.

They not only knew the beginning, but they knew the end. They knew that life had one path and one road. They knew that the path, grass-grown and narrow, filled with thorns and nettles, infested with vipers, wet with tears, stained by bleeding feet, led to heaven, and that the road, broad and smooth, bordered with fruits and flowers, filled with laughter and song and all the happiness of human love, led straight to hell. They knew that God was doing his best to make you take the path and that the Devil used every art to keep you in the road.

They knew that there was a perpetual battle waged between the great Powers of good and evil for the possession of human souls. They knew that many centuries ago God had left his throne and had been born a babe into this poor world—that he had suffered death for the sake of man—for the sake of saving a few. They also knew that the human heart was utterly depraved, so that man by nature was in love with wrong and hated God with all his might.

At the same time they knew that God created man in his own image and was perfectly satisfied with his work. They also knew that he had been thwarted by the Devil, who with wiles and lies had deceived the first of humankind. They knew that in consequence of that, God cursed the man and woman; the man with toil, the woman with slavery and pain, and both with death; and that he cursed the earth itself with briars and thorns, brambles and thistles. All these blessed things they knew. They knew too all that God had done to purify and elevate the race. They knew all about the Flood—knew that God, with the exception of eight, drowned all his children—the old and young—the bowed patriarch and the dimpled babe—the young man and the merry maiden—the loving mother and the laughing child—because his mercy endureth forever. They knew too, that he drowned the beasts and birds—everything that walked or crawled or flew—because his loving kindness is over all his works. They knew that God, for the purpose of civilizing his children, had devoured some with earthquakes, destroyed some with storms of fire, killed some with his lightnings, millions with famine, with pestilence, and sacrificed countless thousands upon the fields of war. They knew that it was necessary to believe these things and to love God. They knew that there could be no salvation except by faith, and through the atoning blood of Jesus Christ.

All who doubted or denied would be lost. To live a moral and honest life—to keep your contracts, to take care of wife and child—to make a happy home—to be a good citizen, a patriot, a just and thoughtful man, was simply a respectable way of going to hell.

God did not reward men for being honest, generous, and brave, but for the act of faith. Without faith, all the so-called virtues were sins, and the men who practiced these virtues, without faith, deserved to suffer eternal pain.

All of these comforting and reasonable things were taught by ministers in their pulpits—by teachers in Sunday schools and by parents at home. The children were victims. They were assaulted in the cradle—in their mother's arms. Then, the schoolmaster carried on the war against their natural sense, and all the books they read were filled with the same impossible truths. The poor children were helpless. The atmosphere they breathed was filled with lies—lies that mingled with their blood.

In those days ministers depended on revivals to save souls and reform the world.

In the winter, navigation having closed, business was mostly suspended. There were no railways and the only means of communication were wagons and boats. Generally the roads were so bad that the wagons were laid up with the boats. There were no operas, no theaters, no amusement except parties and balls. The parties were regarded as wordly and the balls as wicked. For real and virtuous enjoyment the good people depended on revivals.

The sermons were mostly about the pains and agonies of hell, the joys and ecstasies of heaven, salvation by faith, and the efficacy of the atonement. The little churches, in which the services were held, were generally small, badly ventilated, and exceedingly warm. The emotional sermons, the bad singing, the hysterical amens, the hope of heaven, the fear of hell, caused many to lose the little sense they had. They became substantially insane. In this condition they flocked to the "mourner's bench"—asked for the prayers of the faithful—had strange feelings, prayed and wept and thought they had been "born again." Then they would tell their experience—how wicked they had been—how evil had been their thoughts, their desires, and how good they had suddenly become.

They used to tell the story of an old woman who, in telling her experience, said: "Before I was converted, before I gave my heart to God, I used to lie and steal, but now, thanks to the grace and blood of Jesus Christ, I have quit 'em both, in a great measure."

Of course, all the people were not exactly of one mind. There were some scoffers, and now and then some man had sense enough to laugh at the threats of priests and make a jest of hell. Some would tell of unbelievers who had lived and died in peace.

When I was a boy I heard them tell of an old farmer in Vermont. He was dying. The minister was at his bedside—asked him if he was a Christian—if he was prepared to die. The old man answered that he had made no preparation, that he was not a Christian— that he had never done anything but work. The preacher said that he could give him no hope unless he had faith in Christ, and that if he had no faith his soul would certainly be lost.

The old man was not frightened. He was perfectly calm. In a weak and broken voice he said: "Mr. Preacher, I suppose you noticed my farm. My wife and I came here more than fifty years ago. We were just married. It was a forest then and the land was covered with stones. I cut down the trees, burned the logs, picked up the stone, and laid the walls. My wife spun and wove and worked every moment. We raised and educated our children—denied ourselves. During all these years my wife never had a good dress, or a decent bonnet. I never had a good suit of clothes. We lived on the plainest food. Our hands, our bodies are deformed by toil. We never had a vacation. We loved each other and the children. That is the only luxury we ever had. Now I am about to die and you ask me if I am prepared. Mr. Preacher, I have no fear of the future, no terror of any other world. There may be such a place as hell—but if there is, you never can make me believe that it's any worse than old Vermont."

So, they told of a man who compared himself with his dog. "My dog," he said, "just barks and plays—has all he wants to eat. He never works—has no trouble about business. In a little while he dies, and that is all. I work with all my strength. I have no time to play. I have trouble every day. In a little while I will die, and then I go to hell. I wish that I had been a dog."

Well, while the cold weather lasted, while the snows fell, the revival went on, but when the winter was over, when the steamboat's whistle was heard, when business started again, most of the converts "backslid" and fell again into their old ways. But the next winter they were on hand, ready to be "born again." They formed a kind of stock company, playing the same parts every winter and backsliding every spring.

The ministers, who preached at these revivals, were in earnest. They were zealous and sincere. They were not philosophers. To them science was the name of a vague dread—a dangerous enemy. They did not know much, but they believed a great deal. To them hell was a burning reality—they could see the smoke and flames. The Devil was no myth. He was an actual person, a rival of God, an enemy of mankind. They thought that the important business of this life was to save your soul—that all should resist and scorn the pleasures of sense, and keep their eyes steadily fixed on the golden gate of the New Jerusalem. They were unbalanced, emotional, hysterical, bigoted, hateful, loving, and insane. They really believed the Bible to be the actual word of God—a book without mistake or contradiction. They called its cruelties, justice—its absurdities, mysteries—its miracles, facts, and the idiotic passages were regarded as profoundly spiritual. They dwelt on the pangs, the regrets, the infinite agonies of the lost, and showed how easily they could be avoided, and how cheaply heaven could be obtained. They told their hearers to believe, to have faith, to give their hearts to God, their sins to Christ, who would bear their burdens and make their souls as white as snow.

All this the ministers really believed. They were absolutely certain. In their minds the Devil had tried in vain to sow the seeds of doubt.

I heard hundreds of these evangelical sermons—heard hundreds of the most fearful and vivid descriptions of the tortures inflicted in hell, of the horrible state of the lost. I supposed that what I heard was true and yet I did not believe it. I said: "It is," and then I thought: "It cannot be."

These sermons made but faint impressions on my mind. I was not convinced.

I had no desire to be "converted," but did not want a "new heart" and had no wish to be "born again."

But I heard one sermon that touched my heart, that left its mark, like a scar, on my brain.

One Sunday I went with my brother to hear a Free Will Baptist preacher. He was a large man, dressed like a farmer, but he was an orator. He could paint a picture with words.

He took for his text the parable of "the rich man and Lazarus." He described Dives,* the rich man—his manner of life, the excesses in which he indulged, his extravagance, his riotous nights, his purple and fine linen, his feasts, his wines, and his beautiful women.

Then he described Lazarus, his poverty, his rags and wretchedness, his poor body eaten by disease, the crusts and crumbs he devoured, the dogs that pitied him. He pictured his lonely life, his friendless death.

Then, changing his tone of pity to one of triumph—leaping from tears to the heights of exultation—from defeat to victory—he described the glorious company of angels, who with white and outspread wings carried the soul of the despised pauper to paradise—to the bosom of Abraham.

Then, changing his voice to one of scorn and loathing, he told of the rich man's death. He was in his palace, on his costly couch, the air heavy with perfume, the room filled with servants and physicians. His gold was worthless then. He could not buy another breath. He died, and in hell he lifted up his eyes, being in torment.

Then, assuming a dramatic attitude, putting his right hand to his ear, he whispered: "Hark! hear the rich man's voice. What does he say? Hark! 'Father Abraham! Father Abraham! I pray thee send Lazarus that he may dip the tip of his finger in water and cool my parched tongue, for I am tormented in this flame.' "

"Oh, my hearers, he has been making that request for more than eighteen hundred years. And millions of ages hence that wail will cross the gulf that lies between the saved and lost and still will be heard the cry: 'Father Abraham! Father Abraham! I pray thee send Lazarus that he may dip the tip of his finger in water and cool my parched tongue, for I am tormented in this flame.' "

For the first time I understood the dogma of eternal pain—appreciated "the glad tidings of great joy." For the first time my imagination grasped the height and depth of the Christian horror. Then I said: "It is a lie, and I hate your religion. If it is true, I hate your God."

From that day I have had no fear, no doubt. For me, on that day, the flames of hell were quenched. From that day I have passionately hated every orthodox creed. That sermon did some good.

Dives is the Latin word for "wealthy." (Ed.)

II

From my childhood I had heard and read the Bible. Morning and evening the sacred volume was opened and prayers were said. The Bible was my first history, the Jews were the first people, and the events narrated by Moses and the other inspired writers, and those predicted by prophets were the all important things. In other books were found the thoughts and dreams of men, but in the Bible were the sacred truths of God.

Yet in spite of my surroundings, of my education, I had no love for God. He was so saving of mercy, so extravagant in murder, so anxious to kill, so ready to assassinate, that I hated him with all my heart. At his command, babes were butchered, women violated, and the white hair of trembling age stained with blood. This God visited the people with pestilence—filled the houses and covered the streets with the dying and the dead—saw babes starving on the empty breasts of pallid mothers, heard the sobs, saw the tears, the sunken cheeks, the sightless eyes, the new-made graves, and remained as pitiless as the pestilence.

This God withheld the rain—caused the famine—saw the fierce eyes of hunger—the wasted forms, the white lips, saw mothers eating babes, and remained ferocious as famine.

It seems to me impossible for a civilized man to love or worship, or respect the God of the Old Testament. A really civilized man, a really civilized woman, must hold such a God in abhorrence and contempt.

But in the old days the good people justified Jehovah in his treatment of the heathen. The wretches who were murdered were idolators and therefore unfit to live.

According to the Bible, God had never revealed himself to these people and he knew that without a revelation they could not know that he was the true God. Whose fault was it then that they were heathen?

The Christians said that God had the right to destroy them because he created them. What did he create them for? He knew when he made them that they would be food for the sword. He knew that he would have the pleasure of seeing them murdered.

As a last answer, as a final excuse, the worshipers of Jehovah said that all these horrible things happened under the "old dispensation" of unyielding law, and absolute justice, but that now under the "new dispensation," all had been changed—the sword of justice had been sheathed and love enthroned. In the Old Testament, they said, God is the judge—but in the New, Christ is the merciful. As a matter of fact, the New Testament is infinitely worse than the Old. In the Old there is no threat of eternal pain. Jehovah had no eternal prison—no everlasting fire. His hatred ended at the grave. His revenge was satisfied when his enemy was dead.

In the New Testament, death is not the end, but the beginning of punishment that has no end. In the New Testament the malice of God is infinite and the hunger of his revenge eternal.

The orthodox God, when clothed in human flesh, told his disciples not to resist evil, to love their enemies, and when smitten on one cheek to turn the other, and yet we are told that this same God, with the same loving lips. uttered these heartless, these fiendish words: "Depart ye cursed into everlasting fire, prepared for the devil and his angels."

These are the words of "eternal love."

No human being has imagination enough to conceive of this infinite horror.

All that the human race has suffered in war and want, in pestilence and famine, in fire and flood,—all the pangs and pains of every disease and every death—all this as nothing compared with the agonies to be endured by one lost soul.

This is the consolation of the Christian religion. This is the justice of God—the mercy of Christ.

This frightful dogma, this infinite lie, made me the implacable enemy of Christianity. The truth is that this belief in eternal pain has been the real persecutor. It founded the Inquisition, forged the chains, and furnished the fagots. It has darkened the lives of many millions. It made the cradle as terrible as the coffin. It enslaved nations and shed the blood of countless thousands. It sacrificed the wisest, the bravest, and the best. It subverted the idea of justice, drove mercy from the heart, changed men to fiends, and banished reason from the brain.

Like a venomous serpent it crawls and coils and hisses in every orthodox creed.

It makes man an eternal victim and God an eternal fiend. It is the one infinite horror. Every church in which it is taught is a public curse. Every preacher who teaches it is an enemy of mankind. Below this Christian dogma, savagery cannot go. It is the infinite of malice, hatred, and revenge.

Nothing could add to the horror of hell, except the presence of its creator, God.

While I have life, as long as I draw breath, I shall deny with all my strength, and hate with every drop of my blood, this infinite lie.

Nothing gives me greater joy than to know that this belief in eternal pain is growing weaker every day—that thousands of ministers are ashamed of it. It gives me joy to know that Christians are becoming merciful, so merciful that the fires of hell are burning low—flickering, choked with ashes, destined in a few years to die out forever.

For centuries Christendom was a madhouse. Popes, cardinals, bishops, priests, monks, and heretics were all insane.

Only a few—four or five in a century were sound in heart and brain. Only a few, in spite of the roar and din, in spite of the savage cries, heard reason's voice. Only a few in the wild range of ignorance, fear, and zeal preserved the perfect calm that wisdom gives.

We have advanced. In a few years the Christians will become—let us hope—humane and sensible enough to deny the dogma that fills the endless years with pain. They ought to know now that this dogma is utterly inconsistent with the wisdom, the justice, the goodness of their God. They ought to know that their belief in hell gives to the Holy Ghost—the Dove—the beak of a vulture, and fills the mouth of the Lamb of God with the fangs of a viper.

12

The West Turning Infidel

"W."

The influential *Blue Grass Blade* was founded by Charles C. Moore (1837–1906) in Lexington, Kentucky, in 1884. Moore later moved it to Cincinnati, and then back to Lexington. Like other freethought editors, Moore faced charges of publishing obscenity, for which he was convicted in 1899 and sent to prison. He described this experience in his autobiography, *Behind the Bars: 31498*, following his release. Afterward, the *Blade* appeared at irregular intervals until the early 1900s.

The correspondence columns of most freethought newspapers make for lively reading, and indicate the broad geographical extent of freethinking individuals across the United States. Though "W." tries to make a case that the employment and social standing of the infidel is not jeopardized by his lack of religious belief, he appears to find it prudent not to identify himself further.

Rev. John Watson (Ian Maclaren), the celebrated Scotch preacher and novelist, who is making a tour of this country, has this to say of our great West:

From *The Freethought Ideal,* June 15, 1899

I defy any man to go through that great Western land and not
be impressed with the wonderful future that lies there, not only
in the marvelous possibilities that are of nature herself, but in man,
humanity. There lies the strength of your country. Not only is brawn
and strength and indomitable will impressed on those people of
the far western states, but their growing thought, increasing intellect
and a desire to learn, to conquer the secrets of society as well
as nature. The tendency to materialism, however, is the one serious
drawback to the situation. Churches are fast losing their hold upon
the people. Sunday is losing its beautiful significance, and is a day
of rest no longer, far less a day of worship. The gospel is being
supplanted by faith in self. The result is strong character, but a
lack of finer sensibilities. The outcome of it all is through natural
causes, and the remedy for it is strong-minded men to teach pure
faith, not to preach doctrines or lay down dogmatic laws but to
implant in those minds a faith they can appreciate. Let them be
talked to by men of breadth and liberality. There is work to be
done out there. Important work it is, too. It should be done at
once for again I say, the strength of the states lies west. The resources
of the country lie there both in men and natural wealth. Cultivate
both, they [are] worthy of cultivation.

The principle points to be noted in the above are, that the strength
of the country lies in the West—that the intellectual drift of the people
is towards materialism—that the churches are fast losing their hold
upon the people, that the religious Sunday is dying out, that faith
in self is supplanting faith in Jesus, that strong character is taking
the place of finer sensibilities—that is, religious emotion.

What with the governor of New Hampshire declaring that religion
is dying out in the East, and this great foreign preacher is telling
us that the West is drifting to materialism and strong character, why
should any Infidel be afraid to speak out and make his belief known?

If every freethinker in this country would boldly express his sen-
timents, Christians would be compelled to look up to us. They would
be as cautious how they arraign us as we are now to oppose them.
They would fear that they would lose our trade, even as we now
keep silence lest we lose their patronage. We should not wait for preachers to tell us that the country is going to materialism. We should
assert our own individuality and impart the information ourselves.

It is no disgrace to say you are an Infidel. Say it and say it
proudly. To be known as an Infidel is not nearly so dangerous as
many im aine. If you come out boldly and manfully about it, the
masses will respect you and your trade will suffer but little.

Last week the Supreme Medical Examiner of a great Fraternal Insurance company for which I am local medical examiner, visited me for several days. In the course of one of our talks he said: "Doctor, to what church do you belong?" I judged that he was a pious man, and my first thought was to say, "Well, I was raised a Methodist"; but then again I thought, why should I be evasive just for policy, and I replied: "I am happy to say that I belong to the big church, the church of the world, the church to which fifty out of the seventy millions of people in this country belong. I am an Infidel, an uncompromising Infidel. Now to what church do you belong?

"Well," he said, "I am a Methodist!" "And are you not just a little bit ashamed of it?" said I. "In this day of enlightenment and progress are you fully in accord with your best reason, when you say you are a Methodist?" The conversation that followed proved that he was almost as much a heretic as myself, and he respected my frankness, though the bold admission at first shocked him. He was unaccustomed to hear men speak out in such manner, but I was glad I did, for he liked to talk on that subject when he met a man with whom he could freely converse.

I will admit, my frankness might have cost me my position with the company, but it didn't. The fact is that a man's trade is not greatly affected nowadays by the open declaration of Infidel views.

Why should it when "faith in self," as Ian MacLaren says, "is supplanting faith in Christ"; when Infidelity is making "strong character." Is not strong character without the finer sensibilities, far preferable to a weak character with the finer sensibilities?

13

Editorials Condemning Censorship

Lois Waisbrooker

Lois Waisbrooker, born in 1826 to a working class family, had little formal schooling, and labored as a domestic servant. She later recalled: "I have worked in people's kitchens year in and year out when I never knew what it was to be rested." She became a teacher in black schools, then an activist in the women's rights, free love, and spiritualist movements after the Civil War. "I never was popular," she remembered. "When I first began to act as an itinerant speaker, my work was mostly done in back neighborhoods in school houses among people who could gather my life force but could give me very little in exchange." She soon published several pamphlets and books, and Ezra Heywood remembered meeting her for the first time at an 1875 convention: "I met what seemed to be a Roman Sibyl, Scott's Meg Merrilies, enacted by Charlotte Cushman, Margaret Fuller, and Sojourner Truth rolled into one. I sat in a pew looking into her eyes and listening to what seemed to be her talking, awhile, when she rose, went up the aisle, mounted the platform, and the tall, angular, weird, quaint kind of a she Abraham Lincoln was introduced to the audience as 'Lois Waisbrooker.' "

In 1891 Moses Harman,* editor of the anarchist weekly *Lucifer the Light-Bearer,* published out of Topeka, Kansas (and previously from Valley Falls), asked her to serve as co-editor because he was passing

---

*See selection 18 of this volume.

through a series of trials and jail sentences for publishing obscene literature. Harman had welcomed correspondence on a wide range of subjects, including, as time went on, letters revealing spouse abuse in the most intimate details, which aroused the antagonism of postal authorities. During a period when Harman was in jail, Waisbrooker published a section of a U.S. Department of Agriculture book on diseases of the horse, comparing it to a passage from one of the objectionable letters. The post office then confiscated the entire issue, returning it only after protests. This entire dispute has come to be known as the Horse Penis Affair. Waisbrooker published subsequent issues of *Lucifer* under an ornate streamer on the front page: "Published under Government Censorship." She later moved to an anarchist community at Home, Washington, where, in 1902, she was convicted and fined for again publishing obscenity. Lois Waisbrooker died in 1909, after publishing her final article, "The Curse of Christian Morality."

A DIVIDED HOUSE

It is said: "A house divided against itself cannot stand." What then shall we think of the condition of things at Washington at the present time, the head of one governmental department defying the law that it is the business of the head of another department to enforce?

In the extract taken from the *Arena,* the editor says of the proposed law now under consideration: "Under this law," etc. Mr. Wanamaker does not have to wait for the more stringent law in order to have Mr. Rusk don the striped attire, *provided* he can find a judge as much of a "lion" as the one who sentenced the editor of *Lucifer* to five years imprisonment, to act upon the case. It will not do to plead that Mr. Rusk's intentions are good, for in Mr. Harman's case the intention was ruled out.

I presume they will hardly arrest the *Lucifer's* editor if he permits a place in his paper for a portion of that which was mailed to him from a leading governmental department; therefore, I will make an extract or two for *Lucifer* readers. In the special report on diseases of the horse, sent out by the Agricultural Department at Washington, there are pages of description, which, if sent out by an editor in relation to the human generative organs, would give Mr. Comstock and his pharisaical coadjutors spasms, unless they could shut up that

---

"A Divided House," from *Lucifer, The Light-Bearer,* April 15, 1892

same editor inside stone walls. That would stop inquiry you know(?) But to the quotation; I take one paragraph of five on page 138:

> As the result of kicks or blows, or of forcible striking of the yard on the thighs of the mare which it has failed to enter, the penis may become the seat of effusion of blood from one or more ruptured blood vessels. This gives rise to more or less extensive swelling on one or more sides, followed by some heat and inflammation and, on recovery, a serious curving of the organ. The treatment in the early stages may be the application of lotions of alum, or other astringents, to limit the amount of effusion and favor absorption. The penis should be suspended in a sling.

Now compare the above with this from the "Markland letter" published by Moses Harman, and for which a Kansas jury indicted him for sending "obscene literature" through the United States mails, and a Kansas judge sentenced him to five years imprisonment at hard labor and $300 fine.

> A man may stab his wife to death with a knife and they will hang him, but if he stabs her to death with the penis they cannot touch him.

The object of Mr. Harman in publishing the "Markland Letter" was to awaken the public to a sense of the wrongs that wives endure from brutal husbands. Which is the worst, degenerated human stock, or degenerated horse stock, that all about horse generation can be sent broadcast, while the knowledge of human generation is tabooed? The ancient lawgiver, the Jew Moses, put woman on a level with oxen and asses, but it is the work of our modern lawgivers to place her below the horse. Hypocrites! How can ye escape the damnation (condemnation) of the fast awakening people, when they are once entirely awake, and see the enormity of your crimes against humanity!

Another case which illustrates the wrong done to the unborn, and to that society which lawgivers(?) talk so much about protecting. In Chicago about a year ago, a case of "bastardy" was brought into court. The man (brute) did not deny the parentage of the child, but said the woman tempted him to the deed. Now any man who can be *tempted* to make a woman a mother who is as degraded as he claimed she was, will make a woman a mother who could use such language and make such exhibitions of herself—such a man should be confined at hard labor for life where he could never make another woman a mother and the proceeds of his labor should go for the support of his child—the child against which he had committed the unspeakable wrong of starting it on the road to existence. Was this done? Of course not. The fact that she tempted him (if she did) would excuse him in the eyes of *men,* such as lawyers, judges, and the like.

O righteous law, that tolerates such men, and imprisons good and true men for trying to stem the tide of lustful damnation! As to the quotation taken from the book sent out by Mr. Rusk I have not taken the most objectionable of the five paragraphs named, to say nothing of what is found on adjacent pages.

DETAINED

Number 426 of the *Light-Bearer* went to press on time Friday, April 15th; was printed, folded, wrapped, delivered to the postal clerks; weighed and postage paid as usual. Saturday the 16th, the editor was informed by the Asst. P.M.† that the paper was detained in the P.O., by order of the U.S. district attorney, Ady, and U.S. postal inspector Brush. Mr. Brush was seen, also Dept. Dist. Attorney Soper. From them it was learned that the articles condemned by these officials are "A Divided House," on [the] second page, and, on [the] fourth page, the advertisements of Cupid Yokes, "A Discussion of the Social Question, and the Law of Population."

Believing that these men have no moral or legal right to stand between our subscribers and the paper they have paid for and tell them what they may read and what they shall not, we make our appeal to the justice-loving people of the United States, and ask them to rebuke these obscene-minded meddlers in other people's business, and restore to us our natural right of FREE PUBLICATION including the use of the common mails, and to our readers their natural right to CHOOSE THEIR OWN READING. Topeka, April 18, '92.

[Since the above was in type we have asked for and received the condemned issue from the post office, with the postage we had paid.]

"Detained," from *Lucifer, The Light-Bearer,* April 22, 1892
   † Assistant postmaster (Ed.)

14

Letters to *The Truth Seeker*

D. M. Bennett, the founder of *The Truth Seeker*, was born in Springfield, New York, in 1832 and spent thirteen years of his youth as a member of a Shaker colony, where he was placed in charge of the community's seed garden. In 1846, Bennett became dissatisfied with Shakerism and left the community, but his experience in the garden proved useful when he became an itinerant seed merchant. By 1870, Bennett was living in the small Illinois town of Paris, where he commenced a critical exchange of letters about prayer with local ministers, published in the town newspaper. However, after the newspaper refused to print more of Bennett's letters, even while continuing to print those of the clergymen, Bennett became infuriated and started his own eight-page magazine, *The Truth Seeker*, in 1873. After four issues, Bennett moved to New York City, where he believed the intellectual climate would be more congenial. Thereafter, he expanded circulation to about 6,000, along with an extensive book publishing concern, including all the best-known freethinkers of the era. Beginning in 1877, Bennett faced a series of prosecutions for obscenity instigated by the notorious postal inspector, Anthony Comstock. After Bennett's death in 1882, *The Truth Seeker* continued publication under a succession of editors, up to the present day. It printed detailed accounts of freethought tours by such noted figures as Samuel Porter Putnam, and its correspondence columns were filled with remarkable letters providing first-hand accounts of the experiences of freethinkers at the grassroots level across the country.

IN THE THICK OF THE FIGHT

Salida, Col., June 21, 1892

Mr. Editor, Dear sir: Six years ago I was engaged in teaching school in Missouri. When it became known that I was a radical freethinker the "unco guid" literally "froze me out." Myself and wife were twice turned out by Christians from our boarding place in the dead of winter. For this we could not blame them, as they firmly believed in the inspiration of that book which admonishes all believers that "if any man come unto you and bring not this doctrine, receive him not into your house, neither bid him godspeed." From that hour I resolved to have a home of my own, even if it was little better than a dry-goods box. Acting upon this resolution, we came here and settled on a piece of government land no one else would have. By earnest and untiring labor we (for wife has done her share) have literally "made the desert bloom." We have now a home (humble, 'tis true) from which no bigot can drive us because we cannot see the mirage of his dreams. As soon as I get my debts paid, which I hope to do this summer, I intend to devote a portion of my time to the spreading of the gospel of humanity. Let no one deceive himself with the view that the destructive power of freethought is no longer needed. Christianity is *not* dead! Neither does it sleep! Long and bitter will be the conflict before science gains the final victory. It is almost impossible to reach those who most need the light. We need more pioneers, more miners and sappers to work with "pick and crow" at the foundations of the Christian citadel. If the facts that bear against the church, the "terrible facts of history," were universally known, Christianity would die for want of nourishment. All honor to the "apostles of liberty" who are already in the field! I hope in the near future to join your ranks and strike a blow for man.

> The fight for freedom once begun,
> Bequeathed from bleeding sire to son,
> Though baffled oft, is ever won.

Well, we (H. Murray, Otis White, E. R. Naylor, myself, and others) have been stirring up the orthodox camp, and as a natural and necessary result "it smells to heaven." First we had a debate with a lawyer, the only champion of Christianity we could find who

---

"In the Thick of the Fight," from *The Truth Seeker,* June 30, 1892

was willing to "stand up for Jesus"—and he was not a member of the church. Then I published a challenge to any person in the county to discuss the divinity of the Bible. Instead of coming to the scratch like men, one of these Rev. (revenue) gents made a scurrilous attack upon the freethinkers of this vicinity from the "cowards' castle." This moved me to "go out and do battle with the Philistines"; therefore, I delivered my lecture, "Hard Knocks at Christianity," at the Opera House, Salida. To the surprise of myself and friends, the Methodist Episcopal "sky-pilot" who has been "called" to labor in this portion of the vineyard made his appearance, and endeavored to defend the marvelous performance of his master by quoting the spurious passage in Josephus. He also took me to task for asserting that John Wesley believed in witchcraft. So you can see how far advanced orthodoxy is in this community.

We have since been struck by a puritanical wave of Sunday closing and Temperance Reform. The editors of this city wear the Christian gag and collar and refuse to publish anything that "hurts the Christian religion," or I would throw hot shot into the orthodox camp until it became too warm to hold them. I am not able at present to bear the expense, or I would have a lot of handbills struck and distribute them "within the walls."

When I reflect on the condition of man in the ages when superstition reigned supreme—when I consider that this giant evil still afflicts the human race—when I consider the greed, the power, the resolution of the church—when I realize how much I owe to "those immortal dead who live again in minds made better by their presence," I cry aloud, O martyred man! this day, this hour, I consecrate my life to thee! Yours for humanity,

R. WHEELER

CLEANLINESS AHEAD OF GODLINESS

Trinidad, Col. June 29, 1895.

Mr. Editor: Enclosed please find "three of a kind," for renewal of subscription to *The Truth Seeker.* I haven't succeeded as yet in getting the Women's Christian Temperance Union to subscribe for it, but one member of this renowned organization, a neighbor of mine, greatly

"Cleanliness Ahead of Godliness," from *The Truth Seeker,* July 20, 1896

enjoys reading it, and so I hope, through her instrumentality, to obtain the consent of the Union to have *The Truth Seeker* appear in the holy shrine of their "free reading room."

Since the disturber of orthodoxy (Mr. Putnam) was here, your paper has been at a premium. A great many people are anxious to read it, but lack the moral courage to take it in their own name, fearful lest their conduct offend some pious mind. This class of humanity are improving, because a few years ago they would not peruse the columns of a Liberal periodical for fear of provoking divine wrath. God would, in infinite anger, see to it that they had appendicitis or an ingrowing toenail.

Verily I say unto you, Trinidad is a great town—a sort of zoological garden. You find a variety of nationality, not unlike a seaport city, and consequently all forms of religious worship. The Catholic, Baptist, Methodist, Christian, Presbyterian, Congregational, Lutheran, Seventh-Day Adventist, and the irrepressible Salvationist, are all well fed here by credulous, admiring votaries. And, just to think of it! among these holy of holies there live a few for whom Reason has promulgated its emancipation proclamation—a few who have the manhood and womanhood to think for themselves, a few who have peeped under the veil of history, and gathered some damaging truths about Christianity and its terrible career of torture and blood, a few who disbelieve in dreams and the astronomical feat of Joshua, a few who believe that, if the biblical injunction, "Be baptized and be saved," had been, "Bathe semiweekly and be saved," and all theological Santa Claus worshipers as thoroughly imbued with its importance, there would be more health and happiness, and lucrative employment furnished all the unemployed of our land in the manufacture of soap.

E. F. SQUIRES

15

Cartoons

Watson Heston

Though he came to be widely praised as the foremost freethought artist in the United States, surprisingly little is presently known concerning the life of Watson Heston. The main source of information is an obituary which appeared in *The Truth Seeker* in 1905; this informs us that Heston was born in Ohio, circa 1846. In his fortieth year, he began contributing illustrations to *The Truth Seeker*, which were soon collected into *The Freethinkers' Pictorial Textbook*, featuring 185 full-page designs, "with copious citations of facts, history, statistics, and opinions of scholars." The designs were grouped in categories such as "Uncle Sam and the Priests," "Studies in Natural History," "Piety in Our Penitentiaries," and "Some Allegories." The *Freethinkers' Magazine* called it "a most extraordinary publication. We venture the assertion that nothing like it has ever before appeared in this country, and it is very doubtful if another one like it will ever again be published. We must give the Truth Seeker Company the credit of putting the book in the reach of all. At twice the price it would have been a cheap book. Artist Heston as a portrait painter and designer is a wonderful success, and we judge from our own feelings that nearly every Liberal in America will desire a copy of this most wonderful volume." Similarly, the *Boston Investigator* declared: "Mr. Heston deserves to be called the artist hero of Liberalism. He has dedicated his genius to Freethought, and has done faithful and noble work for the cause of right and truth. But the pictures do not make up the whole of this volume. There are nearly two hundred pages of reading matter that serve first as explanations of the illustrations, and secondly as texts to prove the utter falsity of the church's professions and the hypocrisy of those who uphold them. Altogether the book is one of the best weapons against Christianity and the church that has ever been put in the hands of Freethinkers."

The Truth Seeker obituary acknowledges that its connection with Heston was not always smooth: "Mr. Heston had a brilliant mind, and had his execution been equal to his conceptions would have taken a place among the best caricaturists of his day. It was his misfortune not to be docile under instruction. *The Truth Seeker* brought him to New York once that he might attend some art school and improve his touch, but the venture was not a gratifying success, and the 'coarseness' of his work, of which many readers complained, was not modified. He was satisfied with the degree of skill he possessed, and seemed to regard attempt at improvement as waste of strength and time." It appears that Heston wanted to retain the rough, rustic vigor of his art; indeed, the scores of "untrained" artists filling the pages of other grassroots hinterland newspapers of the same period had strikingly similar crude and exuberantly satirical styles.

Around 1898, *The Truth Seeker* discontinued Heston's pictures on the grounds that "though praised, they brought no returns corresponding to their cost." However, his books remained on their lists; by 1900, his *Old Testament Comically Illustrated*, "one of the most popular Freethought books ever issued . . . 400 pages, 200 pictures," was going for only $1.00, and had sold 8,000 copies. Heston did another volume on the New Testament, and both series were also published in a combined volume, *The Bible Comically Illustrated*. For all their popularity a hundred years ago, Heston's books are now of the greatest rarity.

In his later years, Heston did a few illustrations for Etta Semple's *Freethought Ideal*. He died at his home in Carthage, Missouri, on January 27, 1905. "He was not robust," recalled *The Truth Seeker*;

> ill health made him somewhat irritable, and he had a rather impulsive way of expressing his views to and about those who did not agree with him. He made a host of friends among readers of *The Truth Seeker*, some of whom did not prove to be good advisers. He was a genial and companionable man, an able writer as well as artist, and a poet of considerable merit. He was fortunate in being happily married to the woman who survives him, and they never ceased to be inseparable lovers. His work was unique. What he did was

never so successfully attempted by any other man, and had there been a larger field for his labor he might have won fortune as well as fame. No doubt orthodoxy would have paid him well but Freethought has few rewards to offer its votaries. He has passed from a world that did not appreciate him, and with which he was himself dissatisfied. But he left it better than he found it. He did something to lessen the sum total of religious superstition, and to illustrate the benefits of Freethought. It is with genuine sorrow that we contemplate his life, which was embittered by ill health, disappointment, and at times with poverty; and his death, which removes one who was capable of good service to the Liberal cause and other reforms. To his devoted wife is extended that sympathy which is due to all who mourn.

In his biblical illustrations, Heston seized on a simple but effective technique of depicting a scene from scripture as happening literally, and thus appearing absurd. In one cartoon, "Yahweh Gets Mad Again and Slings Filth," God pours garbage, including a dead cat, onto the heads of surprised mortals below. In another, the "Almighty Lunatic" chases and beats a horrified herd of goats. In some, there is an almost Goyaesque quality, as when a mysterious robed woman lifts a torch over a darkened globe, causing weirdly sinister clerical birds and bats to take flight.

Heston had a notable compassion for the poor and outcast. His Jesus—"not Christ but mankind"—is a common working man plundered by church and state, closely paralleling the "Labor Crucified" tableau in S. P. Dinsmoor's Garden of Eden.* The miserable and barren shanties, cabins, and sod houses of the poor are sharply contrasted with the ornate and opulent "houses of superstition." In the heart of the Gilded Age, a demented crowd eagerly worships "The Almighty," an enormous glowing silver dollar mounted on an altar of money bags.

"A Criticism of the Critics" is Heston's response to those, probably including his own editors on *The Truth Seeker*, who chided him for being shockingly crude. His concept of the contemporary world of freethought is one of violent struggle: an army attacks under a black banner inscribed "Death to Freethought"; at the behest of a physician a boy tears down a poster for an Ingersoll lecture; and Freethought is depicted as a pure and virtuous woman, menaced by a sword-wielding mob of priests and puritans, or pounced on by a fierce tiger called Religion. Here and elsewhere, Heston illustrates the world of violent conflicts and contradictions Freethought faced in nineteenth-century America.

---

*See selection 33 in this volume.

Heston's strong sympathies for women are evident throughout his work. His figure of Freethought clearly derives from such typical nineteenth-century heroine models as the Statue of Liberty. Always she is menaced, but always she is steadfast. Her opposite, Christianity, is depicted as a dour Queen Victoria type, trailing devastation and death. In "Coming Out at the Little End of the Horn," a corpulent pope enters the horn at A.D. 1500, to emerge at A.D. 2000 so tiny and diminished that a grown-up Freethought must use a magnifying glass to see him. Even if, as we now approach that date, science and truth have not advanced so far as Heston believed they would, his art retains its power and essential integrity.

Advertisement for *The Freethinker's Pictorial Text-Book*. By permission of the Kansas Collection, University of Kansas Libraries.

THE ALMIGHTY LUNATIC GETS AFTER THE GOATS.

Mine anger was kindled against the shepherds, and I punished the goats; for the Lord of hosts hath visited his flock the house of Judah, and hath made them as his goodly horse in the battle.—Zech. x, 3.

By permission of the Kansas Collection, University of Kansas Libraries

YAHWEH GETS MAD AGAIN AND SLINGS FILTH.

And I will cast abominable filth upon thee, and make thee vile, and will set thee as a gazingstock.—Nahum iii, 6.

By permission of the Kansas Collection, University of Kansas Libraries

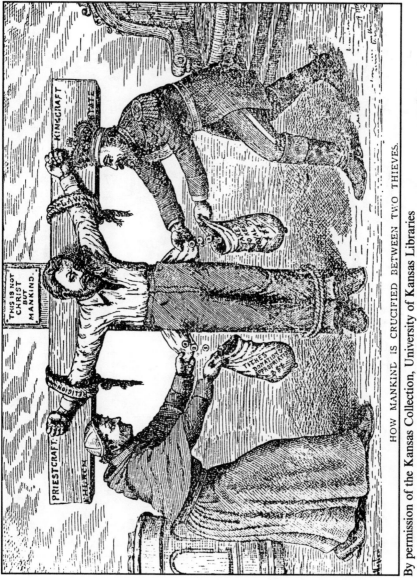

HOW MANKIND IS CRUCIFIED BETWEEN TWO THIEVES.

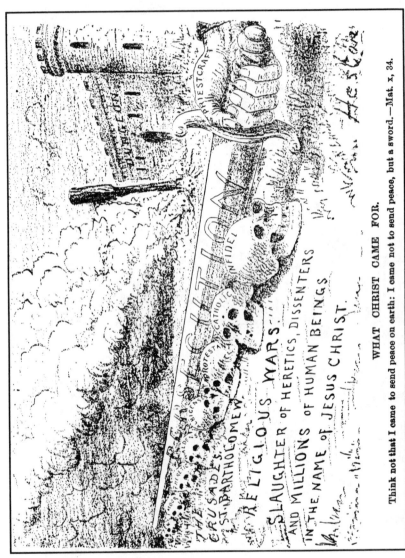

By permission of the Kansas Collection, University of Kansas Libraries

CASTING PEARLS BEFORE SWINE.

WHAT CHRISTIAN MISSIONARIES HAVE TO OFFER THE HEATHEN.

By permission of the Kansas Collection, University of Kansas Libraries

THE TAXED HOMES OF THE POOR AND THE UNTAXED HOUSES OF SUPERSTITION.

By permission of the Kansas Collection, University of Kansas Libraries

By permission of the Kansas Collection, University of Kansas Libraries

THE CHIEF OBJECT OF CHRISTIAN WORSHIP.

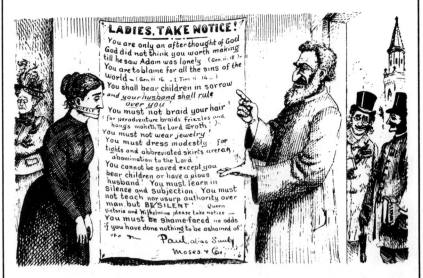

From *The Freethought Ideal* 7, no. 13 (January 1, 1901). By permission of the Kansas State Historical Society.

WHAT CHRISTIANITY CLAIMS.

SOME OF THE DANGERS THAT HAVE MENACED FREETHOUGHT.

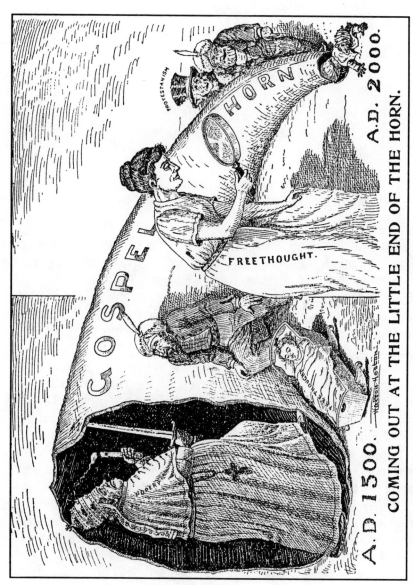

16

Poems of Leisure

G. H. Walser

"We have neither priest, preacher, justice of the peace, or other peace officer, no church, saloon, prison, drunkard, loafer, beggar, or person in want, nor have we a disreputable character. This cannot be truly said of any Christian town on earth." Such was the official "creed" of the unusual town of Liberal, Missouri, founded by G. H. Walser. After serving as an officer in the Union Army during the Civil War, Walser went to Lamar, Missouri, 125 miles south of Kansas City, where he established a successful law practice. He was elected for two terms as a state legislator as well. His reading of Ingersoll led Walser to start a small local group of agnostics called "The Sacred Brotherhood." Lamar's establishment brought economic and social pressure on Walser, so in 1880 he determined to found an entirely new town nearby, on Freethought principles, which he called Liberal. Within three years, Liberal had a diverse, if somewhat eccentric, population of 300 persons. Among the town's institutions were a normal school, a Sunday school for children, a Freethought newspaper, Universal Mental Liberty Hall, and Freethought University. The Reverend Clark Braden, a fire-and-brimstone Methodist minister, who allegedly had once been an "infidel," decided to attack and expose the hotbed of heathenism at Liberal, for permitting dancing and supposed similar "free love" practices. Braden purchased a lot in a town addition and began erecting a church, prompting Walser and others to build a quarter-mile fence right through the middle of town, to keep out the Christians. This feud continued for some years. Walser's downfall began with the dramatic exposure of one Dr. J. B. Buton, whom he supported. Buton, a spiritualist medium, conducted many seances, until one night, after his house caught fire, its secret trap doors, masks, and costumes were revealed. Walser, however, continued in a spiritualist direction, and, in 1902, moved to Nebraska and became a Presbyterian. He died quietly in 1910. While Walser's Victorian style of poetry may seem quaint today, it is representative of his era.

RATIONAL THINKING

I

Our national chief has ordered this day
    Set apart from our daily vocations.
We're ordered to thank, give praise and to pray
    To the Lord for his kind applications
        Of manifold blessings untold.
The rich render thanks for a plethoric purse,
    The well, for their health and vigor of frame;
The poor may thank God, that things are no worse,
    The sick may thank him for not having more pain
        Than their feeble bodies can hold.

II

The preachers thank God and claim that He willed
    Turkeys well fatted and chickens all dressed;
Houses neat furnished and larders well filled
    With luxuries of life, for money possessed
        And other things had for mere asking.
He's thanked for our laws and wealth of our nation,
    For bountiful crops and peace through the land,
For Independence He's paid adoration—
    Our freedom, it is said, came by his command,
        And all other things by his tasking.

From G. H. Walser, *Poems of Leisure* (Lamar, Mo.: South-West Missourian Print, 1890)

III

If preachers for chickens to God are indebted,
    If He's the provider of what they admire,
Who should the chickens thank for being beheaded?
    Who should the turkeys thank for not roosting higher,
        And saving themselves from the pot?
If God gave us peace and plenty of mammon,
    And gladdened our hearts with provisions in store;
Who should the thousands thank dying from famine?
    Who should the nations thank bleeding from war?
        Or a soldier wounded by shot?

IV

If the rich should thank God because they're not poor,
    For their gold in the bank and government bonds;
For ships on the sea and railroads on shore,
    For great lowing herds and rich fertile lands,
        With a life of pleasure and ease;
Who should the poor thank for poverty's wage;
    For hollow-eyed Want, that stands at the door;
For hunger and rags and homeless old age;
    For the kicks and cuffs that fall to the poor,
        And other sweet morsels like these?

V

Who should we thank for the wars of the crusades,
    For the blood that was spilled, for the lives that they cost,
For the woe that marked the dreary dark ages,
    When learning was banished and the sciences lost,
        And their votaries hunted like beasts;
Who should we thank for the Lord's long sable reign,
    When witches were burned and heretics slaughtered;
When the sky was begrimed with fagot and flame;
    When infants were murdered and mothers were quartered,
        To hallow the church for the priests?

VI

If God gives us health and vigor of frame,
    Making us hearty, hale, active and strong,
Who sends our distresses, sickness and pain,

And burdens the millions struggling on,
    Contending with fate and diseases?
Who should the deformed, the crippled from birth,
    The sickly, the blind, halt, helpless and lame,
Praise for their ailments and crosses of earth?
    If God controls all things, who should they blame
    For sending those ills when he pleases?

VII

If God commands plenty and pleasure at will,
    And holds all the good things of life in his hand,
Who brings the scourges, all pestilence and ill
    Luck to the people, throughout the broad land,
    To vex us and curse us through life?
Why force on a being our homage and praise,
    For sending more evil to mankind than good;
For sending the curses of war and disease,
    Earthquakes and storms, cyclones, fire and flood,
    Seasoned with crime, bloodshed and strife?

VIII

A mother must thank God for her prattling babe,
    For the pleasure and joy it brings to her heart;
Then thank him again when its dear form is laid
    In the cold chilly ground and she must depart,
    With her heart in the grave buried there.
Who should we thank when death comes to the door,
    And takes from the circle our loveliest bloom,
And bears it away to be with us no more,
    And renders its memory our saddest gloom,
    And its death an infliction severe.

IX

We could thank with more grace if God would but turn
    His business affairs into more even channels;
If he'd equalize things and give more concern
    To the wails of distress, and less to the trammels
    That curse the whole human race.
If he would but change his manner of doing,
    Make pleasure the rule and not the exception

To life; render us happy and not be sowing
    The seeds of sorrow, woe, strife and contention;
    To bring us down to disgrace.

X

"Render to Caesar the things which are Caesar's,
    And to the Lord which belong to the Lord,"
Is a rule of his own, and very well pleases
    My sense of duty, and ought to accord
        With the author's conception of right.
Then should we e'er meet in the world yet to come,
    I'll risk my whole case on the rule he made here,
And render to Caesar that which is his own,
    Although it deprives the good Lord over there
        Of thanks from my heart here tonight.

XI

Who should we thank for the flag that waves o'er us,
    For the glow of its stripes and its glittering stars;
Who bore it aloft in conflicts before us,
    Who brought us to victory in all of our wars;
        Was it God? No. But our fathers.
Who spilled their blood in Old Revolution,
    And left their bones bleaching on many a field;
Who laid down their lives with patriot's devotion,
    And sank in the conflict rather than yield.
        Was it God, or our forefathers?

XII

Who severed the chains that bound us as slaves?
    Who gave us our rights as a nation of free men?
Whose weatherbeat bones lie in unknown graves,
    That we have the rights of free men and women,
        Was it God? I answer no.
Who sent her last son to the battles' fierce brawl,
    Who kissed his fair cheek and bade him to go
To return to her, only when tyranny's pall
Should cover the form of our country's last foe?
        Was it God? A thousand times no.

XIII

Whose bones dot the sun-scorched fields of the South?
Who met the foe when rebellion had risen?
Who read his own death in the cannon's dark mouth?
Who was it that famished in Anderson prison?
Was it God? My heart responds no.
Who struck the fetters from three million slaves?
Who saved this nation intact, as a whole?
Who rightly deserves our devotion and praise?
Whose name shall be written on Honor's bright scroll?
Is it God's? The world should say no.

XIV

Who furrows the face of the deep raging sea,
And sails every ocean, around and around?
Who causes our flag to float easy and free
In every part of the world to be found?
Is it God? You know it is not.
Then let us not thank him for what he's not done,
Nor force our obeisance upon him again;
'Tis better his name remain ever unsung,
Than those be forgotten who made us free men
And gave us the land we have got.

Written in contradiction of a Rev. Bigot, who asserted that there was no religion in

THE BROTHERHOOD

And no religion thou has said,
    In bitterness of mind,
Can come from noble acts and deeds
    Which in fraternity we find;
No religion where friendship lives,
    Where truth is held most dear,
Where love abides with charity;
    Where is it then, Oh! where?

We seek the widow in her grief,
    And dry the tears up there;
We clothe the orphans in our charge,
    And hunger drive from there;
The anguish of a brother sick,
    We feel, and with him share,
And yet you tell us in cold words,
    Religion is not there.

In all the varied walks of life,
    Our acts we circumscribe;
In social glee, in business strife,
    Excesses are denied.
To fit man for his sphere as such
    Is our great aim and care;
And yet you tell us in your wrath,
    Religion is not there.

Then where, among the scenes of earth
    Is your religion found.
Secluded in some structure made
    To worship God by sound?
Oh, no! my friends, vain, empty words
    Will never catch His ear;
Though you may pray both loud and long
    Is not there, not there.

You compass both the land and sea
    To make one proselyte,*
And when he's made, he's nearer hell
    Than when you gave him light.
You build for God a gorgeous house
    And vend the gospel there;
The rich go in, the poor pass on,
    Religion is not there.

Religion dwells where love abounds,
    Where friendship never dies,
Where neighbor feels a neighbor's pain

---

*"For ye compass sea and land to make one proselyte, and when he is made,
ye make him two-fold more the child of hell than yourselves."—Matthew xxii, 15.

Through pure fraternal ties.
God smiles upon the golden chain
    Which links men near and far
In one great work of mutual aid,
    He's with such everywhere.

Then hail, all hail the Brotherhood,
    Your mission fill—go on,
Press forward in your noble work,
    Though vaunting bigots frown;
Press on! press on and falter not;
    Proclaim it everywhere;
Let every tongue and kindred know
    Religion dwelleth here.

17

Texas and Intolerance: Cranfill Supersedes Christ

William Cowper Brann

William Cowper Brann (1855–1898) was born in Coles County, Illinois, the son of a Presbyterian minister; however, after his mother died when he was only two, he was taken to be raised by a local farm family. Brann left the farm at age thirteen, carrying a single box of his belongings, and worked a variety of jobs until his natural talent for language secured him a position as a newspaper reporter, and then an editorial writer. Though the first thirty-nine years of Brann's life were marked by "the harassing annoyances of extreme poverty," a love of reading richly equipped his mind, which, combined with a fiery temperament, produced "an inexhaustible vocabulary, from which he could always find the words best fitted to convey his meaning at the moment they were most needed, and every sentence was resplendent with an order of wit, humor, and satire peculiar to a style original with himself." Brann moved to Texas, where, after further work on newspapers, he commenced the publication in 1891 of a monthly magazine called *The Iconoclast*, which lasted only two faltering years. Successful engagements as a lecturer convinced Brann to revive *The Iconoclast* in Waco in 1895. Fiercely independent, and sharply critical of many Texas and national institutions as well as outworn attitudes, this magazine soon attained a circulation of 90,000, with subscribers across the country, and around the world.

Paralleling the ferment of the Populist movement of that era, Brann attacked "plutocrats," the Associated Press ("the champion toad-eater of the universe"), and the anti-Catholic American Protective Association (the "Aggregation of Pusillanimous Asses"), as well as the locally power-ful Baylor University, a theological center of the Baptist Church. Dr. J. B. Cranfill, editor of the monthly *Baptist Standard,* was a leader of the anti-Brann faction.

Brann had an unusually colorful, complex, and contradictory per-sonality: he was a self-proclaimed freethinker, but had little use for atheism; he defended Catholics and Jews, but expressed a pathological hatred of African-Americans. Finally, Brann's feud with Baylor provoked a beating and near-lynching at the hands of an enraged mob of students in 1897, and the next year, his assassination on the streets of Waco. Brann's marble monument, featuring a carved profile and a lamp of "Truth," was later defaced by bullets.

A subscriber at Savannah, Ga., sends me a newspaper containing an account of the attempt made by the ministers of Hoboken, N.J., to prevent Col. Robert G. Ingersoll delivering a lecture in that city, and asks, "Can't you touch up those intolerant Jerseyites?" I could, and it would afford me some satisfaction to do so; but it would be firing away ammunition without effect. Professing Christians who believe that God Almighty needs their guardianship—that he can be injured by the ablest agnostic on the earth—are not amenable to reason, and *The Iconoclast* is not so well provided with pearls that it can afford to cast them before swine. When ministers imagine that the religion planted by the toil and watered by the tears of the Immaculate Son of God can be uprooted by a single scoffer; that it cannot stand the fierce light which beats upon Reason's forum and defy all the ballistae and battering rams of human logic; that it must be sheltered from the puny attacks of mortal men lest they prove it a fraud and make it a byword and a shaking of the head to the nations, their faith must be woefully weak or their lives a brazen fraud. Truth does not hide away in dark corners, but seeks the garish light of the noonday sun. It does not fear the attacks of Falsehood, but stands ever in the world's arena, courting the con-flict. The Christian religion is true or it is false. It is of God or

From vol. 1 of *Brann the Iconoclast: A Collection of the Writings of W. C. Brann,* *in Two Volumes, with Biography by J. D. Shaw* (Waco, Tex.: Herz Brothers, 1911)

William Cowper Brann. By permission of the Texas Collection of Baylor University.

it is of the Devil. If true it will stand the severest test. If of God it is indestructible as the law of gravitation. Then why do its ordained defenders take refuge behind long forgotten laws born of brutish ignorance, and with the policeman's bludgeon strive to close the mouth of honest criticism? The poet assures us that "Thrice armed is he who hath his quarrel just"; yet the leaders of the armies of the Lord will not fight, even on compulsion. Instead of meeting logic with logic and the fallible reason of man with the authoritative decrees of God, they answer every attack of infidelity with a tirade of foul calumny, then appeal to the laws of the land to protect them in their pitiful weakness. They shriek "infidel" when it was infidels whom Christ toiled and suffered to save. They howl "blasphemer," when their great Master forgave even those who nailed him to the cross and mocked his agonies. The tactics adopted by the church to crush those who presume to question or dare to differ is making infidels by the million. The day has gone by when men of intelligence were content to close their eyes, open their mouths, and swallow without question every foolish assertion of clerical fatheads. Formerly they builded their Reason on their Faith; now they are grounding their Faith upon their Reason—that infinitesimal fragment of Godhood which burns, more or less brightly, in every human brain. They are demanding that the Christian religion be cast into the crucible where every assumption of science is tried by fire, and either comes forth in deathless splendor or is relegated to the rubbish heap.

Yes, it were a real comfort to "touch up those intolerant Jersey-ites"; but my correspondent must excuse me. There's an old adage to the effect that those who live in glass houses should not throw stones—and Texas can furnish forth more hidebound dogmatists, narrow-brained bigots, and intolerant fanatics in proportion to population than can any other section of these United States. That is why *The Iconoclast* located in Texas. It came, not to call the righteous, but sinners to repentance. When it has thoroughly reformed the Texas ministry it will be time enough for it to tackle that of other states. We are somewhat inclined to sneer at the old-time Puritans of New England and the exuberant cranks of Kansas. Ever and anon some able editor mounts to the roof garden of his donjon keep and thanks God that we are not as other people; but the cold hard fact remains that Massachusetts and Kansas combined cannot furnish so large a contingent whom it were unsafe to trust with power to persecute for religious opinion's sake. Of course Texas has many as broad-gauged and progressive people as any land or clime can boast; but she is cursed with a grand army of Me-and-god creatures of the Cranfillian type, who would, if invested with plenary power, establish a strict censorship of the press and permit nothing to be published that was not considered ultra-orthodox—that did not begin with hypocritical groans and end with blasphemous "amens"; who would require Jews and Catholics to recant on pain of death and place heretics under harrows of iron. In most states the church has made grand progress, broadened, become more tolerant, more Christ-like—calling science, art, and education to its aid while casting nonessentials aside; has realized that

> New occasions teach new duties,
>   Time makes ancient good uncouth;
> They must upward still and onward
>   Who would keep abreast of truth.

But the Texas division seems to have become hopelessly stuck in the Serbonian bogs of a brainless bigotry. It is not content to care for the spiritual welfare of man, but insists upon usurping the functions of the state and providing for his temporal well-being also. It would make him devout, not by God's love, but by due process of law. Having made it a criminal offense for him to pursue his usual vocation on Emperor Constantine's "holy Sabbath," it now aspires to close all fairs and other places of instruction on that day, and we may soon expect it to send a constable after those who fail to attend divine service and cannot furnish a doctor's certificate of inability so to do. It has banded itself together in a political party with the avowed purpose of dictating what man shall drink, and will doubtless next prescribe the cut of his clothing and limit his library to Slattery's and Sam Jones's sermons, a Protestant Bible, and the *Baptist Standard*. And the most remarkable phase of it all is that Cranfill has become infinitely more sacred than Christ, the political tenets of the church militant holier than the Ten Commandments. You may declare the Garden of Eden episode a myth, and even hint that the Immaculate Conception is but an old pagan legend in a new dress, and be allowed to live; but one doubt regarding the efficiency of Prohibition were sufficient to damn you, while to suggest that either Cranfill, Jones, or Slattery are out for the long green and have as little religion as a rabbit, were rankest blasphemy—a sin against the Holy Ghost.

Fortunately the liberal element dominates in Texas, as it does in every civilized country, and the fiendish wolf of fanaticism can only tug at its chain and show its venomous teeth. Not being permitted to put men and women to the torture for uttering their honest convictions in a land of so-called religious liberty; to flay them alive for daring to dissent from some ridiculous dogma cooked up by half-crazed dunderheads during the Dark Ages; to drag them at the cart's tail and bore their tongues with hot irons in the name of a beneficent Deity, these professed followers of the Man of Galilee resort to sneaking

Advertisement for Brann's *Iconoclast*

boycotts, petty annoyances, and cowardly calumnies. They prove in every way possible that their hearts, instead of being full to overflowing with the grace of God and the catholic charity of Christ, are bitter little pools in whose poisonous waters and fetid scum writhe and wriggle unclean reptiles such as Dante saw in the desolate regions of the damned. That the picture is not overdrawn everyone who has chanced to provoke the ire of the ultra-religious element of Texas knows too well. It were equivalent to invading a den of rattlesnakes or stirring up a rabid skunk. Tom Paine was a devout Deist. At the shrine of the Most High God he humbly bowed the knee. He never penned an irreligious line nor uttered an immoral sentiment. He was an intellectual Colossus, towering head and shoulders above even the Titans of his time. He was the unfaltering champion of freedom, the guide, philosopher, and friend of the newborn nation. But for his fearless pen, whose path of fire led on to liberty, the sword of Washington might have slumbered in its sheath. Paine did more than all the preachers of his day to nerve the eagle's wing for its imperial flight—to fling Freedom's banner, like a burst of glory, into the leaden sky. But he chanced to disagree with the orthodoxy of his day, and for a hundred years he has been denounced and damned as an enemy of God and a curse to mankind. Even his dying bed has been heaped with brutal lies, and across his grave still beat and break the accursed waves of "Christian" calumny. In many portions of the county the church has ceased to belittle and belie Tom Paine; but the ultra-orthodox of Texas still insist that he was an atheist and an outlaw who repented of his foul crimes too late to escape the horrors of hell.

The New England Puritans who hanged witches and persecuted Quakers felt that they were discharging a disagreeable duty. They were the creatures of an ignorant and superstitious but God-fearing age, and their cruelties, which have left so dark a stain upon the annals of the Christian church, were performed more in sorrow than in anger. If they inflicted tortures in the name of religion they were willing to suffer death in its most terrible form in defense of their faith. With them religion was a serious thing and morality its synonym. If ignorant they were honest, and if brutal they were brave. They despised the rewards of this world, trampled its frivolities beneath their iron-shod feet, loved God with their whole hearts, and hated a liar and a hypocrite as they did the imps of hell. How is it with the Texas intolerant? Instead of fixing their eyes steadfastly upon the kingdom of God, they are the most persistent seekers after the almightly dollar, the most eager for social preferment and political advancement of any class in the commonwealth. They will give blows, but will not stand to receive them, and instead of regarding with kingly contempt that man who would swerve one iota from the truth to preserve his life, they have made of lying a powerful lever with which they hope to overthrow religious liberty, transform the state into a theocracy, and force freeborn American citizens to submit to the petty slavery of sumptuary laws. Their preachers, instead of serving without salary and looking forward to a heavenly reward as did the Apostles, are ever seeking "calls" to fatter financial pastures. When the legislature is to select a brace of chaplains to insult Almighty God with perfunctory prayers—paid for at the rate of $5 a minute by men glad of an opportunity to earn a dollar a day—there's a wild rush of the sanctified time-servers to the capital city, and the methods they adopt to corral the succulent sinecure would disgrace a railroad lobby or cause a bunco-steerer to blush. They have divorced morality from religion and substituted unadulterated gall for the fear of God. Had the religious fervor of the Puritans dominated the world we would have had men of mistaken methods but of iron mold; should the fashionable politico-religiosity of Texas prevail we would have, to borrow from Macaulay, "the days of dwarfish talents and gigantic vices, the paradise of cold hearts and narrow minds, the golden age of the coward, the bigot, and the slave."

Unquestionably there are many worthy church communicants in Texas, as elsewhere; but they appear to be in a hopeless minority— a few grains of sound corn in a pile of compost. There are broad-gauged men in the Protestant ministry here—men who serve the Lord in spirit and in truth, and by their kindly acts, progressive ideas, and noble tolerance dignify his cause; but they are the exception instead of the rule and are almost invariably unpopular with the great body of church communicants, whose ideal appears to be a preacher "with just ability enough to deceive and just religion enough to persecute." During the recent Prohibition campaign in McLennan county a minister of the gospel, believing sumptuary laws violative both of the spirit of the Christian Bible and the American Constitution, spoke and worked against it. What happened? Did a committee of his brethren in Christ wait upon him and strive by kindly argument to convince him that he was wrong? Did the other preachers offer up public prayers that he be brought within the pale of their political party? Not a bit of it. They poured out upon him the seven vials of their wrath—attacked him with the vindictive hatred of a pack of demons torturing a lost soul, or a drove of mangy jackasses kicking a dead lion. They belabored him from the pulpit and the rostrum, and turned the sectarian press into a reeking sewer that emptied

William Cowper Brann's tombstone. By permission of the Texas Collection of Baylor University.

upon him the foulest filth. These "Christians," these professed followers of the meek and lowly Nazarene, who was all love and charity and gentleness, reached for his vitals with beaks and claws like famished vultures, then served him as the unclean Yahoos did the hapless Gulliver when they found him beneath their roost in Houyhnhnm land. And so they serve every man who declines to permit them to do both his religious and political thinking for him; who refuses to take his place among the intellectual goslings and trail blindly in the wake of some flat-headed old ministerial gander, squawking when he squawks and fluttering when he flies. There are ministers occupying prominent Texas pulpits who haven't originated an idea in forty years, and who would not recognize the Incarnate Son of God if they met him in the road. It is not necessary that a man should possess an iota of intellect to become a popular preacher. In fact, brains are but in his way, for in orthodoxy there is absolutely no room for reason. He needs only to become a prohibitionist—not necessarily a teetotaler—cultivate a sanctified whine calculated to curdle milk, grab the crank of some pitiful little gospel mill, and begin to grind. Let him but select the heavenly turnpike on which he suspects there will be the most travel, set up his little tollgate, do the Jeremiah act, and he'll soon have a mob of sanctified non-entities about him who shame the devil at his own game on weekdays and try to bunco the blessed Savior on Sunday. I have noticed that those who were most fearful that I could commit the awful sin of blasphemy, or "desecrate the Christian Sabbath" by playing ball with the boys or dancing with the girls were the people I had to watch closest in a trade; but those who sat up nights to agonize lest the young be led astray by some awful atheist, could tell the smoothest falsehood with the straightest face; that those who wept the most copiously because the heathen of foreign lands had no Bible, were a trifle backward in supplying the heathen right here at home with bread; that those who cried "awmen" the loudest at camp-meetings were usually expert circulators of calumnies. If we could trade our ham-fat preachers for Good Samaritans at a ratio of 16 to 1, our brass-collar orthodoxy for pure morality, and about three hundred thousand brainless bigots and canting hypocrites for a yaller dog and lose him, Texas would be infinitely better off.

18

Reaction in Kansas

Moses Harman

Born in western Virginia in 1830, Moses Harman grew up in the heart of the Ozarks, near Leasburg, Missouri. An avid reader, he became a licensed preacher in the Methodist Church (South) by the age twenty, and a school teacher. Encounters with traveling Universalists drew him away from Methodism and further into the path of heresy and nonconformist thinking. After witnessing Confederate brutality during the Civil War, Harman finally moved in 1879 to Valley Falls, Kansas, where he became involved with the local organization of the Liberal League.* After practically being driven out of the State of Kansas, Harman moved to Chicago, where he continued his journal. However, he kept in touch with events in the West. Always interested in sexual problems, Harman came to advocate eugenics; he died in 1910.

For a small land-grant college, the Kansas State Agricultural College (now Kansas State University) had a stormy beginning in the late nineteenth century. In February of 1874, a Presbyterian minister named John A. Anderson became president, and immediately fired several professors who favored both a liberal arts and basic sciences curriculum as a foundation for further studies in agriculture. Anderson favored a strictly vocational school. One of those fired, Professor of Science Benjamin Franklin Mudge, had risen to world prominence as a collector

---

*For information on Harman's journal *Lucifer*, see the introduction to the selection from Lois Waisbrooker.

of fossils from the chalk beds of western Kansas; it is said that his dismissal set back the teaching of science some forty years. However, after being forced out of the College, Mudge continued his contributions to scientific advancement, through the support of Professor O. C. Marsh of Yale.

Another controversy arose during the Populist era of the 1890s, in a complex struggle between advocates of Populism and Socialism on the one hand, and supporters of the Republican party on the other. The pro-Populist Thomas Elmer Will had been named president of the College in 1897, and had added new faculty. But several of these teachers were ousted in 1899 after the Republicans returned to political power, and it is this phase of the dispute that Harman addresses here, emphasizing the freethought versus conservative orthodox aspects of the entire affair. As with "W." writing to the *Blue Grass Blade*, it is notable that the local correspondent Harman quotes at length feels obliged to remain anonymous, a fact which in itself suggests both the bitterness of the dispute, and the brutality of the victors, insofar as they were likely to retaliate against anyone associated with Freethought, Populism, or Socialism.

The state, or geographical division, called Kansas, in the middle western part of the United States of America, has been for some years a battleground for the contending forces in the field of politics, of economics, in educational methods, and in what are called moral reform movements. It was there that "populism" as a political reform achieved its greatest triumphs, and now we read that ex-Senator Pfeffer, once a leader of that political faith, has written a series of articles for a leading Chicago daily, to show that populism is now dead and buried. It is in Kansas that the battle between the champions of paternalistic prohibition of the liquor traffic, on the one hand, and the advocates of the right to manage one's own affairs, has been fought out with a persistence and determination never perhaps witnessed elsewhere. In educational matters, likewise, the conflict for mastery between the forces of evolutionary progress and of reactionary or medieval methods and principles, has been persistent and determined. One of the leaders on the side of reason and of progress has sent us a letter containing the following paragraph concerning this ages-old and worldwide conflict as it is now witnessed in the Sunflower State:

From *Lucifer, The Light-Bearer*, June 24, 1899

Moses Harman with baby. By permission of the Kansas State Historical Society.

"The reaction in Kansas goes merrily on. The splendid work, comprehensively radical, being done at the Kansas State Agricultural College is being undone in a ruthless and illegal manner by the party now in power.

"Leedy, the Populist governor, appointed a board of regents of that institution containing some really progressive men, among them C. B. Hoffman, known to many of our readers. This board infused vitality into the preacher-ridden school. It extended the course of agriculture and mechanics and also had the temerity to devote more time to the study of history, sociology, and political economy.

"Progressive men, Parsons of Boston, Bemis of Chicago, Ward of New York, Will of Wisconsin, and others like them were employed. Students were encouraged to think for themselves. Books of even radical tendencies were examined and discussed; the search for truth, no matter where it might lead, was made the prime object. Professors, who under the intolerant spirit which generally prevails at our institutions, would have kept still as mice on religious, economic, and sociological subjects, gradually came out of their shells and gave expression to ideas which were shocking to the plutocrats and to their most efficient allies, the orthodox preachers.

"Thus when the Republicans carried the state last fall and put into the governor's chair a canting, sniveling, goody-goody Sunday School teacher, the reaction set in. In order to get control of the board of regents it was necessary to remove two of the regents. To do this it was necessary to commit perjury, override law, and violate every decency. But such small matters would not lie in the way of the patriots. So Hoffman and Limbocker were removed and subsequently the 'redeemed' board dismissed President Will and Professors Parsons, Bemis, and Ward. These men have legal contracts of employment for a period extending to July 1, 1901. The bosses, however, do not care for contracts, they being in control of the state government and the courts, and can hence soon wear out private individuals who undertake to defend their rights in the courts.

"Other dismissals will no doubt follow, as many of the professors are heretics in religion and politics. The preachers of Manhattan waited in a body upon the board and demanded the removal of Ward, Parsons, Emch, Will, and others, on the ground that these men did not believe in the divinity of Jesus.

"It is also proposed to change the course of study by cutting out much if not all study of sociology and political economy. According to the bosses the farmers' and mechanics' sons and daughters have no business to know anything about the laws that govern society and economics. They should be taught how to produce cheaply and effectively, so that we can compete in the world's markets with rat-fed Chinese labor on the one hand and make millionaires on the other. Thus in the closing days of the nineteenth century do the forces of darkness and reaction raise their reptile heads and show their poisonous fangs.

"Let the Liberals of Kansas and of the nation stand together as a man to destroy the theo-plutocratic party led by such hypocrites and weaklings as McKinley and such bosses as Hanna and Quay."

The Kansas State Agricultural College is one of the largest, and has long been considered one of the most successful schools of its kind in the United States, or in the world. Having been an occasional visitor at that institution, while a citizen of Kansas, I much regret to learn that the good work of the friends of the newer and the truer educational methods is now being nullified by the political leaders elected to office last November. It is sincerely to be hoped, however, that the admonitions of our correspondent will not pass unheeded, and that the "Liberals of Kansas and of the nation will stand together as one man," and will continue the fight until victory perches upon the banner of reason and right.

19

Freethought Editorials

Etta Semple

Etta Semple was an editor, writer, and osteopathic physician in Ottawa, Kansas, from the 1890s to past the turn of the century, publishing first *The Free-Thought Vindicator*, and then *The Free-Thought Ideal*. In part, she continued the tradition of Harman and Waisbrooker's *Lucifer* in that section of the country. When a local opposition paper criticized Semple's loose grammar, she tartly responded: ". . . if upon good grammar depended the betterment of the world, we fear progress would be slow; not that we are against good language by any means, but that often thoughts ignore grammar, and those with something to say often use 'any old word' to express it." She took up a broad range of ideas and issues, including the ardent defense of women's rights, and the plea for more respect to be shown to women in the liberal movement. She demonstrated her sympathy for the cause of Labor in a novel, *The Strike*, published in 1894. Semple criticized college football as "old Druid worship and gladiatorial feats," and wrote: "We feel a little disappointed over the fact that our State Universities here in Kansas both turn out these bloodthirsty semi-barbarian, half man, half monster species."

Despite the criticisms launched against her use of English, Semple's prose became notable for its quick wit, ability to turn a phrase, and clarity of expression. Her paper, co-edited for a time by Laura Knox, also became a vehicle for the expression of her skeptical and anti-religious views. By 1901, each issue of her paper was carrying a streamer on the front page: "A Reward of $1,000 will be Given to the Man, Woman or Child, who will Furnish Positive Proof Of A God, the Holy Ghost, Jesus Christ, (as a savior) the Soul, the Devil, Heaven or Hell, or the Truth of the Bible." She had a large house in Ottawa which served as a "Natural Cure Sanitarium," and while she survived an apparent assassination attempt (another woman being killed instead), her funeral in 1914 was reported to be the largest ever held in Ottawa to that time.

THE FREE-THOUGHT VINDICATOR

To many it may seem strange that the K.F.A.* has brought this little sheet into existence, yet when the facts are brought out there is nothing strange about it. It is just the reflex of Christian tyranny. Last winter, sample copies of *The Free-Thought Ideal* were sent to hundreds of citizens of Ottawa and vicinity. A severe arraignment, containing considerable abuse, appeared shortly afterward in the *Ottawa Bulletin*—a criticism of the principles of this little paper. The article covered almost one column; it was also given a prominent position in the *Bulletin.* In justice to our cause and in defense of *The Free-Thought Ideal* we answered said article. With all due respect we submitted it to the editor and asked that justice be done the "underdog in the fight"; we argued that we had no paper through which to defend ourselves; that we deemed it cowardly to close his columns against us after making the attack; that every fair-minded reader of his paper would be willing to hear both sides, yet all to no avail, the copy was returned and everyone thought we were afraid to answer said article. Again after a meeting here ending Aug. 12, we kindly asked the editor of the *Daily Republican* to publish a set of resolutions passed by our convention to offset a set passed by the First Baptist Church of Ottawa, said resolutions condemning the Santa Fe railroad management for running its own trains, these resolutions appearing in said *Daily.* We sent our resolutions to the editor of the *Daily* but were again met with a refusal. Like all Christian bigots these editors know they have the means of partiality and ofttimes abuse in their own hands, and therefore can afford to crush out anything like truth and justice. Hence this paper.

"The Free-thought Vindicator," from *The Free-Thought Vindicator* 1, no. 1 (August 1895)
    *Kansas Freethought Association (Ed.)

Etta Semple and Laura Knox. By permission of the Kansas State Historical Society.

RESOLUTIONS PASSED BY THE
KANSAS FREE-THOUGHT ASSOCIATION

WHEREAS, the rights of the great engineer of this universe (God) aided by his fireman, Jesus Christ, and conductor, the Holy Ghost, is considered holy enough, wise enough, omnipotent enough to run his train upon the holy day known as Sunday, will allow his sun to shine, his rain to fall, his vegetation to grow, nay, even the entire universe, sweeping, whirling, thundering through space on each and every Sunday. Therefore be it

Resolved, That, as a body advocating free thought, free speech, and free press, we offer to the managers of the Santa Fe system our sympathy in their Christian persecution. And

Resolved, That we wish to accord to the managers of the Santa Fe system the same privilege as the church now possesses, namely, the right of running their own trains on Sunday, providing the people want to travel. And be it further

Resolved, That the taking off of the Sunday trains would be an insult to the traveling public as well as an abridgement of personal liberty.

FREETHOUGHT

At the close of the seventeenth century there seems to have been a great strife raised over the terms "Freethought" and "Freethinkers." The excitement reached a higher pitch then than has been known since. Letters or papers written upon the subject were written in secret and signed "anonymous." The worst feature was that Freethinkers were unable to tell who their friends were; so much danger was embodied in exposure that brother feared to trust his brother and parents their children.

The word Freethought did not mean then what it implies now. Any little doubt or disbelief, or even a desire to investigate the prevailing religion, was then considered Freethought. Many Freethought writers claimed that Protestant religion was one branch of Freethought, or in other words, claimed that the spirit of inquiry had led them out of Catholicism. Years prior to this, however, Protestants were called infidels, and often those more bigoted by their strict

---

"Resolutions Passed by the Kansas Free-Thought Association" and "Freethought," from *The Free-Thought Ideal,* November 15, 1898, and May 1, 1899, respectively

Catholic training called them atheists. In fact, Polycarp was called an atheist—now recognized as one of the Christian fathers, and held in high esteem because of his tenacity in clinging to his infidel or Christian faith. After the period known as the "Dark Ages," namely, the fifth to the fifteenth century, there seemed to dawn gradually upon certain minds that Protestant religion was a step in advance, and if out of a few protests such as Martin Luther and others made there could grow such a broadening of religious views, then there was still room to expand.

Then began Freethought in earnest. Bruno,* Anthony Collins,† and many others were noted Freethinkers. Bruno paid the penalty with his life, having been burned at the stake at Rome February 17, 1600. Collins did not begin his Liberal writing until after the middle of the same century.

The mode of conducting reform then was quite different from what we see now. Never allowing a member of their own family even to know their opinions, they were nevertheless called Freethinkers. Now one has to be outspoken and not ashamed to face the world before he is entitled to the name.

The Catholic Inquisition, embracing a period of about 200 years, begat many Freethinkers, and now some of our boldest and best Freethinkers come out of the Roman Catholic Church. Next came a period of witch burning, which in its turn bred infidels by the thousands. The Christian faith seemed to harden the hearts of its followers so that they resisted all progress—all mental activity—all things which were "out of faith in Christ and denouncing all pleasure and happiness."

It is not generally known what constituted witchcraft 200 years ago. Personal dislike, jealousy, and fear were formidable enemies and used as weapons against witches; but this was not all: if anyone (especially women, for they were like women of today) possessed intuitive powers a trifle out of the ordinary, he or she was suspected and burned at the stake; hence our occult powers were stunted for 200 years and over. We of this age are just beginning to rally from the blow.

We see the same spirit flash up often yet. Mind reading, clairvoyance, finding lost articles, and the art of what some term "second sight," are all subject to being stunted by the tyrannical spirit which

---

*Giordano Bruno. 1548–1600. Philosopher and scientist who championed the Copernican over the Aristotelian universe. (Ed.)

†Anthony Collins. 1676–1729. English deist and rational philosopher. (Ed.)

existed then, only the spirit seems somewhat subdued or modified simply because Freethought has spread; and no more do we fear the dungeon, the rack, the guillotine, or the burning out of tongue and eyes, nor do we fear arrest as of old, and being burned at the stake.

Freethought, then, means liberty of thought, science, mental activity, and justice. It teaches that no written creed is elastic enough to stretch into the next century—it teaches freedom of the mind as relating to religion—it teaches morality—it teaches truth and is willing to go over rough and dangerous paths when in search of it—it teaches its true followers to do good to all, because of the happiness it affords both the doer and the receiver—not for the sole purpose of shunning an endless hell; it offers no reward here or hereafter save the reward of a good conscience. True conscience is being sacrificed every day by a spirit which tends to destroy it, just as our occult powers were destroyed years ago. It is the same tyrannical, bigoted, oppressive spirit. Our consciences are so trained that what is absolutely right is thought of with "fear and trembling." The mandate, "thus far and no farther," "thou shalt not," and "obey my laws," are so constantly before the mind that conscience is almost driven out or crushed. Freethought strives to reinstate conscience—dispel fear—shut out superstition—ease the mind when death comes, and even robs the grave of its terror. It cries out NOW, NOW, NOW! Happiness and joy here on earth now—not waiting until death robs us of our consciousness and nature claims our body to mingle again with the elements as unconscious matter.

AN ENTERPRISING WORLD

We live in an enterprising world. Commerce and manufacturing exist all about. Kansas has long been noted for its enterprise. Ottawa has several factories and manufacturing establishments, some of local note, others of widespread fame. Among the last named is the preacher factory, where they take the raw material and trim it down, and if there is enough left, make a Reverend or Divine of it. They place their trademark upon all goods shipped out of this factory and call it "Baptist." North of here about fourteen miles is another preacher shop. Its trademark is "Methodist." Coming down on the train the other day three bundles of this raw material, now in the process

"An Enterprising World," from *The Free-Thought Ideal,* May 1, 1899

of being cut down, sat in front of us. We have long had the name of mother, also the reputation of trying to mother everybody near us; so acting under this motherly influence we gave each young bundle a copy of the last *Free-Thought Ideal* with a simple request that they put it into their pockets and when at leisure read it. Neither of the three put the papers in their pockets but each sat diligently to work to read the "Women of the Bible." Number one read a few lines, looked back at us with a pair of lovely brown eyes, turned the paper over to the last page, read a few of the advertisements, Paine, Voltaire, Ingersoll, etc., folded the paper up and without looking at us gave it back. Number two read the article through, folded the paper up and jammed it down on the seat, and left it when he got off. Number three read his awhile, shook his head sadly and put the *Ideal* along with his other papers in his bundle. If we had a straw god, and people's opinion of him would injure him, we would set fire to him and hunt up another god. We want a god that is not afraid of infidels. Our god must withstand all investigation, all inspection, all exposure. Our god must be able to prove himself a god beyond all gibberish of a little 2×4 freethought paper. If not, and we fear lest the light of day dispel the misty cobwebs of superstition, then give us a better god.

20

Social and Religious Writings

Mark Twain

Mark Twain's fame today rests mostly on his novels about two Missouri boys, Tom Sawyer and Huckleberry Finn, based on his life in the Mississippi River town of Hannibal, Missouri. Born in 1835, the son of a freethinking father and a devout Christian mother, Twain's mind reflected religious tensions and contradictions throughout his long life. He once declared: "Mine was a trained Presbyterian conscience and knew but one duty—to hurt and harry its slave upon all pretexts and on all occasions, particularly when there was no sense nor reason in it." However, even in his famous novels, there are many passages that should give the attentive reader much to ponder on concerning religion and orthodoxy. Tom Sawyer's Sunday School "prize" is attained through purchase and deceit; Huck's Miss Watson is stultified by pious gloom, and the hilarious camp-meeting passage is followed by the one presenting Huck with the great, epoch-making dilemma of choosing between turning his runaway slave friend Jim in and going to heaven, or hiding Jim and going to hell. Huck chooses the latter, and marks a turning-point in the history of American culture. Indeed, it was for such passages that *Huck Finn* was banned from various public libraries.

Twain evolved a concept of humor as a vital weapon against hypocrisy, corruption, and greed. *The Man Who Corrupted Hadleyburg* (1900) is a bitter and incisive exposure of such vices in a typical American small town. It is sometimes said that Twain became cynical and pessimistic in his old age, but such a view ignores Twain's social activism, including his participation in the Anti-Imperialist League which responded to such events as the U.S. takeover of the Philippines in 1898–1899, during which time he wrote: "I bring you the stately matron named Christendom, returning bedraggled, besmirched, and dishonored from pirate-raids in Kaio-Chow, Manchuria, South Africa, and the Philippines, with her soul full of meanness, her pocket full of boodle, and her mouth full of pious hypocrisies. Give her soap and a towel, but hide the looking-glass." In addition, Twain wrote a searing attack on the Belgian rape of the Congo, *King Leopold's Soliloquy* (1905).

Shortly before his death in 1910, Twain wrote and dictated a number of essays, fables, and enigmatic parables which were suppressed, either by himself, his literary executor, or his family—some almost to the present day. The first selection here is a "creed" written in a notebook of 1887. The second is a version of a famous hymn, inscribed in a friend's book in 1901. The third is from *Letters to the Earth*, a series of amusing "biblical" soliloquies, this one in the "voice" of Satan.

MARK TWAIN'S CREED

I believe in God the Almighty.

I do not believe He has ever sent a message to man by anybody, or delivered one to him by word of mouth, or made Himself visible to mortal eyes at any time in any place.

I believe that the Old and New Testaments were imagined and written by man, and that no line in them was authorized by God, much less inspired by Him.

I think the goodness, the justice, and the mercy of God are manifested in His works: I perceive that they are manifested toward me in this life; the logical conclusion is that they will be manifested toward me in the life to come, if there should be one.

I do not believe in special providences. I believe that the universe is governed by strict and immutable laws. If one man's family is swept away by a pestilence and another man's spared it is only the law working: God is not interfering in that small matter, either against the one man or in favor of the other.

I cannot see how eternal punishment hereafter could accomplish

"Mark Twain's Creed" and "Another Version of the 'Battle Hymn of the Republic,' " from Philip S. Foner, *Mark Twain, Social Critic*, 2d ed. (New York: International Publishers, 1966). Reprinted by permission of the publisher.

any good end, therefore I am not able to believe in it. To chasten a man in order to perfect him might be reasonable enough; to annihilate him when he shall have proved himself incapable of reaching perfection might be reasonable enough; but to roast him forever for the mere satisfaction of seeing him roast would not be reasonable—even the atrocious God imagined by the Jews would tire of the spectacle eventually.

There may be a hereafter and there may *not* be. I am wholly indifferent about it. If I am appointed to live again I feel sure it will be for some more sane and useful purpose than to flounder about for ages in a lake of fire and brimstone for having violated a confusion of ill-defined and contradictory rules said (but not evidenced) to be of divine institution. If annihilation is to follow death, I shall not be aware of the annihilation and therefore shall not care a straw about it.

I believe that the world's moral laws are the outcome of the world's experience. It needed no God to come down out of heaven to tell men that murder and theft and the other immoralities were bad, both for the individual who commits them and for society which suffers from them.

If I break all these moral laws I cannot see how I injure God by it, for He is beyond the reach of injury from me—I could as easily injure a planet by throwing mud at it. It seems to me that my misconduct could only injure me and other men. I cannot benefit God by obeying these moral laws—I could as easily benefit the planet by withholding my mud. (Let these sentences be read in the light of the fact that I believe I have received moral laws *only* from man—none whatever from God.) Consequently I do not see why I should be either punished or rewarded hereafter for the deeds I do here.

ANOTHER VERSION OF THE "BATTLE HYMN OF THE REPUBLIC"

I have read this bandit gospel writ in burnished rows of steel,
As ye deal with my pretentions, so with you my wrath shall deal,
Let the faithless sons of freedom, crush the patriot with his heel.
    Lo, Greed is marching on.

Mine eyes have seen the orgy of the launching of the Sword;
He is searching out the hoardings where the stranger's wealth is stored;
He has loosed his fateful lightning, & with woe & death has scored;
    His lust is marching on.

I have seen him in the watch-fires of a hundred circling camps;
They have builded him an altar in the Eastern dews & damps;
I have read his doomful mission by the dim & flaring lamps—
    His might is marching on.

We have legalized the Strumpet & are guarding her retreat;
Greed is seeking out commercial souls before his judgment seat;
Oh, be swift, ye clods, to answer him! be jubilant my feet!
    Our god is marching on!

In a sordid slime harmonious, Greed was born in yonder ditch;
With a longing in his bosom—for other's goods an itch;
Christ died to make men holy, let men die to make us rich;
    Our god is marching on.

THE CHRISTIAN HEAVEN

This is a strange place, an extraordinary place, and interesting. There is nothing resembling it at home. The people are all insane, the other animals are all insane, the earth is insane, Nature itself is insane. Man is a marvelous curiosity. When he is at his very very best he is a sort of low grade nickel-plated angel; at his worst he is unspeakable, unimaginable; and first and last and all the time he is a sarcasm. Yet he blandly and in all sincerity calls himself the "noblest work of God." This is the truth I am telling you. And this is not a new idea with him, he has talked it through all the ages, and believed it. Believed it, and found nobody among all his race to laugh at it.

    Moreover—if I may put another strain upon you—he thinks he is the Creator's pet. He believes the Creator is proud of him; he even believes the Creator loves him; has a passion for him; sits up nights to admire him; yes, and watch over him and keep him out of trouble. He prays to Him, and thinks He listens. Isn't it a quaint idea? Fills his prayers with crude and bald and florid flatteries of Him, and thinks He sits and purrs over these extravagancies and enjoys them. He prays for help, and favor, and protection, every day; and does it with hopefulness and confidence, too, although no prayer of his has ever been answered. The daily affront, the daily defeat, do not discourage him, he goes on praying just the same. There is something almost fine about this perseverance. I must put one more strain upon you: he thinks he is going to heaven!

He has salaried teachers who tell him that. They also tell him there is a hell, of everlasting fire, and that he will go to it if he doesn't keep the Commandments. What are the Commandments? They are a curiosity. I will them you about them by and by.

"I have told you nothing about man that is not true." You must pardon me if I repeat that remark now and then in these letters; I want you to take seriously the things I am telling you, and I feel that if I were in your place and you in mine, I should need that reminder from time to time, to keep my credulity from flagging.

For there is nothing about man that is not strange to an immortal. He looks at nothing as we look at it, his sense of proportion is quite different from ours, and his sense of values is so widely divergent from ours, that with all our large intellectual powers it is not likely that even the most gifted among us would ever be quite able to understand it.

For instance, take this sample: he has imagined a heaven, and has left entirely out of it the supremest of all his delights, the one ecstasy that stands first and foremost in the heart of every individual of his race—and of ours—sexual intercourse!

It is as if a lost and perishing person in a roasting desert should be told by a rescuer he might choose and have all longed-for things but one, and he should elect to leave out water!

His heaven is like himself: strange, interesting, astonishing, grotesque. I give you my word, it has not a single feature in it that he *actually values.* It consists—utterly and entirely—of diversions which he cares next to nothing about, here in the earth, yet is quite sure he will like in heaven. Isn't it curious? Isn't it interesting? You must not think I am exaggerating, for it is not so. I will give you details.

Most men do not sing, most men cannot sing, most men will not stay where others are singing if it be continued more than two hours. Note that.

Only about two men in a hundred can play upon a musical instrument, and not four in a hundred have any wish to learn how. Set that down.

Many men pray, not many of them like to do it. A few pray long, the others make a short cut.

More men go to church than want to.

To forty-nine men in fifty the Sabbath Day is a dreary, dreary bore.

Of all the men in a church on a Sunday, two-thirds are tired when the service is half over, and the rest before it is finished.

The gladdest moment for all of them is when the preacher uplifts his hands for the benediction. You can hear the soft rustle of relief that sweeps the house, and you recognize that it is eloquent with gratitude.

All nations look down upon all other nations.

All nations dislike all other nations.

All white nations despise all colored nations, of whatever hue, and oppress them when they can.

White men will not associate with "niggers," nor marry them.

They will not allow them in their schools and churches.

All the world hates the Jew, and will not endure him except when he is rich.

I ask you to note all those particulars.

Further. All sane people detest noise.

All people, sane or insane, like to have variety in their life. Monotony quickly wearies them.

Every man, according to the mental equipment that has fallen to his share, exercises his intellect constantly, ceaselessly, and this exercise makes up a vast and valued and essential part of his life. The lowest intellect, like the highest, possesses a skill of some kind and takes a keen pleasure in testing it, proving it, perfecting it. The urchin who is his comrade's superior in games is as diligent and as enthusiastic in his practice as are the sculptor, the painter, the pianist, the mathematician, and the rest. Not one of them could be happy if his talent were put under an interdict.

Now then, you have the facts. You know what the human race enjoys, and what it doesn't enjoy. It has invented a heaven, out of its own head, all by itself: guess what it is like! In fifteen hundred eternities you couldn't do it. The ablest mind known to you or me in fifty million eons couldn't do it. Very well, I will tell you about it.

1. First of all, I recall to your attention the extraordinary fact with which I began. To wit, that the human being, like the immortals, naturally places sexual intercourse far and away above all other joys— yet he has left it out of his heaven! The very thought of it excites him; opportunity sets him wild; in this state he will risk life, reputation, everything—even his queer heaven itself—to make good that opportunity and ride it to the overwhelming climax. From youth to middle age all men and all women prize copulation above all other pleasures

combined, yet it is actually as I have said: it is not in their heaven; prayer takes its place.

They prize it thus highly; yet, like all their so-called "boons," it is a poor thing. At its very best and longest the act is brief beyond imagination—the imagination of an immortal, I mean. In the matter of repetition the man is limited—oh, quite beyond immortal conception. We who continue the act and its supremest ecstasies unbroken and without withdrawal for centuries, will never be able to understand or adequately pity the awful poverty of these people in that rich gift which, possessed as we possess it, makes all other possessions trivial and not worth the trouble of invoicing.

2. In man's heaven *everybody sings!* The man who did not sing on earth sings there; the man who could not sing on earth is able to do it there. This universal singing is not casual, not occasional, not relieved by intervals of quiet; it goes on, all day long, and every day, during a stretch of twelve hours. And *everybody stays;* whereas in the earth the place would be empty in two hours. The singing is of hymns alone. Nay, it is of *one* hymn alone. The words are always the same, in number they are only about a dozen, there is no rhyme, there is no poetry: "Hosannah, hosannah, hosannah, Lord God of Sabaoth, 'rah! 'rah! 'rah! siss!—boom! . . . a-a-ah!"

3. Meantime, every person is playing on a harp—those millions and millions—whereas not more than twenty in the thousand of them could play an instrument in the earth, or ever wanted to.

Consider the deafening hurricane of sound—millions and millions of voices screaming at once and millions and millions of harps gritting their teeth at the same time! I ask you: is it hideous, is it odious, is it horrible?

Consider further: it is a *praise* service; a service of compliment, of flattery, of adulation! Do you ask who it is that is willing to endure this strange compliment, this insane compliment; and who not only endures it, but likes it, enjoys it, requires it, *commands* it? Hold your breath!

It is God! This race's God, I mean. He sits on his throne, attended by his four and twenty elders and some other dignitaries pertaining to his court, and looks out over his miles and miles of tempestuous worshipers, and smiles, and purrs, and nods his satisfaction northward, eastward, southward; as quaint and naïve a spectacle as has yet been imagined in this universe, I take it.

It is easy to see that the inventor of the heaven did not originate the idea, but copied it from the show-ceremonies of some sorry little sovereign State up in the back settlements of the Orient somewhere.

All sane white people hate noise; yet they have tranquilly accepted this kind of a heaven—without thinking, without reflection, without examination—and they actually want to go to it! Profoundly devout old gray-headed men put in a large part of their time dreaming of the happy day when they will lay down the cares of this life and enter into the joys of that place. Yet you can see how unreal it is to them, and how little it takes to grip upon them as being fact, for they make no practical preparation for the great change: you never see one of them with a harp, you never hear one of them sing.

As you have seen, that singular show is a service of praise: praise by hymn, praise by prostration. It takes the place of "church." Now then, in the earth these people cannot stand much church—an hour and a quarter is the limit, and they draw the line at once a week. That is to say, Sunday. One day in seven; and even then they do not look forward to it with longing. And so—consider what their heaven provides for them: "church" that lasts forever, and a Sabbath that has no end! They quickly weary of this brief hebdomadal Sabbath here, yet they long for that eternal one; they dream of it, they talk about it, they *think* they think they are going to enjoy it—with all their simple hearts they think they think they are going to be happy in it!

It is because they do not think at all; they only think they think. Whereas they can't think; not two human beings in ten thousand have anything to think with. And as to imagination—oh, well, look at their heaven! They accept it, they approve it, they admire it. That gives you their intellectual measure.

4. The inventor of their heaven empties into it all the nations of the earth, in one common jumble. All are on an equality absolute, no one of them ranking another; they have to be "brothers"; they have to mix together, pray together, harp together, hosannah together—whites, niggers, Jews, everybody—there's no distinction. Here in the earth all nations hate each other, and every one of them hates the Jew. Yet every pious person adores that heaven and wants to get into it. He really does. And when he is in a holy rapture he thinks he thinks that if he were only there he would take all the populace to his heart, and hug, and hug, and hug!

He is a marvel—man is! I would I knew who invented him.

5. Every man in the earth possesses some share of intellect, large or small; and be it large or be it small he takes a pride in it. Also his heart swells at mention of the names of the majestic intellectual chiefs of his race, and he loves the tale of their splendid achievements. For he is of their blood, and in honoring themselves they have honored

him. Lo, what the mind of man can do! he cries; and calls the roll of the illustrious of all the ages; and points to the imperishable literatures they have given to the world, and the mechanical wonders they have invented, and the glories wherewith they have clothed science and the arts; and to them he uncovers, as to kings, and gives to them the profoundest homage, and the sincerest, his exultant heart can furnish—thus exalting intellect above all things else in his world, and enthroning it there under the arching skies in a supremacy unapproachable. And then he contrives a heaven that hasn't a rag of intellectuality in it anywhere!

Is it odd, is it curious, is it puzzling? It is exactly as I have said, incredible as it may sound. This sincere adorer of intellect and prodigal rewarder of its mighty services here in the earth has invented a religion and a heaven which pay no compliments to intellect, offer it no distinctions, fling to it no largess: in fact, never even mention it.

By this time you will have noticed that the human being's heaven has been thought out and constructed upon an absolutely definite plan; and that this plan is, that it shall contain, in labored detail, each and every imaginable thing that is repulsive to a man, and not a single thing he likes!

Very well, the further we proceed the more will this curious fact be apparent.

Make a note of it: in man's heaven there are no exercises for the intellect, nothing for it to live upon. It would rot there in a year—rot and stink. Rot and stink—and at that stage become holy. A blessed thing: for only the holy can stand the joys of that bedlam.

21

A Portrait of His Father

Clarence Darrow

Clarence Darrow, one of the best-known activist criminal attorneys of the twentieth century, was born in 1857 and grew up in Kinsman, Ohio, the son of a local miller who was both an intellectual and an abolitionist; the family home was a station on the "underground railroad" conveying slaves to freedom in the North. Darrow attended the University of Michigan Law School for a year, and, after being admitted to the bar, became an attorney first for the City of Chicago, then for a large railroad, and, finally, a law partner of Edgar Lee Masters.

Though he became, perhaps, most famous for his searching and relentless cross-examination of William Jennings Bryan at the great Scopes evolution trial in Tennessee in 1925, Darrow also took on many other labor and progressive cases. His philosophy was deterministic, if not almost fatalist; he made penetrating criticisms of contemporary socialist ideas, yet steadfastly defended radicals in many trials. In addition to writing an autobiography, *The Story of My Life* (1932), Darrow published several titles in the Blue Books series under the able editorship of his friend Emanuel Haldeman-Julius. This excerpt is drawn from one of these, *The Wisdom of Clarence Darrow.*

As I grew up, I learned that there are all sorts of people in the world, and that selfishness and greed and envy are, to say the least, very common in the human heart; but I never could be thankful enough that my father was honest and simple, and that his love of truth and justice had grown into his being as naturally as the oaks were rooted to the earth along the little stream.

All my life I have felt that Nature had some grudge against my father. If she had made him a simple miller, content when he was grinding and dipping the small toll from the farmer's grist, he might have lived a fairly useful, happy life. But day after day and year after year he was compelled to walk the short and narrow path between the little house and the decaying mill, while his mind was roving over scenes of great battles, decayed empires, dead languages, and the starry heavens above. To his dying day he lived in a walking trance; and his books and their wondrous stories were more real to him than the turning water wheel, the sacks of wheat and corn, and the cunning, soulless farmers who dickered and haggled about his hard-earned toll.

Whether or not my father had strong personal ambitions, I never really knew; no doubt he had, but years of work and resignation had taught him to deny them even to himself, and slowly and pathetically he must have let go his hold upon that hope and ambition which alone make the thoughtful man cling fast to life.

Often, too, he wrote, sometimes night after night for weeks together; but I never knew what it was he put down—no doubt his hopes and dreams and loves and doubts and fears, as men have ever done since time began, as they will ever do while time shall last, and as I am doing now; but these poor dreams of his were never destined to see the light of day. Perhaps, with no one to tell him that they were good, he despaired about their worth, as so many other doubting souls have done before and since. It is not likely that any publisher could have been found ready to transform his poor cramped writing into print. Whatever may have been the case, if I could only find the pages that he wrote I would print them now with his name upon the title page, and pay for them myself.

It must be that my father gave me little chance to tarry long from one single book to another, for I remember that at a very early age I was told again and again that John Stuart Mill began studying Greek when he was only three years old. I thought then,

From *The Wisdom of Clarence Darrow* (Girard, Kans.: Haldeman-Julius Publications, 1947)

as I do today, that he must have had a cruel father, and that this unnatural parent not only made miserable the life of his little boy, but thousands of other boys whose fathers could see no reason why their sons should be outdone by John Stuart Mill. I have no doubt that my good father thought that all of his children ought to be able to do anything that was ever accomplished by John Stuart Mill; and so he did his part, and more, to make us try.

But, after all, I feel today just as I did long years ago, when with reluctant ear and rebellious heart I heard of the great achievements of John Stuart Mill. I look back to those early years, and still regret the beautiful play-spells that were broken and the many fond childish schemes for pleasure that were shattered because John Stuart Mill began studying Greek when only three years old.

My father must have been quite advanced in years before he wholly gave up his ambitions to do something in life besides grinding the farmers' corn. Indeed, I am not sure that he ever gave them up; but doubtless, as the task seemed more hopeless and the chain grew stronger, he slowly looked to his children to satisfy the dreams that life once held out to him; and so this thought mingled with the rest in his strong endeavor that we should all have the best education he could get for us, so that we need not be millers as he had been. Well, none of us are millers! The old family is scattered far and wide; the last member of the little band long since passed down the narrow road, and out between the great high hills into the far-off land of freedom and opportunity of which my father dreamed. But I should be glad to believe today that a single one over whom he watched with such jealous care ever gave as much real service to the world as this simple, kindly man whose name was heard scarcely farther than the water that splashed and tumbled on the turning wheel.

I started bravely to tell about my life—to write my story as it seems to me; and here I am halting and rambling like a garrulous old man over the feelings and remembrances of long ago. By a strange trick of memory I seem to stand for a few moments out in the old front yard, a little barefoot child. The long summer evening is at hand. Beyond the black trees I hear the falling water spilling over the wooden dam; and farther on, around the edges of the pond, the hoarse croak of the frogs sounds clear and harsh in the still night air. Above the little porch that shelters the front door in my father's study window, I look in and see him sitting at his desk with his shaded lamp; before him is the everlasting book, and his pale face and long white hair bend over the infatuating pages with all the confidence and trust of a little child. For a simple child he was, from the time when he first saw the light until his friends and comrades lowered him into the sandy loam of the old churchyard. I see him through the little panes of glass, as he bends above the book. The chapter is finished and he wakens from his reverie into the world in which he lives and works; he takes off his iron-framed spectacles, lays down his book, comes downstairs and calls me away from my companions with the old story that it is time to come into the house and get my lessons. For the thousandth time I protest that I want to play—to finish my unending game; and again he tells me no, that John Stuart Mill began studying Greek when he was only three years old. And with heavy heart and muttered imprecations on John Stuart Mill, I am taken away from my companions and my play, and set down beside my father with my book. I can feel even now my sorrow and despair, as I leave my playmates and turn the stupid leaves. But I would give all that I possess today to hear my father say again, as in that far-off time, "John Stuart Mill began studying Greek when he was only three years old."

My parents were not members of the church; in fact, they had little belief in some of its chief articles of faith. In his youth my father was ambitious to be a minister, for all his life he was bent on doing good and helping his fellow man; but he passed so rapidly through all the phases of religious faith, from Methodism through Congregationalism and Universalism to Unitarianism and beyond, that he never had time to stop long enough at any one resting spot to get ordained to preach.

My father seldom went to church on Sunday. He was almost the only man in town who stayed away, excepting a few who were considered worthless and who managed to steal off with dog and gun to the woods and hills. But Sunday was a precious day to my father. Even if the little creek had been swollen by recent rains, and the water ran wastefully over the big dam and off on its long journey through the hills, still my father never ran his mill on Sunday. I fancy that if he had wished to do so the people would not have let him save the wasted power. But all through the week my father must have looked forward to Sunday, for on that day he was not obliged to work, and was free to revel in his books. As soon as breakfast was over he went to his little room, and was soon lost to the living world. I have always been thankful that the religion and customs of the community rescued this one day from the tiresome monotony of his life. All day Sunday, and far into the night, he lived with those rare souls who had left the records of their lives and spirits for the endless procession of men and women who come and go upon the earth. . . .

The old preacher, as he stood before us on Sunday morning, never seemed quite like a man—we felt that he was a holy being, and we looked on him with fear and reverence and awe. I remember meeting him in the field one day, and I tried to avoid him and get away; but he came to me and talked in the kindest and most entertaining way. He said nothing whatever about religion, and his voice and the expression of his face were not at all as they seemed when I sat in front of him in the hard pew during the terrible "long prayer."

But my father never feared him in the least, and often these two old men met for an evening to read their musty books, although I could not understand the reason why. After I had gone to bed at night I heard them working away at their Greek, with more pains than any of the scholars at the school. I wondered why they did these tasks, when they had no parents to keep them at their work. I was too young to know that as these old men dug out the hard Greek roots, they felt the long stems reaching back through the toilsome years and bringing to their waning lives a feeling of hope and vigor from their departed youth.

To the kind old miller the condition of the water in the pond was doubtless quite another thing, and every revolution of the groaning wheel must have meant bread to him—not only bread for the customers whose grain he ground, but sorely needed bread for the hungry mouths of those who had no thought or care whence or how it came, but only unbounded faith that it would always be ready to satisfy their needs.

It is only by imagination, through the hard experience life has brought, that I know these familiar things had a different meaning to the old miller and to me. Yet even now I am not sure that they had for him a deeper or more vital sense. Perhaps the water for my swimming hole was as important as the water for his bread. For after all both were needed, in their several ways, to make more tolerable the ever illusive game of life.

As to my father, I am sure I never thought he was a man of extraordinary power. In fact, from the time I was a little child I often urged him to do things in a different way—especially as to his rules about my studies and my schooling. I never believed that he ran the mill in the best way; and I used to think that other men were stronger or richer, or kinder to their children, than father was to us. It was only after years had passed, and I looked back through the hazy mist that hung about his ambitions and his life, that I could realize how great he really was. As a child, I had no doubt that any man could create conditions for himself; the copy-books had told me so, and the teachers had assured us in the most positive way that our success was with ourselves. It took years of care and toil to show me that life is stronger than man, that conditions control individuals. It is with this knowledge that I look back at the old miller, with his fatal love of books; that I see him as he surveys every position the world offers to her favored sons. He knows them all and understands them all, and he knows the conditions on which they have ever been bestowed; yet he could bury these ambitions one by one, and cover them so deep as almost to forget they had once been a portion of his life, and in full sight of the glories of the promised land could day by day live in the dust and hum of his ever-turning mill, and take from the farmers' grist the toll that filled the mouths of his little brood. To appreciate and understand the greatness of the simple life, one must know life; and this the child of whatever age can never understand.

I could not then know why my father took all this trouble for me to learn my grammar; but I know today. I know that, all unconsciously, it was the blind persistent effort of the parent to resurrect his own buried hopes and dead ambitions in the greater opportunities and broader life that he would give him child. Poor man! I trust the lingering spark of hope for me never left his bosom while he lived, and that he died unconscious that the son on whom he lavished so much precious time and care never learned Latin after all, and never could.

Almost unconsciously I grew into sympathy with his ideals and his life, seeing faintly the grand visions that were always clear to him, and bewailing more and more my own indolence and love of pleasure that made them seem so hard for me to reach. I learned to understand the tragedy of his obscure and hidden life, and the long and bitter contest he had waged within the narrow shadow of the stubborn little town where he had lived and struggled and hoped so long. It was many years before I came to know that the smaller the world in which we move, the more impossible it is to break the prejudices and conventions that bind us down. And so it was many, many years before I realized what must have been my father's life.

As a little child, I heard my father tell of Frederick Douglass,*

---

*Frederick Douglass. 1817–1895. American writer and abolitionist. (Ed.)

Parker Pillsbury,* Sojourner Truth,† Wendell Phillips,‡ and the rest of that advance army of reformers, black and white, who went up and down the land arousing the dulled conscience of the people to a sense of justice to the slave. They used to make my father's home their stopping-place, and any sort of vacant room was the forum where they told of the black man's wrongs. My father lived to see these disturbers canonized by the public opinion that is ever to follow in the wake of a battle fought to a successful end. But when his little world was ready to rejoice with him over the freedom of the slave, he had moved his soiled and tattered tent to a new battlefield and was fighting the same stubborn, sullen, threatening public opinion for a new and yet more doubtful cause. The same determined band of agitators used still to come when I had grown to be a youth. These had seen visions of a higher and broader religious life, and a fuller measure of freedom and justice for the poor than the world had ever known. Like the despised tramp, they seemed to have marked my father's gatepost, and could not pass his door. They were always poor, often ragged, and a far-off look seemed to haunt their eyes, as if gazing into space at something beyond the stars. Some little room was found where a handful of my father's friends would gather, sometimes coming from miles around to listen to the voices crying in the wilderness, calling the heedless world to repent before it should be too late. I cannot remember when I did not go to these little gatherings of the elect and drink in every word that fell upon my ears. Poor boy! I am almost sorry for myself. I listened so rapturously and believed so strongly and knew so well that the kingdom of heaven would surely come in a little while. And though almost every night through all these long and weary years I have looked with the same unflagging hope for the promised star that should be rising in the east, still it has not come; but no matter how great the trial and disappointment and delay, I am sure I shall always peer out into the darkness for this belated star, until I am so blind that I could not see it if it were really there.

After these wandering minstrels returned from their meetings to our home, they would sit with my father for hours in his little study, where they told each other of their visions and their hopes. Many a time, as I lay in my bed, I listened to their words coming through the crack with the streak of lamplight at the bottom of

---

*Parker Pillsbury. 1809–1898. New England reformer and abolitionist. (Ed.)
†Sojourner Truth. 1797–1883. American evangelist and reformer. (Ed.)
‡Wendell Phillips. 1811–1884. American reformer and abolitionist. (Ed.)

the door, until my weary eyes would close in the full glow of the brilliant rainbow they had painted from their dreams.

After all, I am glad that my father and his footsore comrades dreamed their dreams. I am glad they lived above the sordid world, in that ethereal realm which none but the blindly devoted ever see; for I know that their visions raised my father from the narrow valley, the dusty mill, the small life of commonplace, to the great broad heights where he really lived and died.

And I am glad that as a youth and a little child it was given me to catch one glimpse of these exalted realms, and to feel one aspiration for the devoted life they lived; for however truly I may know that this ideal land was but a dream that would never come, however I may have clung to the valleys, the fleshpots, and the substantial things, I am sure that some part of this feeling abides with me, and that its tender chord of sentiment and memory reaches back to that hallowed land of childhood and of youth, and still seeks to draw me toward the heights on which my father lived.

22

Dawn

Theodore Dreiser

Throughout his long, colorful life, Theodore Dreiser never forgot his poverty-blasted beginnings in Terre Haute, Indiana, in 1871, as the son of a fervently Catholic father who was a skilled but unsuccessful woolen-mill operator. His mother had been a pietistic Mennonite who converted to Catholicism at her husband's demand. Growing up in a large family, frequently having to move one step ahead of the bill-collector, ill at ease with his physical looks and the family's chronic desperation, young Theodore yet maintained a rather dreamy nature. After a series of odd jobs and a year at Indiana University given him by a former teacher, Dreiser became a newspaper reporter, and gravitated toward writing as a livelihood.

Ever restless and curious, Dreiser evolved a philosophy of determinism based on Herbert Spencer, and a naturalistic literary style. "We were taught persistently," he wrote, "to shun most human experience as either dangerous or degrading or destructive. The less you knew about life the better; the more you knew about the fictional heaven and hell ditto. People walked about in a kind of sanctified daze or dream, hypnotized or self-hypnotized by an erratic and impossible theory of human conduct which had grown up heaven knows where or how, and had finally cast its amethystine spell over all America, if not over all the world."

Dreiser's first novel, *Sister Carrie,* was, for all practical purposes, repressed by its publisher, in part on grounds of immorality. A reviewer for the *Chicago Tribune* noted, "Not once does the name of the Deity appear in the book, except as it is implied in the suggestion of profanity," but went on to say such a book had been long awaited. Eventually the novel was republished, and Dreiser was acknowledged to be a major figure in modern American literature. Even after attaining success, he remained a maverick; just before his death in 1945, Dreiser resolved many of his moral and political conflicts by joining the Communist party.

The various mental and inward stages of my youth are somewhat clouded or slightly greyed in part by heavy introspective and moralistic inquiries, which seemed a bent with me as they were naturally a mental condition with my father, and, by force of circumstances, with my mother also.

Also, America, and especially the Middle West, was at that time miasmatically puritanic as well as patriotic, twin states bred of ignorance and what mental or economic lacks I am not able to discern. At any rate, quite all of the old was bad, all the new good. The enlightenment of the world, as I was to learn by degrees, dated from the Declaration of Independence. The United States of America constituted the greatest country in the world, the strongest and only free one. Catholicism, in our family, was the true religion; some form of Protestantism in all of the homes of our neighbors. The darkness and intolerance in which they were held! An atheist was a criminal. Anyone who doubted that Christ died on the cross to save all men or that men were truly saved thereby, or that there was a specific heaven, a definite hell, and so forth, was a scoundrel, a reprobate, a lost soul. Just how people were to live and die had all been fixed long before. There were no crimes greater than adultery, atheism, and theft. And so it went. I picture this atmosphere because some phases of it were at times so stern and destructive. . . .

I have described my father as a religious enthusiast. At that time he was a morose and dour figure, forlorn and despondent, tramping about the house, his hands behind his back and occasionally talking to himself. One of his worst phases was the conviction that there was refuge in religion, more and more self-humiliation before a Creator who revealed Himself only through the forms and ceremonies of the Catholic Church. He believed implicitly that the least

---

From Theodore Dreiser, *A History of Myself: Dawn* (New York: Horace Liveright, Inc., 1931). By permission of The Dreiser Trust, Harold J. Dies, Trustee.

neglect or infraction of such forms and ceremonies as were ordered by the Church was sufficient to evoke disfavor or at least neglect on the part of the Universal Ruler. This being true, the rather indifferent religious conduct of his wife and children was sufficient to convince him that they were evil to a degree and in need of driving. Even before this time, my mother had been prone to suspect, and to voice her suspicion, that because of his insistence on the Catholic school as opposed to the public or free school, her children had not been given the proper educational advantages and so were already greatly handicapped in their race for place and position. But none too well grounded in her revolt and still overawed by the ponderous material flummery of the faith she had adopted, she doubted and protested one minute and was the next awed into silence, and even acquiescence, by the uproar that invariably ensued. I rise to testify, for I have heard these arguments with my own ears, almost daily, nightly, or both—what should be said or done for the children when there was so little of any value that was being done for any one of them!

True, as my father once told me, during the period when he was managing the mill of his former rivals in Terre Haute, and before trade misfortune overtook them too, he had urged both of his eldest sons to permit him to teach them the technique of woolen manufacture, since he believed that such manufacture was destined to a future in America. But they would not hear of it, feeling that their interests lay elsewhere. But apart from that, I could never see that he offered any directive suggestions of value.

But in this connection I would like to say that I have no fixed theories as to the best method of educating children. It seems to me an almost inscrutable problem, a system applicable under some conditions being by no means suitable under others. But having had opportunity later to contrast the American public school with the Catholic parochial system, I now regard the first as in the main a real aid to intelligence and freedom of spirit and the second as an outrageous survival of a stultifying medievalism which should be swept away to its last detail.

The inanity of teaching at this day and date, and as illustrated by the Holy Roman Catechism, the quite lunatic theories and pretensions of that entirely discredited organism to divine inspiration and hence leadership and of putting that unscratched tablet, the mind of a child, into its possession or care! Fie! Faugh! The alleged intelligence of a maundering world! And the brassy insouciance and tongue-in-cheek "authority" with which the alleged "princes of the

Church," their factotums or "fathers," step forward not only to receive but to demand the care of the young! No wonder it became the first business of the Russian Communists to rip out root and branch the eastern or Asiatic extension of this same designing and serpentine organization!

To what end, then, the work of a Galileo, a Newton, a Darwin, a Lamarck,* a Huxley,† a Faraday,‡ a Tyndall,§ a Helmholtz,** a Jeans,†† a Millikan,‡‡ in truth the entire army of distinguished and substantiated students who have labored and meditated on behalf of reality, if these sacrament and indulgence salesmen are to be allowed to seize upon the child—in the protectory, the orphan asylum, the school and Catholic home—and corrupt its reason with unverifiable dogma or just plain lies? A bishop has a palace while a scientist lacks a laboratory! Churches to St. Joseph, St. Anthony, the Immaculate Conception; monasteries, nunneries, convents, homes, and hospitals erected in honor of the same, but also for what profit can be had out of the psychopathic balderdash they represent! Billions in real estate untaxed, and science, whether it conflicts with dogma or not, even called in to help—in the profit-taking but no further!

I often think of the hundreds of thousands of children turned out of the Catholic schools at twelve or thirteen years of age, with not a glimmer of true history or logic, no efficient mechanical training, not a suggestion even of such comparatively simple and yet enormously valuable things as rudimentary botany, chemistry, or physics. For in these realms, you see, you come upon strange facts and paradoxes which might endanger an inculcated belief in the infallibility of the pope, the sanctity of the priests, the importance of the confessional, the presence of a definite hell and a specific heaven. My father died firm in his belief of these dogmas. My mother was troubled by them to the day of her death. They continue, I believe, to influence at least one of my brothers to such an extent that were he to read this he would regard it as blasphemous, my soul in danger of hell.

At any rate, here was I, at six years of age, along with Trina

---

*Jean-Baptiste Lamarck. 1744–1829. French naturalist. (Ed.)
†Thomas Henry Huxley. 1825–1895. English biologist. (Ed.)
‡Michael Faraday. 1791–1867. English physician and chemist. (Ed.)
§John Tyndall. 1820–1893. Irish physician and popularizer of science. (Ed.)
**Hermann Ludwig Ferdinand von Helmholtz. 1821–1894. German anatomist and physiologist. (Ed.)
††Sir James Hopwood Jeans. 1877–1946. English physicist and astronomer. (Ed.)
‡‡Robert Millikan. 1868–1953. American physicist. (Ed.)

and later my brother Ed, installed in St. Joseph's German Catholic school, an adjunct of St. Joseph's Roman Catholic church, in Ninth Street in Terre Haute—a pay school, you may be sure, although right around the corner was a free public school where an at least fairly liberal and honest brand of information concerning life was being dispensed. The schoolroom contained forty or fifty hard wooden benches, much scarred, as I recall, by knives and pencils and much bespattered with ink. The other children, mostly of my own age and sex—hardy little jiggers, in the main—may not have been disturbed as much as myself by the meager and to me forbidding regimen prescribed. (There are temperaments and temperaments, minds and minds!) The floor was bare, the walls covered with blackboards. On a dais which faced us sat—as she then seemed to me—the Nemesis or Gorgon of the place, an outlandish figure of a woman clad in black, with a flaring white hood or bonnet.

Once the business of inducting me into a seat was over, I along with others was called upon to register and apprehend my A, B, C's—a long line of curious-looking German symbols—which were pointed at with a long, thin wand by this hooded figure, herself articulating the letters and ordering us to do the same. Impressed, terrified even, I did so. The remainder of her requests, for that day at least if I recall aright, were principally for silence and order. But the uniform overawed me, as did that of the black-cassocked priest who occasionally on this first day, and almost regularly on every other day thereafter, strutted or prowled amongst us.

Daily we were led into church—attendance at which was compulsory—to hear a mass. At twelve o'clock, after prayers, we were turned out to play and eat until one. If we encountered a priest anywhere, we had to lift our hats and say: "Praised be Jesus Christ!" to which he replied, lifting his hat, "Amen!" And it was our bounden duty, as we soon learned, to appear at mass at least once on Sunday (high mass, preferably) and at Vespers on Sunday afternoon. A number of the boys were selected to do church duty—serve as altar boys, ring the bell, or run errands for the priest. At the age of eight or ten we were supposed to begin to go to confession. At twelve, having mastered the Catechism (the rules of the Catholic Church covering our relation to it and God), we were ready for our First Holy Communion. After that our parents could put us to work if they chose. However deficient in other respects our education might be, we were good Catholics, or were supposed to be, and beyond that, what mattered? . . .

[Dreiser was later enrolled in a Catholic school in Evansville, Indiana.]

It was after I had been in this school for two years and was by then twelve years old that the Very Reverend Dudenhausen appeared one morning, his eyes commanding and yet not unfriendly, and announced that from now on until the end of school all those who were twelve years of age were to report to him in an adjoining room between eleven and twelve every morning and there receive such instruction as would fit them for their First Communion and subsequent confirmation.

You may well guess with what a mixture of surprise, fear, and doubt this announcement was received by these poor scrubs of boys who had no more conception of what it meant to be instructed in the tenets of the Catholic Church than they had of what it would mean to be called upon to sail to the moon. Literally, outside of *hearing* what was said and then going to the altar and going through certain motions and genuflections, they knew nothing of what was meant. Catechism? What was that? "And the Word was made flesh and dwelt among men"—how might the import of that be imparted to a child, and a dull one at that? What could the elevation of the Host or the body and blood of Jesus Christ mean to them? Yet it was the business of these heavy religionists, regardless of the mental equipment of these silly lads, to "instruct" or rather demand acceptance (and all unexplained), of all of the obscurities of dogmatic theology, or failing that, catch them by threatened ills and the hopes of the possible remission of the same providing they agreed or came to look upon the Holy Catholic Church as insuperable and so absolutely necessary to their future spiritual salvation. In other words, assure a man that he has a soul and then frighten him with old wives' tales as to what is to become of it afterwards, and you have a hooked fish, a mental slave! And so once more I ask, why permit this dogged insistence on religious theory which cannot be proven but must be accepted on faith—especially in the case of children? Why not confine it to the grown mind? There are libraries enough for all, and we can all theorize for ourselves when the time comes.

I wish you might have been with me, though, to see the Reverend Anton Dudenhausen as he was at that time. Fat, domineering, albeit honestly (possibly) and blindly convinced. And before him, in that big, bare classroom, these fumbling, duncy boys being instructed for an hour each day in the mysteries and subtleties of the Catholic faith. Their mental inefficiency, their lack of interest, and yet their fear of being punished for any noted inattention! And the Reverend Anton so broad and solemn and stern, towering above them, himself so bigoted and deficient. Yet there was at the same time something so bland, so smug, so oilily affectionate about him. In short, I actually believe of this porker that he was of the very stuff of zealotry. He believed in so far as he could understand, and what he did not understand he accepted on hearsay and faith, and demanded, most violently at times, that these others do likewise. For instance, how he dwelt on the horrors of hell and the punishment awaiting all who failed to conform to what the Church had ordained as necessary to salvation! But no plausible explanations and none there capable of understanding had any been made. No honest presentation of the history of the Church as such; mere rules and regulations and then denunciations of all Protestantism and infidelity and of all those who dared to think otherwise than did Rome!

At this time lived the redoubtable Ingersoll, traveling, lecturing, writing, making a hash of the dogmatic as well as spiritual pretensions of quite all of the sectarian religions of his day, and him the Reverend Anton excoriated with fiery zeal. This demon! This actual devil in men's clothing, dragging these foolish and mistaken souls down into hell with him! And for what? Well, he, the very Reverend Anton, would tell you for what! And here and now! For the crime, no less, of listening to this demon sent here by the Devil and then daring to believe him, when here at hand, free to the wish and will of everybody, was Holy Church, with its Christ-given authority and its holy laws and sacraments ordained by God himself and confirmed by Peter, the first pope; by no less a person than Jesus himself, the Almighty Ruler of the Universe! Only to think of this scoundrel in a high hat attempting to persuade inattentive souls to the notion that the divine teachings of the Holy Church were not true!! But wait! Wait until he died! Wait until at his very bedside in death the Devil himself appeared and seized him! For God still ruled. And what he ordained the Devil had to obey. And for his sins against the Church, he and all of his victims here on earth would be properly punished! Just wait. . . .

I leave you to disentangle this fine bundle of logic and dogma as well as its probable effect on these immature and gaping and altogether fearful minds, the while I conclude the picture of the noble Anton and his labors. For while he talked, there was something iron in his eye, something dictatorial and final about his fat paunch. In cassock and lace and chasuble—for effect, I presume—he strolled among these children and either glared or laid a soft, white, priestly hand on a tousled head here and there, and talked, and talked, and talked.

I have often thought it a pity that this man, with all of his native force and enthusiasm for his work, was without mental understanding or equipment of any kind. He was probably not a bad man, just a fool, a narrow bigot like my father, his one idea being to make good Catholics of these children and nothing more. Years later he was found dead in his bedroom—kneeling at his bedside, so I was told, his head upon his hands which clasped (or had) a cross. He had died praying! In short, he was a good Catholic. But why such a lunatic firebrand in charge of the minds of children? Why?

23

The Reserved Section

Wilbur D. Nesbit

William D. Nesbit was born in Xenia, Ohio, in 1871, and educated in nearby Cedarville, where he began a career in newspaper journalism. He later worked as a columnist and feature writer in Indianapolis and Baltimore. From there Nesbit moved into advertising, and became a vice president of the Rankin Advertising Company in Chicago. He published many volumes of poetry, including poems for children, in the sentimental, homespun tradition of Eugene Field and James Whitcomb Riley. Nesbit died in 1927.

(At the time of the great anthracite coal strike in 1902, George F. Baer, head of the coal trust, was quoted as declaring: "The rights and interests of the laboring man will be protected and cared for, not by labor and agitation, but by the Christian men to whom God in his infinite wisdom has given control of the property interests of this country.")

From *The Cry for Justice: An Anthology of the Literature of Social Protest*, edited by Upton Sinclair with an introduction by Jack London. Published 1921 by Upton Sinclair.

In the prehistoric ages, when the world was a ball of mist—
A seething swirl of something unknown in the planet list;
When the earth was vague with vapor, and formless and
     dark and void—
The sport of the wayward comet—the jibe of the asteroid—
Then the singing stars of morning chanted soft: "Keep
     out of there!
Keep off that spot which is sizzling hot—it is making
     coal for Baer!"

When the pterodactyl ambled, or fluttered, or swam, or jumped,
And the plesiosaurus rambled, all careless of what he bumped,
And the other old-time monsters that thrived on the
     land and sea,
And did not know what their names were, any more than
     today do we—
Wherever they went they heard it: "You fellows keep
     out of there—
That place which shakes and quivers and quakes—it is
     making coal for Baer."

The carboniferous era consumed but a million years;
It started when earth was shedding the last of her baby tears,
When still she was swaddled softly in clumsily tied on clouds,
When stars from the shop of nature were being turned out in crowds;
But high o'er the favored section this sign said to all:
     "Beware!
Stay back of the ropes that surround these slopes—they
     are making coal for Baer!"

24

Poems

Robert Service

Because of the tremendous popularity of his poetry in the United States during the first two decades of this twentieth century, many people probably believe that Robert Service was an American. Yet Service was actually born in England (in 1874), raised largely in Scotland, and while part of his vagabond years were indeed spent in the United States, the crucial period of his sub-Arctic experiences was in the Yukon Territory of Canada between 1901 and 1912. *The Spell of the Yukon,* containing his poems of most enduring popularity, appeared in 1907, selling hundreds of thousands of copies within a very short period of time.

Service's poetry seemed to capture not only the wild, rough-edged life of the far northwest frontier, in memorable ballad forms, but also detonated the polite esthetic standards of later Victorian society. In short, there were overtones of theological scandal, as when Dan McGrew is described as "a hound of hell," and the Yukon is "The Land God Forgot." Service's "Wage Slave" hopes neither for heaven nor hell, and addresses God: "Well, 'tis Thy world, and Thou knowest I blaspheme and my ways be rude;/ But I've lived my life as I found it, and I've done my best to be good." In a harsh and unyielding land, described in similar terms by Jack London, the bonds of society are expressed in something so simple as a man's word, as in "The Ballad of Blasphemous Bill," where Bill's pal finds himself sworn to fulfill his final wish, and has to saw up Bill's frozen body to fit him into a coffin.

Although Service also wrote novels and an autobiography, his real fame rests on his early poetry. That he continued to write well is evidenced by "The Ballad of Salvation Bill," along with two late poems which reflect his continuing interest in a healthy, earth-centered life. Service did tend to write more orthodox religious poetry toward the end of his life, which came in 1958; yet he remained a thoughtful and questioning, if unpretentious, artist.

THE SKEPTIC

My Father Christmas passed away
When I was barely seven.
At twenty-one, alack-a-day,
I lost my hope of heaven.

Yet not in either lies the curse:
The hell of it's because
I don't know which loss hurt the worse—
My God or Santa Claus.

MY MADONNA

I haled me a woman from the street,
    Shameless, but, oh, so fair!
I bade her sit in the model's seat
    And I painted her sitting there.

I hid all trace of her heart unclean;
    I painted a babe at her breast;
I painted her as she might have been
    If the Worst had been the Best.

She laughed at my picture and went away.
    Then came, with a knowing nod,
A connoisseur, and I heard him say:
    "Tis Mary, the Mother of God."

So I painted a halo round her hair,
    And I sold her and took my fee,
And she hangs in the church of Saint Hillaire,
    Where you and all may see.

THE BALLAD OF SALVATION BILL

'Twas in the bleary middle of the hard-boiled Arctic night,
    I was lonesome as a loon, so if you can,
Imagine my emotions of amazement and delight
    When I bumped into that Missionary Man.
He was lying lost and dying in the moon's unholy leer,
    And frozen from his toes to fingertips;
The famished wolf pack ringed him; but he didn't seem to fear,
    As he pressed his ice-bound Bible to his lips.

'Twas the limit of my trapline, with the cabin miles away,
    And every step was like a stab of pain;
But I packed him like a baby, and I nursed him night and day,
    Till I got him back to health and strength again.
So there we were, benighted in the shadow of the Pole,
    and he might have proved a priceless little pard,
If he hadn't got to worrying about my blessed soul,
    And a-quotin' me his Bible by the yard.

Now there was I, a husky guy, whose god was Nicotine.
    With a "coffin nail" a fixture in my mug;
I rolled them in the pages of a pulpwood magazine,
    And hacked them with my jackknife from the plug.
For, oh to know the bliss and glow that good tobacco means,
    Just live among the everlasting ice. . . .
So judge my horror when I found my stock of magazines
    Was chewed into a chowder by the mice.

A woeful week went by and not a single pill I had,
    Me that would smoke my forty in a day;
I sighed, I swore, I strode the floor; I felt that I would go mad:
    The gospel-plugger watched me in dismay.
My brow was wet, my teeth were set, my nerves were rasping raw;
    And yet that preacher couldn't understand:
So with despair I wrestled there—when suddenly I saw
    The volume he was holding in his hand.

Then something snapped inside my brain, and with an evil start
The wolf man in me woke to rabid rage.
"I saved your lousy life," says I; "so show you have a heart,
And tear me out a solitary page."
He shrank and shriveled at my words; his face went pewter white;
'Twas just as if I'd handed him a blow;
And then . . . and then he seemed to swell, and grow to
    Heaven's height,
And in a voice that rang he answered: "No!"

I grabbed my loaded rifle and I jabbed it to his chest:
"Come on, you shrimp, give up that Book," says I.
Well sir, he was a parson, but he stacked up with the best,
And for grit I got to hand it to the guy.
"If I should let you desecrate this Holy Word," he said,
"My soul would be eternally accurst;
So go on, Bill, I'm ready. You can pump me full of lead
And take it, but—you've got to kill me first."

Now I'm no foul assassin, though I'm full of sinful ways,
And I knew right there the fellow had me beat;
For I felt a yellow mongrel in the glory of his gaze,
And I flung my foolish firearm at his feet.
Then wearily I turned away, and dropped upon my bunk,
And there I lay and blubbered like a kid.
"Forgive me, pard," says I at least, "for acting like a skunk,
But hide the blasted rifle. . . ." Which he did.

And he also hid his Bible, which was maybe just as well,
For the sight of all that paper gave me pain;
And there were crimson moments when I felt I'd go to hell
To have a single cigarette again.
And so I lay day after day, and brooded dark and deep,
Until one night I thought I'd end it all;
Then rough I roused the preacher, where he stretched
    pretending sleep,
With his map of horror turned towards the wall.

"See here, my pious pal," says I, "I've stood it long enough. . . .
Behold! I've mixed some strychnine in a cup;
Enough to kill a dozen men—believe me it's no bluff;
Now watch me, for I'm gonna drink it up.

You've seen me bludgeoned by despair through bitter days
    and nights,
And now you'll see me squirming as I die.
You're not to blame, you've played the game according
    to your lights. . . .
But how would Christ have played it?—Well, good-bye. . . .

With that I raised the deadly drink and laid it to my lips,
But he was on me with a tiger-bound;
And as we locked and reeled and rocked with wild and wicked
    grips,
The poison cup went crashing to the ground.
"Don't do it, Bill," he madly shrieked. "Maybe I acted wrong.
See, here's my Bible—use it as you will;
But promise me—you'll read a little as you go along. . . .
You do! Then take it, Brother; smoke your fill."

And so I did. I smoked and smoked from Genesis to Job,
And as I smoked I read each blessed word;
While in the shadow of his bunk I heard him sigh and sob,
And then . . . a most peculiar thing occurred.
I got to reading more and more, and smoking less and less,
Till just about the day his heart was broke,
Says I: "Here, take it back, me lad, I've had enough, I guess.
Your paper makes a mighty rotten smoke."

So then and there with plea and prayer he wrestled for my soul,
And I was racked and ravaged by regrets.
But God was good, for lo! next day there came the police patrol,
With paper for a thousand cigarettes. . . .
So now I'm called Salvation Bill; I teach the Living Law,
And Ballyhoo the Bible with the best;
And if a guy won't listen—why, I sock him on the jaw,
and preach the Gospel sitting on his chest.

GRANDAD

Heaven's mighty sweet, I guess;
Ain't no rush to get there;
Been a sinner, more or less;
Maybe wouldn't fit there.
Wicked still, bound to confess;
Might jest pine a bit there.

Heaven's swell, the preachers say:
Got so used to earth here;
Had such good times all the way,
Frolic, fun, and mirth here;
Eighty Springs ago today,
Since I had my birth here.

Quite a spell of happy years.
Wish I could begin it;
Cloud and sunshine, laughter, tears,
Livin' every minute.
Women, too, the pretty dears;
Plenty of 'em in it.

Heaven! that's another tale.
Mightn't let me chew there.
Gotta have me pot of ale;
Would I like the brew there?
Maybe I'd get slack and stale—
No more chores to do there.

Here I weed the garden plot,
Scare the crows from pillage;
Simmer in the sun a lot,
Talk about the tillage.
Yarn of battles I have fought,
Greybeard of the village.

Heaven's mighty fine, I know. . . .
Still, it ain't so bad here.
See them maples all aglow;
Starlings seem so glad here:
I'll be mighty peeved to go,
Scrumptious times I've had here.

Lord, I know You'll understand.
With Your Light You'll lead me.
Though I'm not the pious brand,
I'm here when You need me.
Gosh! I know that Heaven's GRAND,
But dang it! God, *don't speed me.*

REPTILES AND ROSES

So crystal clear it is to me
That when I die I cease to be,
All else seems sheer stupidity.

All promises of Paradise
Are wishful thinking, preacher's lies,
Dogmatic dust flung in our eyes.

Yea, *life's* immortal, swift it flows
Alike in reptile and in rose,
But as it comes, so too it goes.

Dead roses will not bloom again;
The lifeless lizard writhes in vain;
Cups shattered will not hold champagne.

Our breath is brief, and being so
Let's make our heaven here below,
And lavish kindness as we go.

For when dour Death shall close the door
There will be darkness evermore;
So let us kneel in prayer before

Each day and let our duty be
To fight that Mankind may be free . . .
There is our Immortality.

Part Three

The Revolt from the Village

25

Poems

Vachel Lindsay

Though many times he traveled far afield from his home in Springfield, Illinois, Vachel Lindsay (1879–1931) always returned there, bound to the city in an intense love-hate relationship. The son of a local doctor, Lindsay was strongly influenced by his mother, who envisioned for him a career as an artist. Both his parents were devout members of the Campbellite church, based on a revival of primitive Christianity. Lindsay later observed: "There was always a cold second thought, a double consciousness, among the 'Campbellite' theologians. They breathed fire, but they thought in granite. Scotch heads, Red Indian and Kentucky blood." Consequently, Lindsay's own long struggle with God may have arisen from this divided heritage.

Lindsay attended college and art schools, but failed to graduate from any of them. He hoboed across the country several times, often exchanging poems for a bed of hay, and recalled: "I found an extraordinary responsiveness in cultured and uncultured. It seemed the only time I ever lived. I will never forget those log houses of the Blue Ridge, those rings of faces lit only by the fire on the hearth." Lindsay was restless, discontented, and prophetic; as his friend and biographer Edgar Lee Masters phrased it: ". . . he saw life with the exuberance of Whitman and nothing less, and with the imagination of Coleridge, plus Joseph Smith, plus Jacob Boehme, and plus Swedenborg."

While still a young man, Lindsay gave away his writing on the streets of Springfield, proclaiming in his *War Bulletin No. 1* of 1909: "I have spent a great part of my years fighting a soul battle for absolute liberty, for freedom from obligation, ease of conscience, independence of commercialism. . . . The things that go into the War Bulletin please me only, to the Devil with you, Average reader. To Gehenna with your stupidity, your bigotry, your conservatism, your cheapness and impatience." For this and similar utterances, Lindsay was dropped from the rolls of the Y.M.C.A. and the Anti-Saloon League.

Inconsistent and touchingly naive, Lindsay extolled "Christ the Socialist, the Beautiful, the personal savior from sin, the singing Immanuel." He wrote a new Gospel of Beauty and thought that civics should be America's religion. But, like Carl Sandburg, Lindsay dropped socialism during the hysteria of World War I. In part, it was his dependence on popularity as a performer that led to his tragic end, because by the late 1920s, as his popularity waned, he sank into a paranoid illness, and committed suicide in 1931 by drinking disinfectant.

THE TRAMP'S REFUSAL
ON BEING ASKED BY A BEAUTIFUL GYPSY
TO JOIN HER GROUP OF STROLLING PLAYERS

Lady, I cannot act, though I admire
God's great chameleons, Booth-Barret men.
But when the trees are green, my thoughts may be
October-red. December comes again
And snowy Christmas there within my breast
Though I be walking in the August dust.
Often my lone, contrary sword is bright
When every other soldier's sword is rust.
Sometimes, while churchly friends go up to God
On wings of prayer to altars of delight
I walk and talk with Satan, call him friend,
And greet the imps with converse most polite.
When hunger nips me, then at once I knock
At the near farmer's door and ask for bread.
I must, when I have wrought a curious song,
Pin down some stranger till the thing is read.

From *The Poetry of Vachel Lindsay*, volumes 1 and 2, Dennis Camp, ed. (Peoria, Ill.: Spoon River Poetry Press, 1984). Reprinted by permission of the publisher.

When weeds choke up within, then look to me
To show the world the manners of a weed.
I cannot change my cloak except my heart
Has changed and set the fashion for the deed.
When love betrays me, I go forth to tell
The first kind gossip that too-patent fact.
I cannot pose at hunger, love or shame.
It plagues me not to say: "I cannot act."
I only mourn that this unharnessed *me*
Walks with the devil far to much each day.
I would be chained to angel-kings of fire.
And whipped and driven up the heavenly way.

THE SONG OF THE TEMPLE SPARROWS
AFTER THE TEMPLE FELL

Gone are the roofs and the eaves of Jehova.
There no longer the sparrow fledges.
Let us go, let us sing in the Highways and Hedges.
For the Priests are dead. There is naught to find
But dogs of the street—all starved, unkind:
They eat the burnt flesh of the martyr's cold bones.
And the night mists that rise from the overthrown stones
Poison the birds from the highways and hedges.
Oh Sparrows dear, and swallows kind
Let us play in the dust with the halt and the blind,
Beside their paths there are crumbs to find,
And the Lord lives yet in the roots of the grass
That are soft to the foot through the Autumn hours
And warm to the taste while the blown snows pass.
And the Lord lives yet in the Summer flowers—
Yea, the Lord comes down in Springtime showers,
Let us live content in the Highways and Hedges.

FACTORY WINDOWS ARE ALWAYS BROKEN

Factory windows are always broken.
Somebody's always throwing bricks,
Somebody's always heaving cinders,
Playing ugly Yahoo tricks.

Factory windows are always broken.
Other windows are let alone.
No one throws through the chapel window
The bitter, snarling, derisive stone.

Factory windows are always broken.
Something or other is going wrong.
Something is rotten, I think, in Denmark.
End of the factory-window song.

THE UNPARDONABLE SIN

This is the sin against the Holy Ghost:—
To speak of bloody power as right divine,
And call on God to guard each vile chief's house,
And for such chiefs, turn men to wolves and swine:—

To go forth killing in White Mercy's name,
Making the trenches stink with spattered brains,
Tearing the nerves and arteries apart,
Sowing with flesh the unreaped golden plains.

In any Church's name, to sack fair towns,
And turn each home into a screaming sty,
To make the little children fugitive,
And have their mothers for a quick death cry,—

This is the sin against the Holy Ghost:
This is the sin no purging can atone;—
To send forth rapine in the name of Christ:—
To set the face, and make the heart a stone.

DREAMS IN THE SLUM

Some men, not blind, still think amid the filth.
Some scholars see vast cities like the sun:
Bright hives of power, of justice and of love,
In brains like these our Zion has begun.
What will you do to make their thought come true?
Or will you tread their pearls into the earth?
Friends, when such voices rise despite the time,
What are your shabby, rich man's temples worth?

BLOWING UP HELL-GATE

While I wait for you to dress,
I sit and drink my coffee straight,
And think up what we may yet do,
Toward blowing up Hell-Gate.

The little harbor Hell-Gate here,
Was blown up by electric wires,
That led to pits of dynamite,
And small machines adjusted right
For giving Hell-Gate dynamite.

But in the harbor of all souls
Where we would blow up Hell-Gate reef,
We must dive much deeper down,
We must place more marvelous wires,
Or all our tricks will come to grief.

Yet we have hoped to blow up Hell
And give mankind relief.

I TURNED MY HEAD AWAY

I turned my head away,
Reviling not the man,
And I forgave him soon.
I walked in happiness all afternoon.
I slept that night
A sleep like death
And killed him in my dream.

I turned my head away.
I loved my neighbor's wife.
Looking not again
I bade that love good-by.
Forgot her shining eye.
Most pious of young men.
I slept that night
A sleep like death
And killed her in my dream.

I turned my head away.
I would not curse my God.
Or look upon the crime
That made me doubt his name,
And very holy fame.
I loved my God, and sang
Throughout the afternoon.
Sang with all my life and breath.
Till I saw the stars agleam.
I slept that night
A sleep like death
And cursed God in my dream.

26

Poems

Carl Sandburg

Next to the railroad tracks in Galesburg, Illinois, the small frame house where Carl Sandburg (1878–1967) grew up still stands, preserved as a literary memorial. The son of a railroad blacksmith, Sandburg never forgot his modest origins. He early showed signs of rebelliousness, drifting around the country and working a variety of odd jobs, gaining first-hand experience of the American land and people. He enlisted in the army during the Spanish-American War, and after that, attended Lombard College, but did not graduate. Within a few years Sandburg made his way to Chicago, where he formed his gritty, realistic style of poetry, as well as his socialist politics. When Milwaukee elected a socialist mayor, Sandburg served as his secretary. However, during the anti-radical hysteria of World War I, Sandburg left the socialist movement. Meanwhile, after the publication of "Chicago" in *Poetry* magazine in 1914, his literary reputation began to grow. Sandburg also was sought after as a folksinger, touring the country. He authored a massive biography of Lincoln, and a New Deal poem, *The People Yes,* in 1936. In later years, Sandburg moved more into the "mainstream," retaining his considerable popularity until his death.

BROKEN TABERNACLES

Have I broken the smaller tabernacles, O Lord?
And in the destruction of these set up the greater and massive, the ever-
    lasting tabernacles?
I know nothing today, what I have done and why, O Lord, only I have
    broken and broken tabernacles.
They were beautiful in a way, these tabernacles torn down by strong
    hands swearing—
They were beautiful—why did the hypocrites carve their own names on
    the corner-stones? Why did the hypocrites keep on singing their own
    names in their long noses every Sunday in these tabernacles?
Who lays any blame here among the split corner-stones?

THE HAMMER

I have seen
The old gods go
And the new gods come.

Day by day
And year by year
The idols fall
And the idols rise.

Today
I worship the hammer.

HAMMERS POUNDING

Grant had a sledgehammer pounding and pounding and Lee had a sledge-
    hammer pounding and pounding
And the two hammers gnashed their ends against each other and broke

---

holes and splintered and withered
And nobody knew how the war would end and everybody prayed God his
hammer would last longer than the other hammer
Because the whole war hung on the big guess of who had the hardest
hammer
And in the end one side won the war because it had a harder hammer than
the other side.
Give us a hard enough hammer, a long enough hammer, and we will
break any nation,
Crush any star you name or smash the sun and the moon into small
flinders.

BOOKS MEN DIE FOR

Lights or no lights,
so they stand waiting
. . . books men die for.

For this a man was hanged.
For this a man was burned.
For this two million candles
snuffed their finish.
For this a man was shot.

Open the covers, they speak,
they cry, they come out as from
open doors with voices, heartbeats.

Fools: I say hats off.
Fools: I say, who did better?
Fools: I say with you:
What of it?

You books in the dark now with the lights off,
You books now with the lights on,
What is the drip, drip, from your covers?
What is the lip murmur, the lost winds wandering
from your covers?
Books men die for—
I say with you: what of it?

27

Songs and Poems

Industrial Workers of the World

Rising from the many violent strikes of the Western Federation of Miners led by Big Bill Haywood, the I.W.W. was founded in Chicago in 1905. Opening its first convention, Haywood picked up a slat from the stage of the auditorium, pounded it on the table, and declared: "This is the Continental Congress of the working class." The western miners already possessed a rich cultural heritage: their library in Cripple Creek, Colorado, numbered several thousand volumes. From this social and intellectual matrix, the I.W.W. produced many poets, composers, artists, and storytellers, who proclaimed their roots in peoples' culture as a matter of principle in both ethics and esthetics. There was a strong anarcho-syndicalist strain in the I.W.W. which called for Direct Action—slowdowns on the job, soapbox oratory, and industrial sabotage if necessary. They attracted a number of natural rebels, including, for instance, Father Hagerty, an ex-priest and designer of the famous "Industrial Wheel," which graphically demonstrated the revolutionary reorganization of society according to industrial and agricultural occupations. The I.W.W. was also fond of soapbox orations, in direct competition with the Salvation Army and other evangelists. These confrontations produced many parodies of well-known hymns, and furthermore led to the great "free speech" fights, in which hundreds of "Wobblies" were arrested for such "dangerous activities" as publicly reciting the Declaration of Independence. Because of their forthright revolutionary aims, the I.W.W. faced constant repression, especially during World

War I, when most of their leadership was arrested and convicted for violations of the Espionage Act. Though greatly reduced in numbers, the I.W.W. still exists today, with their headquarters in San Francisco. These selections are taken from their famous *Songs to Fan the Flames of Discontent,* commonly known as "The Little Red Songbook," which has passed through some thirty-five editions.

THE PREACHER AND THE SLAVE
(Tune: "In The Sweet Bye And Bye")
by Joe Hill

Long-haired preachers come out ev'ry night,
Try to tell you what's wrong and what's right;
But when asked about something to eat,
They will answer with voices so sweet:

> Chorus: You will eat bye and bye
> In that glorious land in the sky
> Work and pray, live on hay,
> You'll get pie in the sky when you die
> (That's a lie).

And the starvation army they play,
And they sing and they clap and they pray,
Till they get all your coin on the drum;
Then they tell you when you're on the bum: (chorus).

Holy rollers and jumpers come out;
They holler, they jump and they shout:
Give your money to Jesus they say,
He will cure all diseases today: (chorus).

If you fight hard for children and wife,
Try to get something good in this life,
You're a sinner and bad man they tell;
When you die you will surely go to hell: (chorus).

From *Songs of the Workers to Fan the Flames of Discontent,* 32nd and 35th eds. (Chicago: Industrial Workers of the World, 1968 and 1984). Reprinted with permission.

Workingfolk of all countries unite;
Side by side we for freedom will fight.
When the world and its wealth we have gained
To the grafters we'll sing this refrain:

Chorus: You will eat, bye and bye,
              When you've learned how to cook and to fry;
              Chop some wood, 'twill do you good,
              And you'll eat in the sweet bye and bye
                                                    (That's no lie!).

LUMBERJACK'S PRAYER
(Tune: "Doxology")
by T-Bone Slim

I pray dear Lord for Jesus' sake
Give us this day a T-Bone steak.
Hallowed be Thy Holy Name,
But don't forget to send the same.

Oh, hear my humble cry, O Lord,
And send us down some decent board,
Brown gravy and some German fried
With sliced tomatoes on the side.

Observe me on my bended legs,
I'm asking you for ham and eggs,
And if thou havest custard pies
I'd like, dear Lord, the largest size.

Oh, hear my cry, Almighty Host,
I quite forgot the quail on toast.
Let your kindly heart be stirred
And stuff some oysters in that bird.

Dear Lord, we know Your holy wish,
On Friday we must have a fish.
Our flesh is weak and spirit stale;
You better make that fish a whale.

Oh, hear me, Lord, remove these "dogs,"
These sausages of powdered logs;
The bull beef hash and bearded snouts,
Take them to Hell or thereabouts.

With alum bread and pressed beef butts
Dear Lord, they've damn near ruined my guts;
The whitewash milk and oleorine
I wish to Christ I'd never seen.

Oh, hear me, Lord, I'm praying still,
But if you won't our Union will
Put porkchops on the bill of fare
And starve no workers anywhere.

DUMP THE BOSSES OFF YOUR BACK
(Tune: "Take It To The Lord in Prayer")
by John Brill

Are you cold, forlorn, and hungry?
  Are there lots of things you lack?
Is your life made up of mis'ry?
  Then dump the bosses off your back!
Are your clothes all torn and tattered?
  Are you living in a shack?
Would you have your troubles scattered?
  Then dump the bosses off your back!

Are you almost split asunder?
  Loaded like a long-eared jack?
Boob—Why don't you buck like thunder,
  And dump the bosses off your back?
All the agonies you suffer
  You can end with one good whack—
Stiffen up, you orn'ry duffer—
  And dump the bosses off your back!

Capital and Labor Are Partners—Not Enemies

John D. Rockefeller, Jr.

I.W.W. cartoon by "Dust" Wallin (*One Big Union Monthly,* March 1919)

CHRISTIANS AT WAR
(Tune: "Onward Christian Soldiers")
by John F. Kendrick

Onward, Christian soldiers! Duty's way is plain;
Slay your Christian neighbors, or by them be slain.
Pulpiteers are spouting effervescent swill,
God above is calling you to rob and rape and kill,
And your acts are sanctified by the Lamb on high;
If you love the Holy Ghost, go murder, pray, and die.

Onward, Christian soldiers, rip and tear and smite!
Let the gentle Jesus bless your dynamite.
Splinter skulls with shrapnel, fertilize the sod;
Folks who do not speak your tongue deserve the curse of God.
Smash the doors of every home, pretty maidens seize;
Use your might and sacred right to treat them as you please.

Onward, Christian soldiers! Eat and drink your fill;
Rob with bloody fingers, Christ O.K.'s the bill.
Steal the farmers' savings, take their grain and meat;
Even though the children starve, the Savior's bums must eat.
Burn the peasants' cottages, orphans leave bereft;
In Jehova's holy name, wreak ruin right and left.

Onward, Christian soldiers! Drench the land with gore;
Mercy is a weakness all the gods abhor.
Bayonet the babies, jab the mothers, too;
Hoist the cross of Calvary to hallow all you do.
File your bullets' noses flat, poison every well;
God decrees your enemies must all go plumb to hell.

Onward, Christian soldiers! Blighting all you meet,
Trampling human freedom under pious feet.
Praise the Lord whose dollar sign dupes his favored race!
Make the foreign trash respect your bullion brand of grace.
Trust in mock salvation, serve as tyrant's tools:
History will say of you: "That pack of G - - d - - - fools."

28

The Infidel's Grave

Vance Randolph

The foremost authority on Ozark culture and folklore, Vance Randolph was born in 1892 in Pittsburg, Kansas, where his father was a prominent attorney. After graduating from the State Manual Training Normal School (now Pittsburg State University), Randolph attended Clark University in Massachusetts, where he wrote a master's thesis under the direction of G. Stanley Hall. Subsequently, Randolph worked for the *Appeal to Reason* newspaper in Girard, Kansas, and authored numerous Blue Books, several under pseudonyms. During his long life, Randolph compiled many scholarly collections of Ozark stories, songs, and folklore, the most famous and popular of these being *Pissing in the Snow,* an anthology of "off-color" folktales from the region. Randolph died in 1980.

One time there was a rich infidel died, and the folks buried him without no preacher. Nobody said a prayer, even. That's what the infidel told 'em he wanted, and they done everything just like he said.

The night after the funeral some neighbors got to talking about it, and a old woman says if anybody was to walk on that grave

From *The Devil's Pretty Daughter and Other Ozark Folk Tales,* collected by Vance Randolph (New York: Columbia University Press, 1955). Reprinted by permission.

at midnight, the infidel will reach right up and grab 'em. But a girl named Betty Ream just laughed right in their face. She says a infidel's grave ain't no different than anybody else's grave.

So then the boys wanted to bet she is scared to go out there by herself, at midnight. Betty says it is all foolishness, but she will go just to show 'em. And one fellow says, "If there ain't nobody with you, how will we know you was there?" The young folks had been a-playing croquet, and Betty says, "Fetch me that stake with the red rings painted on it, and one of them mallets." So the fellow done it. "You just go over to the buryin' ground in the morning," says Betty. "You'll find the stake drove right in that infidel's grave, and the mallet a-layin' close by."

It was about half-past eleven when Betty rode off down the road. She had the croquet stake in her hand, and the mallet was tied on her saddle. Two of the boys cut across the pasture unbeknownst, and they seen Betty go in the graveyard. They waited a long time, but she never come out. Them boys wouldn't go no further by theirself, but they run to the tavern and got some more fellows and a couple of lanterns. When the crowd come back they found Betty Ream a-layin' on the infidel's grave, and she was dead as a doornail.

Betty had hunkered down and drove the stake, all right. But girls wore big wide dresses in them days, and the moon was behind her, so it throwed a big black shadow in front. That's how come she drove the stake right through the edge of her skirt. The folks figured that when Betty went to get up, the dress held her fast to the ground. Maybe she thought the infidel sure enough did reach up out of his grave to grab her. Whatever happened, it scared Betty so bad that she died right then and there.

Doc Holton says she must have a bad heart, and maybe wouldn't live long anyhow. But that didn't make the folks feel no better. Betty Ream was mighty good company, and everybody thought a lot of her. It's kind of sad for a young girl to die that way, just on account of some foolishness.*

---

*Told by Mr. Ern Long, Joplin, Mo., August, 1931. He said it was common, in several versions, all over southern Missouri. Rayburn (*Ozark Guide,* Spring 1950, p. 29) prints a related tale from Hot Springs, Ark. See also Earl A. Collins (*Legends and Lore of Missouri,* 1951, pp. 57–59). Cf. *Midwest Folklore* 2 (Summer 1952): 83–84 [Vance Randolph].

This well-known tale, a form of Motif N 384, "Death from fright," is usually vouched for as an actual occurrence. A girl (or boy), to show her bravery, is to jab a fork (or knife, stick, etc.) into a grave, or drive a nail into a coffin;

she accidentally pins her dress, or coat, to the ground or coffin and dies of fear. Smith, *Hoosier Folklore* 6: 107, gives several American and European references. For American versions, see Fauset, *Journal of American Folklore* 41: 548 (Philadelphia; Negro, learned in North Carolina); Boggs, ibid., 47: 295–96 (North Carolina; two variants); White and others, *The Frank C. Brown Collection of North Carolina Folklore*, I, 686; Federal Writers' Project of the Work Projects Administration, *South Carolina Folk Tales*, pp. 103–104 (Negro); Halpert, *Hoosier Folklore Bulletin*, 1: 58–59 (Indiana); Neely and Spargo, *Tales and Songs of Southern Illinois*, pp. 64–67 (four variants); Dorson, *Hoosier Folklore*, VI, 5 (Wisconsin; learned in Hanover, Germany); ibid., p. 5, note 1 (Professor Dorson refers to at least four variants which he heard in Michigan); Baylor, ibid., p. 144 (New Mexico; Spanish; told as religious tale); Klein, *New Mexico Folklore Record*, 6: 27 (New Mexico; from Hungary). Jansen (*Hoosier Folklore Bulletin*, 2: 8) gives a curious Pennsylvania version told in Indiana, in which a grave robber pins his own long coattails to the ground with his shovel, and, of course, dies.

Another version of this tale ends with the man who is proving his courage going mad rather than dying. See Saxon, Dreyer, and Tallant, *Gumbo Ya-Ya*, pp. 276–77 (Louisiana); Law, *Folklore*, 11: 346 (Wiltshire, England); ibid., p. 346, note 2 (from south of Ireland). [Herbert Halpert].

29

From *Spoon River Anthology*

Edgar Lee Masters

Edgar Lee Masters was born in Garnett, Kansas, in 1869, but grew up in the small towns of Petersburg and Lewistown in central Illinois. After attending Knox College for a year, Masters began a law practice in Chicago that lasted thirty years. His famous collection, *Spoon River Anthology*, from which these selections are taken, consists of interrelated imaginary tombstone inscriptions as short life stories, in a small town cemetery such as he knew in his childhood and youth. Published in 1915, after several months of creative effort that almost wrecked his health, the book brought Masters immediate acclaim as a figure in the Chicago Renaissance, along with Dreiser, Sandburg, and Sherwood Anderson. "I must say," wrote Masters, "that if I had my conscious purpose in writing it and *The New Spoon River*, it was to awaken the American vision, that love of liberty which the best men of the Republic strove to win for us, and to bequeath to time."

Through a long life, Masters published many other books, including a pungent defense of fellow poet and free spirit, Vachel Lindsay. In 1942, he told the *New York Times:* "I am a Hellenist. . . . The great marvel of the world is Greek civilization. They thought in universals, as did the Elizabethans. We are provincial in our thoughts." Masters died in 1950, and in recent decades his poetry has suffered an unjust neglect.

WENDELL P. BLOYD

They first charged me with disorderly conduct,
There being no statute on blasphemy.
Later they locked me up as insane
Where I was beaten to death by a Catholic guard.
My offense was this:
I said God lied to Adam, and destined him
To lead the life of a fool,
Ignorant that there is evil in the world as well as good.
And when Adam outwitted God by eating the apple
And saw through the lie,
God drove him out of Eden to keep him from taking
The fruit of immortal life.
For Christ's sake, you sensible people,
Here's what God himself says about it in the book of Genesis:
"And the Lord God said, behold the man
Is become one of us" (a little envy, you see),
"To know good and evil" (The all-is-good lie exposed):
"And now lest he put forth his hand and take
Also of the tree of life and eat, and live forever:
Therefore the Lord God sent Him forth from the garden of Eden."
(The reason I believe God crucified His Own Son
To get out of the wretched tangle is, because it
        sounds just like Him.)

THE VILLAGE ATHEIST

Ye young debaters over the doctrine
Of the soul's immortality,
I who lie here was the village atheist,
Talkative, contentious, versed in the arguments
Of the infidels.
But through a long sickness
Coughing myself to death
I read the *Upanishads* and the poetry of Jesus.

"Wendell P. Bloyd," "The Village Atheist," "Yee Bow," and "Jefferson Howard" from *Spoon River Anthology,* by Edgar Lee Masters. Originally published by the Macmillan Company, copyright by Edgar Lee Masters. Permission by Ellen C. Masters.

And they lighted a torch of hope and intuition
And desire which the Shadow,
Leading me swiftly through the caverns of darkness,
Could not extinguish.
Listen to me, ye who live in the senses
And think through the senses only:
Immortality is not a gift,
Immortality is an achievement;
And only those who strive mightily
Shall possess it.

YEE BOW

They got me into the Sunday-school
In Spoon River
And tried to get me to drop Confucius for Jesus.
I could have been no worse off
If I had tried to get them to drop Jesus for Confucius.
For, without any warning, as if it were a prank,
And sneaking up behind me, Harry Wiley,
The minister's son, caved my ribs into my lungs,
With a blow of his fist.
Now I shall never sleep with my ancestors in Pekin,
And no children shall worship at my grave.

JEFFERSON HOWARD

My valiant fight! For I call it valiant,
With my father's beliefs from old Virginia:
Hating slavery, but no less war.
I, full of spirit, audacity, courage
Thrown into life here in Spoon River,
With its dominant forces drawn from New England,
Republicans, Calvinists, merchants, bankers,
Hating me, yet fearing my arm.
With wife and children heavy to carry—
Yet fruits of my very zest of life.
Stealing odd pleasures that cost me prestige,
And reaping evils I had not sown;

Foe of the church with its charnel darkness,
Friend of the human touch of the tavern;
Tangled with fates all alien to me,
Deserted by hands I called my own.
Then just as I felt my giant strength
Short of breath, behold my children
Had wound their lives in stranger gardens—
And I stood alone, as I started alone!
My valiant life! I died on my feet,
Facing the silence—facing the prospect
That no one would know of the fight I made.

30

The Red Swede

Sinclair Lewis

The son of a small-town doctor in Sauk Centre, Minnesota, Sinclair Lewis (1885–1951) had a troubled yet courageous career as a writer. His novel *Main Street* (1920) was, according to his biographer Mark Schorer, "the most sensational event in twentieth-century American publishing history," attaining a sudden and dramatic success not only among intellectuals, but the reading public in general. Among other things, the novel is a relentless exposé of the smug Puritanism of "Gopher Prairie," which is not only Lewis's hometown, but all similar towns in the Midwest. While Lewis gained a reputation as a cynical observer of the "Roaring Twenties," his work endures as a carefully detailed description of the American scene, with characters and dialogue which almost every thinking reader found devastatingly accurate and representative of the times. The excerpt given here describes an encounter between Carol Kennecott, the wife of the town doctor, and Miles Bjornstam, the town radical. Carol Kennecott represents, in part, the emerging "modern" woman of the professional class, while Bjornstam is Lewis's version of the "Village Atheist" type.

Lewis's novel *Elmer Gantry* (1927) is his most sustained study of the religious personality, and was preceded by a period when he moved to Kansas City in order to gather "material." During that time Lewis made front-page headlines across the country by standing up in a pulpit in Kansas City and giving God ten minutes to strike him down. When nothing happened, he declared, "that settles that." It was this and similar episodes which reinforced Lewis's reputation as a cynic. Throughout the rest of his life, Lewis passed through tragic periods of acute alcoholism, yet produced a number of novels of varying quality. He died in Rome, Italy, and his ashes were returned to be interred in Sauk Centre.

A black February day. Clouds hewn of ponderous timber weighing down on the earth; an irresolute dropping of snow specks upon the trampled wastes. Gloom but no veiling of angularity. The lines of roofs and sidewalks sharp and inescapable. . . .

She fled from the creepy house for a walk. It was thirty below zero; too cold to exhilarate her. In the spaces between houses the wind caught her. It stung, it gnawed at nose and ears and aching cheeks, and she hastened from shelter to shelter, catching her breath in the lee of a barn, grateful for the protection of a billboard covered with ragged posters showing layer under layer of paste-smeared green and streaky red.

The grove of oaks at the end of the street suggested Indians, hunting, snow-shoes, and she struggled past the earth-banked cottages to the open country, to a farm and a low hill corrugated with hard snow. In her loose nutria coat, seal toque, virginal cheeks unmarked by lines of village jealousies, she was as out of place on this dreary hillside as a scarlet tanager on an ice-floe. She looked down on Gopher Prairie. The snow, stretching without break from streets to devouring prairie beyond, wiped out the town's pretense of being a shelter. The houses were black specks on a white sheet. Her heart shivered with that still loneliness as her body shivered with the wind.

She ran back into the huddle of streets, all the while protesting that she wanted a city's yellow glare of shop windows and restaurants, or the primitive forest with hooded furs and a rifle, or a barnyard warm and steamy, noisy with hens and cattle, certainly not these dun houses, these yards choked with winter ash-piles, these roads of dirty snow and clotted frozen mud. The zest of winter was gone. Three months more, till May, the cold might drag on, with the snow ever filthier, the weakened body less resistant. She wondered why the good citizens insisted on adding the chill of prejudice, why they

---

did not make the houses of their spirits more warm and frivolous like the wise chatterers of Stockholm and Moscow.

She circled the outskirts of the town and viewed the slum of "Swede Hollow." Wherever as many as three houses are gathered there will be a slum of at least one house. In Gopher Prairie, the Sam Clarks boasted, "you don't get any of this poverty that you find in cities—always plenty of work—no need of charity—man got to be blame shiftless if he don't get ahead." But now that the summer mask of leaves and grass was gone, Carol discovered misery and dead hope. In a shack of thin boards covered with tar paper she saw the washerwoman, Mrs. Steinhof, working in gray steam. Outside, her six-year-old boy chopped wood. He had a torn jacket, muffler of a blue like skimmed milk. His hands were covered with red mittens through which protruded his chapped raw knuckles. He halted to blow on them, to cry disinterestedly.

A family of recently arrived Finns were camped in an abandoned stable. A man of eighty was picking up lumps of coal along the railroad.

She did not know what to do about it. She felt that these independent citizens, who had been taught that they belonged to a democracy, would resent her trying to play Lady Bountiful.

She lost her loneliness in the activity of the village industries— the railroad yards with a freight train switching, the wheat elevator, oil tanks, a slaughter house with blood-marks on the snow, the creamery with the sleds of farmers and piles of milk cans, an unexplained stone hut labeled "Danger—Powder Stored Here." The jolly tombstone yard, where a utilitarian sculptor in a red calfskin overcoat whistled as he hammered the shiniest of granite headstones. Jackson Elder's small planing mill, with the smell of fresh pine shavings and the burr of circular saws. Most important, the Gopher Prairie Flour and Milling Company, Lyman Cass president. Its windows were blanketed with flour dust, but it was the most stirring spot in town. Workmen were wheeling barrels of flour into a boxcar; a farmer sitting on sacks of wheat in a bobsled argued with the wheat buyer; machinery within the mill boomed and whined; water gurgled in the ice-freed millrace.

The clatter was a relief to Carol after months of smug houses. She wished that she could work in the mill; that she did not belong to the caste of professional man's wife.

She started for home, through the small slum. Before a tarpaper shack, at a gateless gate, a man in rough brown dogskin coat and black plush cap with lappets was watching her. His square face was confident, his foxy mustache was picaresque. He stood erect, his hands in his side-pockets, his pipe puffing slowly. He was forty-five or-six, perhaps.

"How do, Mrs. Kennicott," he drawled.

She recalled him—the town handyman, who had repaired their furnace at the beginning of winter.

"Oh, how do you do," she fluttered.

"My name's Bjornstam. 'The Red Swede' they call me. Remember? Always thought I'd kind of like to say howdy to you again."

"Ye—yes—I've been exploring the outskirts of town."

"Yump. Fine mess, No sewage, no street cleaning, and the Lutheran minister and the priest represent the arts and sciences. Well, thunder, we submerged tenth down here in Swede Hollow are no worse off than you folks. Thank God, we don't have to go and purr at Juanity Haydock at the Jolly Old Seventeen."

The Carol who regarded herself as completely adaptable was uncomfortable at being chosen as comrade by a pipe-reeking odd-job man. Probably he was one of her husband's patients. But she must keep her dignity.

"Yes, even the Jolly Seventeen isn't always so exciting. It's very cold again today, isn't it. Well—"

Bjornstam was not respectfully valedictory. He showed no signs of pulling a forelock. His eyebrows moved as though they had a life of their own. With a subgrin he went on:

"Maybe I hadn't ought to talk about Mrs. Haydock and her Solemcholy Seventeen in that fresh way. I suppose I'd be tickled to death if I was invited to sit in with that gang. I'm what they call a pariah, I guess. I'm the town badman, Mrs. Kennicott: town atheist, and I suppose I must be an anarchist, too. Everybody who doesn't love the bankers and the Grand Old Republican Party is an anarchist."

Carol had unconsciously slipped from her attitude of departure into an attitude of listening, her face full toward him, her muff lowered. She fumbled:

"Yes, I suppose so." Her own grudges came in a flood. "I don't see why you shouldn't criticize the Jolly Seventeen if you want to. They aren't sacred."

"Oh yes, they are! The dollar sign has chased the crucifix clean off the map. But then, I've got no kick. I do what I please, and I suppose I ought to let them do the same."

"What do you mean by saying you're a pariah?"

"I'm poor, and yet I don't decently envy the rich. I'm an old bach. I make enough money for a stake, and then I sit around by myself, and shake hands with myself, and have a smoke, and read history, and I don't contribute to the wealth of Brother Elder or Daddy Cass."

"You—I fancy you read a good deal."

"Yep. In a hit-or-a-miss way. I'll tell you: I'm a lone wolf. I trade horses, and saw wood, and work in lumber camps—I'm a first-rate swamper. Always wished I could go to college. Though I s'pose I'd find it pretty slow, and they'd probably kick me out."

"You really are a curious person, Mr.—"

"Bjornstam. Miles Bjornstam. Half Yank and half Swede. Usually known as that damn lazy big-mouth calamity-howler that ain't satisfied with the way we run things. No, I ain't curious—whatever you mean by that! I'm just a bookworm. Probably too much reading for the amount of digestion I've got. Probably half-baked. I'm going to get in 'half-baked' first, and beat you to it, because it's dead sure to be handed to a radical that wears jeans!"

They grinned together. She demanded:

"You say that the Jolly Seventeen is stupid. What makes you think so?"

"Oh, trust us borers into the foundation to know about your leisure class. Fact, Mrs. Kennicott, I'll say that far as I can make out, the only people in this man's town that do have any brains— I don't mean ledger-keeping brains or duck-hunting brains or baby-spanking brains, but real imaginative brains—are you and me and Guy Pollock and the foreman at the flour mill. He's a socialist, the foreman. (Don't tell Lym Cass that! Lym would fire a socialist quicker than he would a horse thief!)"

"Indeed, no, I sha'n't tell him."

"This foreman and I have some great set-to's. He's a regular old-line party member. Too dogmatic. Expects to reform everything from deforestation to nosebleed by saying phrases like 'surplus value.' Like reading the prayer book. But same time, he's a Plato J. Aristotle compared with people like Ezry Stowbody or Professor Mott or Julius Flickerbaugh."

"It's interesting to hear about him."

He dug his toe into a drift, like a schoolboy. "Rats. You mean I talk took much. Well, I do, when I get hold of somebody like you. You probably want to run along and keep your nose from freezing."

"Yes, I must go, I suppose. But tell me: Why did you leave

Miss Sherwin, of the high school, out of your list of the town intelligentsia?"

"I guess maybe she does belong in it. From all I can hear she's in everything and behind everything that looks like a reform—lot more than most folks realize. She lets Mrs. Reverend Warren, the president of this-here Thanatopsis Club, think she's running the works, but Miss Sherwin is the secret boss, and nags all the easygoing dames into doing something. But way I figure it out—You see, I'm not interested in these dinky reforms. Miss Sherwin's trying to repair the holds in this barnacle-covered ship of a town by keeping busy bailing out the water. And Pollock tries to repair it by reading poetry to the crew! Me, I want to yank it up on the ways, and fire the poor bum of a shoemaker that built it so it sails crooked, and have it rebuilt right, from the keel up."

"Yes—that—that would be better. But I must run home. My poor nose is nearly frozen."

"Say, you better come in and get warm, and see what an old bach's shack is like."

She looked doubtfully at him, at the low shanty, the yard that was littered with cordwood, moldy planks, a hoopless washtub. She was disquieted, but Bjornstam did not give her the opportunity to be delicate. He flung out his hand in a welcoming gesture which assumed that she was her own counselor, that she was not a Respectable Married Woman but fully a human being. With a shaky, "Well, just a moment, to warm my nose," she glanced down the street to make sure that she was not spied on, and bolted toward the shanty.

She remained for one hour, and never had she known a more considerate host than the Red Swede.

He had but one room: bare pine floor, small workbench, wall bunk with amazingly neat bed, frying pan and ash-stippled coffeepot on the shelf behind the potbellied cannonball stove, backwoods chairs—one constructed from half a barrel, one from a tilted plank—and a row of books incredibly assorted; Byron and Tennyson and Stevenson, a manual of gas engines, a book by Thorstein Veblen, and a spotty treatise on "The Care, Feeding, Diseases, and Breeding of Poultry and Cattle."

There was but one picture—a magazine color plate of a steep-roofed village in the Harz Mountains which suggested kobolds and maidens with golden hair.

Bjornstam did not fuss over her. He suggested, "Might throw open your coat and put your feet up on the box in front of the stove." He tossed his dogskin coat into the bunk, lowered himself into the barrel chair, and droned on:

"Yeh, I'm probably a yahoo, but by gum I do keep my independence by doing odd jobs, and that's more 'n these polite cusses like the clerks in the banks do. When I'm rude to some slob, it may be partly because I don't know better (and God knows I'm not no authority on trick forks and what pants you wear with a Prince Albert), but mostly it's because I mean something. I'm about the only man in Johnson County that remembers the joker in the Declaration of Independence about Americans being supposed to have the right to 'life, liberty, and the pursuit of happiness.'

"I meet old Ezra Stowbody on the street. He looks at me like he wants me to remember he's a highmuckamuck and worth two hundred thousand dollars, and he says, "Uh, Bjornquist—"

" 'Bjornstam's my name, Ezra,' I says. *He* knows my name, all rightee."

" 'Well, whatever your name is,' he says, 'I understand you have a gasoline saw. I want you to come around and saw up four cords of maple for me,' he says."

" 'So you like my looks, eh?' " I says, kind of innocent.

" 'What difference does that make? Want you to saw that wood before Saturday,' he says, real sharp. Common workman going and getting fresh with a fifth of a million dollars all walking around in a hand-me-down fur coat! "

" 'Here's the difference it makes,' I says, just to devil him. 'How do you know I like *your* looks?' Maybe he didn't look sore! 'Nope,' I says, 'thinking it all over, I don't like your application for a loan. Take it to another bank, only there ain't any,' I says, and I walks off on him."

"Sure. Probably I was surly—and foolish. But I figured there had to be *one* man in town independent enough to sass the banker!"

He hitched out of his chair, made coffee, gave Carol a cup, and talked on, half defiant and half apologetic, half wistful for friendliness and half amused by her surprise at the discovery that there was a proletarian philosophy.

At the door, she hinted:

"Mr. Bjornstam, if you were I, would you worry when people thought you were affected?"

"Huh? Kick 'em in the face! Say, if I were a sea gull, and all over silver, think I'd care what a pack of dirty seals thought about my flying?"

It was not the wind at her back, it was the thrust of Bjornstam's scorn which carried her though town. She faced Juanita Haydock, cocked her head at Maud Dyer's brief nod, and came home to Bea radiant. She telephoned Vida Sherwin to "run over this evening." She lustily played Tschaikowsky—the virile chords an echo of the red laughing philosopher of the tar-paper shack.

(When she hinted to Vida, "Isn't there a man here who amuses himself by being irreverent to the village gods—Bjornstam, some such a name?" the reform leader said "Bjornstam? Oh yes. Fixes things. He's awfully impertinent.")

31

The Village Atheist

Emanuel Haldeman-Julius

The founder of the world famous Little Blue Books, Emanuel Haldeman-Julius was born in Philadelphia in 1889, and became a socialist while still a teenager. Moving to Girard, Kansas, in 1915, he joined the editorial staff of the *Appeal to Reason* newspaper, the most widely circulating socialist newspaper in the world at that time, with subscribers numbering in the hundreds of thousands. Author Meridel LeSueur tells how her mother, Marian Wharton, who taught correspondence courses at the People's College in nearby Fort Scott, Kansas, urged that the books she referred to in her text be printed in inexpensive format, so that workers and common folk could afford an education. Thus, Haldeman-Julius, who meanwhile had married the daughter of a local banker, commenced his small 3½ × 5-inch booklets in 1919. Combining his advertising skill (especially large, attractive newspaper ads) and courageous editorial spirit, the Little Blue Book sales soon expanded geometrically, and over the next thirty years, hundreds of millions of copies were sold for as little as 5¢ each. Haldeman-Julius had a strong interest in freethought, publishing not only such classics as Paine and Ingersoll, but Darrow, Russell, and other modern writers. One of his most prolific authors, billed as "the world's greatest scholar," was the ex-priest Joseph McCabe. While Haldeman-Julius acquired a slightly scandalous reputation for publishing spicy-sounding booklets on sex and sex education, he also printed the complete plays of Shakespeare, Oscar Wilde, and the Greek tragedians. By the late 1940s, Haldeman-Julius's antagonism to J. Edgar Hoover was such that he published a Blue Book which amounted to a scathing attack on the F.B.I. (described as "a Gestapo in knee pants"). Hoover retaliated, and I.R.S. investigations began. In 1951, Emanuel Haldeman-Julius was found dead in his own swimming pool, an apparent drowning.

After his father's death, Henry Haldeman-Julius retained a stock of Blue Books in the building originally constructed in Girard as the home of the *Appeal* and the book company. This structure, "The Temple of the Revolution," survived until its destruction by fire on July 4, 1978.

In certain quarters, where there is pride of intellect together with a spirit of compromise and policy playing on the subject of religion, it seems to be fashionable to sneer at "the village atheist." Sometimes this "village atheist" is called, by way of mock courtesy, a "curbstone philosopher"; and the suggestion is that he is a very crude, poorly educated, awkwardly reasoning fellow—one who is incapable of perceiving the subtler arguments that, while they may (according to these critics) turn one away from superstition, enable one more clearly to appreciate the value of what is called "true religion." Even so good and usually sound a literary critic as Carl Van Doren, in his preface to a collection of excerpts from Thomas Paine's writings, says that Paine's *The Age of Reason* has long been the "Bible of village atheists."

It is not clear, after a first or second thought, why an atheist in a village should be absolutely inferior to an atheist in a city. Ordinarily we do not think of villages as homes of the highest culture; but it is also a fact that thousands of inhabitants of the city differ only in manners and not really in culture from their village-bred brethren; and it is further true that good books and good ideas can and in a measure do find their way to villages, bringing at least to an individual here and there a more enlightened viewpoint than is shared by the majority.

Atheism, as an attitude toward the problems, fictitious or real, that are posed by religion requires considerable decision and a clearer light of thought for anyone who has been reared in the atmosphere of conventional religion. One would like to ask the critics of the "village atheist" whether they regard him as intellectually a higher or a lower type than the village pulpit-pounder or the village Christian

---

From E. Haldeman-Julius, *The Age-Old Follies of Man,* Little Blue Book No. 1488 (Girard, Kans.: Haldeman-Julius Publications, 1930). Courtesy E. Haldeman-Julius Collection, Axe Library, Pittsburg State University, Pittsburg, Kansas.

E. Haldeman-Julius. By permission of Special Collections, Axe Library, Pittsburg
State University, Kansas.

who believes his Bible from cover to cover or any village (or city)
believer in religion whose belief is a matter of thoughtlessness and
fashion. Whatever the shortcomings of this "village atheist," evidently
his mind has been active and curious enough to rise above the level
of his mental surroundings; it is literally true that he has devoted

more actual thought to religious questions than his pious neighbors; he has not been tamely and incuriously gullible, swallowing as gospel truth whatever the preachers have declared on the bogus authority of a hodge-podge Bible and a hypothetical God.

But we need not for the moment concern ourselves with the refinement, the subtlety and suavity, nor the general culture of "the village atheist." He may be deficient in esthetic sensibilities; as a philosopher he may not be all-embracing in scope; in numerous branches of knowledge his information may not be all that it should be—no layman, for that matter, however intelligent and studious, can match the extensive information and understanding of the specialist in any subject; but in his philosophy of atheism, I maintain that "the village atheist" is sound and that his critics cannot dispose of him derisively with a phrase.

It is usually insinuated by these critics that "the village atheist" is superficial, that his arguments are crude and elementary, and that he is not sufficiently aware of the broader reaches of philosophy. The fact is that his arguments are sound, shrewd, and unanswerable. They may not original with him—they have been repeated innumerale times—but they are still decidedly vital and insistent arguments precisely because, while having been repeated so often, they have never been answered with reason and conviction. There is not a single point in the philosophy of atheism as commonly expounded by "village atheists" which has been shown to be irrelevant or unreasonable; the most roughly educated "village atheist" propounds questions that all the so-called wise men of religion have been unable to answer satisfyingly; his objections to religion may seem elementary—well, indeed they are elementary—which means that they go to the root of the matter and deal with those first principles which must be placed in clarity before religion can justify itself. Assuredly the arguments of "the village atheist" appear quite simple; one might even say that these are questions which a bright child would naturally ask, which is by no means to say that they are foolish questions; on the contrary, they are questions which, first and last, stand centrally challenging to the whole viewpoint and all the conceivable claims and doctrines of religion.

One query, for example, which is shrewdly put forth by every "village atheist" is as follows: If God made the world, who made God? That is looked upon with an amused smile as a childish question by some persons who proudly regard themselves as intellectual without fairly grasping, in the first place, what simple fundamental intelligence is. Here, nevertheless, we see a keen, penetrating objection to theology at its very basis; for all theology assumes divinity and it is this idea of divinity that is basically inconceivable and untenable. To assume the existence and the original creative action of a God is certainly not a simplification or explanation of the mystery of things. It serves only to confuse the issue and the problem of beginnings still remains to be settled.

Naïvely, the Christian says that the world can only be explained by the belief that a God made it and is running it or, as some more tentatively suggest, wound it up so that it runs itself; but in fact this so-called explanation simply demands another explanation, which, indeed, when we try to reconcile the idea of God with the realities of life, lands us in confusion worse confounded. Usually, I believe, the Christian replies that God is eternal and uncreated, that he always existed. And to this the obvious comment of common sense is that the simpler thing is to assume that the universe has always existed, that nobody made it, and that the assumption of divinity is not only unreasonable but unnecessary. It is true that one cannot very well imagine the universe either as having eternally existed or as having been definitely started at some time; life, in other words, still has a good deal of the mysterious about it but there is no sense in adding to the mystery or trying obviously erroneous ways of solving it by religion. We can only take the world, the universe, life as it is and observe it scientifically, leaving aside the vain speculations that are called spiritual.

In essence, religion is a vague belief in something outside the universe which controls, as it has created, the universe; whereas science observes and makes use of what is instead of imagining what is not. As a matter of fact, the most subtle and profound thinkers have dealt most seriously with this very question of the inconceivable existence of a God as the starting point of things; and while they have employed a more refined phraseology and have given a more extensive and unusual display of logic, they are at bottom standing on the same ground and tackling the same difficulty as "the village atheist."

Who made God? Admittedly here is a very simple question— yet it is a question that no believer in religion, not the most pretentious theologian nor the most profoundly intellectual God-defending philosopher, has ever been able to answer clearly and convincingly; it is no answer to say that God always existed; for the idea of God is purely fictitious and is conceived in the first place, supposedly, to solve a problem; but the atheist says, a good deal more simply and sensibly, that the universe cannot be explained by something or somebody outside of the universe—that, in fact, it is far more satisfactory to the reason and far less confusing in dealing with the problem to assume that the universe always existed.

The idea of God is merely a gratuitous and, one may say, even a grotesque complication. The way of intelligence is to start with the observation and the orderly explanation of what we know and from this to clear a field of further knowledge—to proceed, in other words, from what we know to what we do not know but may reasonably hope to know as the result of scientific investigation. But the method of religion is just the opposite; it attempts to dominate and distort knowledge by the overbearing power of sheer ignorance— to begin, ludicrously backwards, with what we do not know and thus explain reality by arbitrary schemes of fantasy. Religion says: Let us assume the idea of a God and try to make the facts of life fit that assumption. Science says: Let us study life and see where it leads us. However crudely he may put his case, "the village atheist" is in harmony with this human (as opposed to divine) and realistic attitude of science.

Again, the assumption of divinity raises many other problems which have been a real vexation to sincere theologians and have rather embarrassingly tried the talent for sophistry which is found in those who insincerely seek to bolster up the case for religion. Deviously and even desperately theologians have attempted to reconcile the conflicting ideas of omnipotence and benevolence as attributes of deity. Some of the most ludicrous intellectual acrobatics known to man have been displayed in trying to solve this problem of evil in its relation to the dogma of an all-ruling and good-purposing God. Is "the village atheist" crude in his remarks about this problem? Maybe, but what matters is that he exposes sharply the illogical, indefensible position of the believer in God.

The evil, planless, and chance-ridden nature of things; the remorseless activity of tooth and claw that obtains throughout the animal world; the sufferings and follies of mankind, all make a mockery of the idea of Providence. Obviously, a God could not at once be the possessor of absolute power to carry out his will and, when one reflects upon the evils of life, be at the same time a good God. Christian theology only gets itself into a worse quandary when it attempts to solve this puzzle by inventing a Devil who is responsible for the world's evils. It follows, from this argument, that the Devil often gets the better of God and is thus in many things more powerful. Either this is true or, which is not much more agreeable to the sensibilities of Christians, God willfully permits the Devil to inflict suffering upon men and lead them astray into sin.

Like the query as to the origin of God, this contradiction as to the assumed nature of deity has been pointed out again and again by atheists, both in the cultured atmosphere of universities and in the humbler sphere of village controversy. And equally this argument, whether made by the philosophical skeptic (more subtly trained in philosophy and logic) or by the "village atheist," has stumped the succeeding generations of mentally gyrating theologians. The argument is dodged in various ways, none of which is very graceful. There is the theory expressed poetically by Tennyson:

For I doubt not though the ages one increasing purpose runs
And the thoughts of men are widened with the process of the suns.

Or, as the "Modernists" in religion say, evolution is simply the method of God. But, after all, does this make sense? The statement is made that an all-powerful, all-wise God has no function through a slow, blundering, cruel process of evolution; that divine wisdom, although foreseeing all, has to err immensely in order to reach perfection; that evil is an unescapable agency through whch somehow good must be achieved, although logically, if there were a God who loved the good and had the power to make it universal and triumphant, he would do so.

Convincingly enough, the facts of evolution show the fallacy of the God idea. We have a world of mixed good and evil, of slow processes and countless blunders, of ignorance and greed and struggle gradually yielding to the more orderly and humane unfolding of man's intelligence—we have such a world precisely because it is planless and is indifferent to moral values save as man has made such plans and cultivated such values in the interests of his own social life. Evolution, fairly understood in its true significance, is absolutely incompatible with the deistical theory. In the light of the evolutionary story, the idea of God is a supreme irony.

Now, the philosopher may set forth a widely reasoned, extensively documented, and very impressive and masterly exposition of this argument for atheism; he may have the material and style of scholarship, to which "the village atheist," cannot pretend; even so, the heart of the argument is perfectly well understood by "the village atheist," and in stating it he is not being crude but rather very cogent and basic. Those who affect an air of superiority and who suggest, with a bland tone of timeless and unworldly wisdom, that it is superficial to apply human judgments and reasoning to such esoteric matters are themselves, in striving for the "spiritually" profound, flying off at a tangent from all meaning and all connection with clear, mundane reality. What other than human reasoning can we use? The notion of a divine reason or viewpoint or standard of judgment is all sheer illusion. It turns out to be, upon examination, simply a particularly lawless and dogmatic kind of human reasoning.

Theologians are not inspired; they are irrational—and that no matter how cleverly they seem to confound reason with their tricks of specious logic. Theology at its most abstruse is no doubt a very intricate game of wits; but it is a child's game after all; theology has never shed any enlightenment or stimulated any progress in life. And as between a highly educated mystic and subtle exponent of Catholic superstition like Cardinal Newman and "the village atheist," the latter is far the more reasonable and sees more clearly in a world of facts.

There is of course one dodge that serves—to the satisfaction of Christians, at any rate—when all others fail. It is said, by way of removing religion out of the sphere of merely human intelligence, that the ways of God are inscrutable. It wouldn't be so bad if Christians would really stick to that attitude—if they would (for that must logically follow from the argument of inscrutability) leave the mention of God out of things. But inconsistently they pretend to know a great deal about God's ways, his nature, his purposes, his commandments to men. Holding strictly to the theory of the inscrutability of God, there could be no theology; for theology is nothing more or less than an assumed explanation of God and his ways; and when the theologian is argumentatively in a corner, his talk of inscrutability is a poor and unimpressive defense. It is true enough indeed, as the atheist sees it—decidedly the theologian, the God-explainer clerical or lay, knows nothing whatever about God. The rub is that he pretends to know when he thinks he can impress the unwary and, contrarily, hunts his hole of esoteric profundity (or the profound secretiveness of a swollen, pious cipher of ignorance) when the argument becomes too strong for him. Whatever his critics may say, it remains the fact that "the village atheist" propounds questions that not all the schools of divinity can answer reasonably or even so as to make apparent, sustained sense.

With regard to the subject of man's means of salvation and the so-called divine plan, "the village atheist" is also sharp and logical in criticism of religion. Is he simply repeating what he has read in Paine's *The Age of Reason?*—very well, we must give him credit for perceiving that Paine is a better reasoner than the preachers. It may seem to a pseudo-intellectual that it is trifling or impolite to suggest that it was very awkward, crude, and even causelessly cruel for God to have his own son turned into a man and force upon him the agony of crucifixion in order that man might have a chance to be saved through believing in Jesus Christ. Yet surely one would have a very poor opinion of the intelligence of a mere human being who should adopt such a fantastic and ludicrous scheme; and, coming from the alleged fountainhead of divine omniscience, such a scheme appears all the more flabbergasting. It is not "the village atheist" who is foolish in deriding this theory of salvation; rather it is the Christian who is foolish in believing that such monkey-shines have any rhyme or reason about them, let alone the egregious notion that they are the eternal, essential, eminently wise, and inspired plan of salvation.

It is urged by "the village atheist" as a legitimate and plainly sensible argument that if there were a God and if there were such a thing as a necessity of salvation, religiously speaking, this God could devise a much simpler and surer scheme. He could put it infallibly in the hearts of men to be saved, so that there could be no chance of a slipup in the spiritual machinery. He could make his divine truth, if any, so clear and simple and impressive that none could doubt it nor fail to take it profoundly and in its full significance. He could have made God-consciousness, so to speak, as natural and as instinctive and as indisputable as breathing or any other natural function. But what—we can imagine "the village atheist" asking the question in sarcastic tone—is the upshot of this curious plan of salvation? Why, it is so obscure and debatable that one-half of the world has always insisted that the other half was headed straight for hell. What should be clearest of all things—God's will and wish toward man—is, ironically, the most dubious question (a question that has its ramifications in endless futile questions upon questions) which has ever puzzled the poor, ill-guided, fantasy-beset wits of man. Naturally enough this is so, for, as "the village atheist" points out repeatedly at the risk of being called superficial and unoriginal, the idea of God—the first principle of religion—primarily sets at defiance the perception and reasoning and sense of reality of rational beings. The idea of God is bunk in a densely opaque state; therefore, all ideas that issue from the idea of God are similarly chips from the same block of bunk.

The conception of free will is another inconsistency of the God-worshipers which the "village atheist" points out, crudely maybe but not the less logically. He has said upon this score exactly what the best thinkers are still saying, and it is a difficulty which Christians

The Temple of the Revolution. Girard, Kansas.
By permission of Special Collections, Axe Library, Pittsburgh State University, Kansas.

have never been able to explain away. It is a perverse notion that a God with any sense of his responsibilities would leave the preference for good or evil an open question with his creatures—his human creatures, for it is not contended by anyone that there is any question of good and evil among the lower animals; and this latter assumption, by the way, is legitimately challenged by "the village atheist," who suggests fairly enough that it is queer indeed that a God would make some creatures with souls and some without souls. God, says the Christian, makes it possible for men to know the difference between good and evil and leaves the responsibility of choice to them. Yet it is not, in the first place, true that there is any absolute unvarying difference between good and evil that is perfectly known to men and agreed upon by men. Even so far as knowledge goes, let alone freedom of action, God has left things in a distressing and perplexing state of obscurity.

Certainly, God should know a great deal more about this troubling question of good and evil than mere men can possibly know; yet he neglects to give men the light of his superior knowledge and leaves them to decide these fine points by their tentative and experimental finite reason; and, with apparent unconcern, God sees men sacrificing themselves to the most ludicrous errors of moral judgment, a prey to fanaticism, to unnatural and poisonous fears, to dogmatic concepts that interfere with a sane life.

Is it argued that God places men on trial and that, by struggle and error, it is his intention to develop them ruggedly in moral character? That would seem an entirely needless proceeding to an all-powerful God; and besides it means that many, who are unable to stand the strain and who are corrupted rather than developed by the moral struggle, have to fall pitiably by the wayside in order that others may reach the goal.

The assumption of a God cannot be applied logically to any phase or problem of life. At the very outset, in trying to reason from the assumption of God, one is landed in a swamp of unreason. We know that some men are weak and others are strong; nature distributes unevenly her favors and defects; so that if God is responsible, he is unfair—and if he is simply permitting such inequalities without willing them (a distinction without a difference, after all) then he must be charged with being criminally indifferent or negligent. Predestination is not a better theory; it would be a cruel and unjust God—a monster of a God—who would condemn some infallibly to hell and reserve to others the privilege of heaven.

True, these are simple objections to religion; but when one says they are simple, one means that they are fundamental; until they are cleared away, no further claims of religion are worth consideration. Philosophy, serving as the handmaiden of religion, may produce some very high-flown arguments. Sophistry may proceed to the cleverest extreme. Fine distinctions may be drawn and subtle points made in favor of this or that view of religion. But first of all these familiar questions asked by the "village atheist" must be answered reasonably— indeed, truth concerning these questions must be demonstrated realistically—and it is this which the defenders of religion have failed utterly to accomplish in all the long, ingenious, powerful history of theology.

As simply as he presses other objections to religion, so does "the village atheist" press his pious neighbors to prove or even intelligibly to explain the dogma of immortality. Here, too, he asks questions that are as pertinent and unanswerable as they were when the first skeptic gave utterance to them. It is evident that the universal way of things is life, growth, decay, and death—and what, asks "the village atheist," has the Christian to offer in proof that man is an exception to this rule? Furthermore, why should he be an exception and, to put it on the simplest ground, what conceivable reasonable point would there be in carefully saving throughout an eternity the souls of individual men, so many of whom are quite unimportant and readily replaced and whom it is hard to believe could be so spiritually vital in an endless scheme of things?

Perhaps "the village atheist" does not go elaborately into philosophic arguments about immortality, but he is certainly logical and sufficiently powerful in his criticism when he asks the simple question: What actual evidence can be shown for immortality? It is, he points out, an idea that rests on pure assumption and which in all the experiences and investigations of men has not been supported by a single fact. So-called "spiritual evidence" is rightly disregarded by "the village atheist." Perhaps he is lacking in subtlety—that is what his intellectual or "spiritual" critics are fond of asserting. But there is such a thing as being too subtle, when that subtlety is merely a mental mirage of sophistry; when it is only fine words strung together and sustained by no concrete image; when the wish is father to the thought.

"The village atheist" makes out a plain case against religion, buttressed by a formidable if rude logic. If he appears insensitive to the finer—and futile—speculations of men who spin webs of wonderful fantasy out of their inner consciousness, he has at any rate a due regard for facts and that, for the purpose of arriving at truth, is better than any amount of nimble fact-dodging logic. Before one goes into abstruse speculation or argument on any subject, there are certain plain, fundamental questions that require an answer. These are the questions which, with regard to the subject of religion, "the village atheist" continues to ask and which not the most skillful theologian can answer, although he may offer various evasive and unsatisfactory replies. In building a philosophy of life, "the village atheist"—at least insofar as an attitude toward religion is involved in a philosophy of life—wants to begin at the foundation. Maybe that is a crude and materialistic method. That is what his "spiritual critics" assert, who ignore the foundation of facts and reason and start in gaily and irresponsibly trying to establish an airy structure in the clouds—indeed, beyond the clouds, entirely out of sight.

What if "the village atheist" does lack originality? It is better to be unoriginal and rational than to be originally fantastic and irrational. Does "the village atheist" repeat the arguments of Paine and Ingersoll? Very well; they are sound, unanswerable, directly pertinent arguments; they strike at the very heart of the assumptions of religion; and it is not a matter of inventing arguments, but of looking at things reasonably, denying oneself the dubious luxury that may be associated in some minds with the refinements of sophistry.

Was Thomas Paine crude when he pointed out that revelation must be direct from God to man and that when coming through an intermediary, prophet or savior so-called, it is but hearsay? Was Paine giving evidence of a lack of culture, or was he exhibiting a good and clear critical insight when he riddled with remorseless logic the inconsistencies of the Bible? Was Ingersoll merely being childish or perversely refusing to see the truth and beauty of religion when he said that man created God in his own image—that the God idea is but a reflection of man's superstition and his unscientific effort to explain things—that the assumptions of religion, God and all the rest, are compounded of pure fallacy? When Ingersoll exposed the absurdities and cruelties of the doctrines of heaven and hell, of the whole mystic notion of a hereafter, was he taking a position inferior in point of wisdom to the high plane of "spiritual" philosophy or was he taking the best vantage ground of common sense, of plain observation and reason, to see the truth of things?

Certainly the preachers have never been able to show anything that was wrong with Ingersoll's (or, similarly, with the "village atheist's") reasoning; in attempting to show that Ingersoll and "the village atheist" are superficial the preachers simply expose their own wide variance from a valid, reasonable, conception of life.

No doubt it is annoying to a preacher when "the village atheist" throws at him questions about heaven—its location, its nature, its appearance and laws, and the like. It doubtless seems a bit of perversity for "the village atheist" to point out that this heaven the preachers mention so assuredly is an imaginary place which nobody has ever seen, with which we have no communication, from which no one has ever returned even for a moment to enlighten us. These are irrelevant details, the preacher may say; but they are not; they are exactly what we should and would know if heaven were a positive, located, comprehended place.

And, again, when the preacher says that men must have faith, "the village atheist" replies that he is merely asking that others believe him without the slightest evidence or show of reason; that in other words the preacher is saying, "Don't bother me with questions, and don't ask me for proof, but just believe what I tell you."

One does not readily understand why "the village atheist" should be accused of crudeness and superficiality because he has an inquiring and independent mind. Of course, we expect him to be condemned by preachers and by Christians of the ordinary type. But it is more of a surprise when we find this attitude among certain intellectuals and critics who have, after all, an unusually thoughtful view of life and who might be expected to recognize the pertinence and logic of "the village atheist's" arguments—who, assuredly, do not have a simple belief in a God or in religion, although by some trick of verbiage and imagery they may persuade themselves that they have a glimpse of "true religion." Such a critic as Carl Van Doren, for instance, may feel that the arguments of "the village atheist" are unoriginal and crudely expressed; but can he produce any arguments for religion that are as sound as the arguments of "the village atheist" against religion? What Van Doren's attitude toward religion is I do not know; he may, for all I know, be an atheist or he may prefer to call himself more tentatively a skeptic; but, surprisingly, now and then a man who is himself utterly a disbeliever in religion speaks slightingly of "the village atheist"; quite often it is no more than a literary objection and is made in forgetfulness of the fact that, after all, "the village atheist" is voicing the prime inquiries that still must be made in approaching the subject of religion.

There is another type of man who, while not able to gull himself with the absurdities of conventional religion, is nevertheless at heart a mystic. This sort of man dislikes "the village atheist" because the latter is realistic and materialistic and because he prefers plain truth to fancy notions. When the strain of mysticism is strong in a man he does not wish to be confined to clear-cut, definite ideas nor does he wish to make direct, detailed inquiries into religion or anything else. He loves, it seems, a sort of thinking—or perhaps it would be better described as feeling—that is without form or real direction, that inspires the mind to function in free fancy regardless of rules of reason. Mystics are impatient with facts. A simple, logical form of thought, based carefully upon observation, is distasteful to this— well, disorderly—type of mind.

Nine times out of ten one will find that it is a man who is enamored with some sort of mysticism who accuses "the village atheist" of arguing crudely, superficially, impertinently and ignoring higher "spiritual" values. And quite effectively "the village atheist" would reply that it is this "spiritual" assumption—the assumption that there is a peculiar order of truth apart from and above the kind of truth that men can know by observation and reason—which is, after all, his main point of attack. What is the "soul"? asks "the village atheist"— and philosophers have asked it and the great skeptics of all ages have asked it and, when all the arguments or attempted explanations of theologians are summed up, one finds that all they can say is that the "soul" is "spiritual" and that "spiritual" truth is the concern of the "soul," pretending to explain one word with another word that is equally meaningless.

Yes—the great skeptics, the great thinkers who have led in the work of enlightenment, have insisted, with reference to religion, upon fundamentally the same inquiries and have stated the same contradictions and difficulties that are directly propounded in the familiar arguments of "the village atheist." There is nothing so devastating as common sense applied to religion; and "the village atheist," if he is lacking in intellectual refinements and cannot argue subtly in a circle of metaphysics, at any rate does, with a few observations and queries of common sense, cut away the bare, unsupported, even unintelligible assumptions that are the stock in trade of religion.

Socrates asked questions—no doubt they seemed to many of his fellows to be perverse or childish questions—and the "village atheist," in confounding interrogatively and argumentatively the wits of the pious, is following an illustrious intellectual example.

32

Essays

Charles Leroy Edson

Charles Leroy Edson was born near Wilber, Nebraska, in 1881, but soon moved to Cuba, Kansas, in the north central section of the state. His early life was one of great deprivation, later chronicled in an anonymously published autobiography, *The Great American Ass* (1926). Here's a typical excerpt:

> I had come out of the Kansas culture, which is a derivation of the Harvard culture because Kansans are derived from the Puritan tribe. And this Kansas culture with its hatred of the superior man, and its belief in magic, clairvoyance, food from the atmosphere, federal aid from governmental Santa Clauses, and its identifying itself with the downtrodden beasts under a cruel master, was a tribal propaganda that forever disgusted me with all tribal propaganda.

Edson attended the University of Kansas, where he almost starved to death, and worked for the *Appeal to Reason* newspaper in Girard, Kansas, as well as other newspapers. In the twenties, he published some small booklets of poetry and prose; during the Depression, Edson was part of the Federal Writers Project in Kansas. His remarkable correspondence from that period is in the collections of the Kansas State Historical Society in Topeka, along with the manuscript of an unpublished novel, *The Biological Jesus*. Although much of Edson's work was bitterly and powerfully satirical with an unusually zesty style, he was most proud that some of his children's verses had passed into the general recital lore of school playgrounds. Edson's later years were marked by poverty and neglect. He died in a nursing home in Topeka, Kansas, in 1975.

TALES FROM THE FOLKLORE OF SOCIALISM

"A romancer" is what George H. Shoaf was called by E. Haldeman-Julius in his autobiography. Newsman Shoaf was the roving reporter for the Socialist *Appeal to Reason,* and he appealed to the imagination. Shoaf "wrote prodigious fairy tales," and sent them in as straight news to the editor in Kansas, who printed them because he believed in magic. The test of the inferior mind, said Freud, is that it believes in magic. None of Shoaf's fantastic news dispatches from Los Angeles in 1911 have been reprinted in the first edition of H-J's autobiography; he only mentions the setup left for the police in George's rooming house in Los Angeles, when George Shoaf went underground after leaving "circumstantial evidence" to indicate he'd been murdered.

Said an anonymous communication: "You socialist editors should have better sense than to send George Shoaf to Los Angeles, the city of beautiful blond angels, because you knew George was susceptible to women." When the letter came to Girard, Kansas, the assistant editor to Fred D. Warren was a clairvoyant writer named Charles Lincoln Phifer. Phifer had already pronounced Shoaf dead and eaten by sharks, and the *Appeal to Reason* had published the story as a fact. Phifer later told me the anonymous letter plainly was written by George Shoaf and it did not come from the spirit world where the clairvoyants supposed their Roving Reporter to be.

Shoaf pretended to have been snatched into Spirit Land while he was honestly reporting a famous murder case in Los Angeles. Labor leaders had dynamited an anti-labor capitalistic daily, the Los Angeles *Times,* incidentally killing a score of fellow workers in the press room and on the reporters' floor. James McNamara, a dynamiter, had gone to a Los Angeles establishment to needle himself up with courage before blowing up the anti-labor newspaper.

"Tales from the Folklore of Socialism," from Frank Swancara et al., *Black Lies as Evangelic Aids: Defamation as an Ingredient of Evangelism* (Girard, Kans.: Haldeman-Julius Publications, 1950). Courtesy E. Haldeman-Julius Collection, Axe Library, Pittsburg State University, Kansas.

Charles Leroy Edson. Photo courtesy of C. W. Gusewelle.

In the establishment the dynamiter probably rubbed elbows with the socialist fairy-story reporter because George Shoaf practically lived there. In the house where Shoaf was comforting peroxide blondes while McNamara was doping himself up for the killing, here is a close-up on the happenings: young McNamara paid the pianist to play "Humoresque," a popular tune with a tug on the emotions. The laborite also tipped one of the blondes to hoochie-cooch while

the Negro pianist played "Humoresque" over and over again. Mc-
Namara and friend were served a strong drink from time to time,
until he got just right. "Now," he told his Lady Lou, "I'm ready."

After the explosion I was in the socialist paper's office at Girard,
Kansas, the McNamara brothers were in jail, and George Shoaf was
in Los Angeles sending back highly imaginative news dispatches about
the cruelly farcical case against these framed young innocents. He
said that labor-baiting Harrison Gray Otis (the hate-crazed capitalist)
dynamited his own capitalistic property to smear labor. Such fact-
reporting reached the common man through the only medium that
would tell such news, and it needled him into a rage. Thousands
of 25-cent subscriptions poured into the office of the Kansas weekly
of an editor who sometimes got his inside information, his news
behind the news, by buying it from gypsy mind-readers. This believer
in clairvoyance had a clairvoyant for sub-editor, the Charles Lincoln
Phifer mentioned laughingly by H.-J. in the first draught of his
autobiography. Editorialist Phifer was shocked on hearing the circumstantial evidence of the murder of Reporter Shoaf. He went into
a physical trance for the benefit of his editorial chief and came up
with this story:

The battered, foot-trampled hat of the murdered socialist reporter
lacked clotted gore from the slaughtered idealist because the hat was
not on the head of slumbering George Shoaf when a Burns detective,
the G-man of that era, pussyfooted into the dreamer's room and
slugged the *Appeal*'s reporter to death, a dastardly deed done purely
in the interests of the "Vested Interests of Capitalism." The Burns
detective's dastardly followers transported the dead body in a motor-
boat out to sea. There was a certain spot in the Pacific Ocean not
far from shore where the salty sea's plutocratic man-eating sharks
awaited the conjunction of these capital agents at the place of rendezvous. The man-eating fish, gosh-dam their barstedly souls, soon
cleaned the bones of the truth-telling reporter as thoroughly as a
barfly polishing off pig's knuckles at the free lunch counter. Shoaf's
deep-sea skeleton can be dredged up and identified, as crystal-gazer
Lincoln Phifer prophesied, by the gold fillings in his front teeth.
The sharks had left untouched the gold deposits which were a loan
from dentistry.

The frightful news of this capitalistic crime (it was enough to
make a saint swear), brought a new rain of tinkling silver to the
only paper that tells the anti-capitalistic TRUTH. And the credulous
newspaper editors really believed their own stuff.

The McNamara brothers ended their siege of persecution by

confessing that persecution is not a one-way street, and the laborites had worked their side against the sunny side of the street where the capitalists thrived.

A preceding paragraph portraying Shoaf and McNamara in the establishment at the same time is doubtless anachronistic instead of chronological. But it gives a true picture of the habits of the two characters; and the dramatic unities of time, place, and action required the superimposing of these scenes one on another. These interesting details were obtained by this old reporter from newsmen who covered the story. Their editors had no use for this material because the press printed stories of actual actions, not the psychopathic reactions. It avoided libel suits.

The McNamara confession that they dynamited the Los Angeles newspaper jarred the workers of America like a blow on the chin. How do these muscular, uneducated, honest workers react mentally? How do men in the hot steel mills, the cool lumbering forests, the diggers in the deep mines, and the pole-climbing linemen on the high Rockies react to such a disillusionment, to such betrayal in the house of their friends?

Subscription cancellations by the thousands flooded the editorial office of the believer-in-magic and his clairvoyant assistant editor. The letters were penciled on the cheapest school tablet paper, which daddy borrowed from daughter Susie. These messages from the muscular workers were all similar in tone, and said: "You liars, you fakers . . . You barstedly s.o.b.'s . . . God dam your sole!" Other letters from men who were not so literate contained commentary-without-words, a few pages with the wiped skite of their bowels on toilet paper—a form of picture writing surviving into the steel-and-oil age of American finance-industrialism. These facts and comments are for the anthropologists.

A depression came upon the circulation of the Kansas socialist weekly, and the slump was not caused by the money economy of a boom-and-bust system in the capitalistic world. These unpleasantries are recorded here only because the picture of the Age of Liberalism would not be quite complete without this phase of the story. The tale of the error in the clairvoyant news dispatches and the resultant storm or repudiation by toilet paper was told, smilingly, by Lincoln Phifer himself. He was laughing it off as a mild error by himself in mental televison and spiritual-guided radio. Psychic Lincoln never predicted that later fools would give birth to video and radio, but he did predict that the slave-driven horse would disappear, leaving the hay crop as an insoluble problem for capitalism. Comrade Phifer said: "When the enslavement of the grass-eating beasts is ended, there will be no market for hay." His prophesy came true on that one; but how he missed it in solving the murder mystery of his friend, George Shoaf!

GOD AS TRIBAL ARTIFACT

In our studies of the more primitive tribes such as the black African, the Totem Pole Indian, and the Australian Bushman, we Nordics have put on our green goggles and our air of scholar, pundit, and savant, and have proceeded to catalogue and analyze the tribal beliefs of these "inferiors," these poor helpless "children of nature." As if our tribe was above nature! As if we, the Snordics (and by Snordics I mean the tribe that embraces all the Anglo-Saxons of all races, black and white), were not beings in nature but were supranatural— or a God race. And that is exactly what we think. But our studies of the Bushman and the Hottentot reveal to us that those tribes also regard themselves as a race of gods (and deem us a degraded race of poor benighted suckers), so there you are.

Then why not turn the green goggled eye of the scholar pundit upon our own Snordic tribe and study it just as we would the voodoo and totem delusions of the Hottentot and Eskimo? That is precisely what the author has done, in an effort to tear off the mask of ceremonial propaganda called Liberty or Democracy and lay bare the tribal soul with all the natural delusions of our tribe—and to prove that our people are "children of nature" like other races and are not above nature any more than a jack rabbit. . . .

In showing our tribal nature thus from the inside, I argue that our tribal nature is the Absolute. There is only one way to get mules, and that is due to the law of nature—an oddity of natural law— that permits the jackass to cross with the domestic horse. The mule is the living embodiment of that law. That mule and the law are one. The mule is the embodied Absolute. You cannot go behind the Absolute. And wisdom does not attempt to go behind the mule.

And since the nature of mules is absolute, and the natures of canine and of feline are also inscrutable, then the tribal nature of the Nordic is the ultimate and the Absolute. You need seek God

"God as Tribal Artifact," from C. L. Edson, *Whale Meat: A Shocking Portrayal of Our Tribal Belief in Free Food from the North Pole* (Charleston, S. C.: Southern Printing and Publishing Co., 1924)

no farther. You see him in action in that chemical-urged organism, man, driven from within. Those inward impulses common to the tribal man are the absolute. They are the face of God. Behind them the human mind cannot search. The mind is a part of tribal nature, hence it cannot go beyond tribal nature. And since the ultimate bound to which mind (or science) can penetrate, like the uppermost limit to which man can fly, must be accepted by man as the limit, we might as well call that limit Absolute. Man need never go farther than his own racial whims to find the Ultimate and the Eternal.

I do not claim that the Nordic is a race, in any scientific sense. I claim indeed that the so-called Nordic race is itself a tribal delusion, a Santa Claus. It is the giver of all gifts to mankind, isn't it? The Nordic, in his desire for a Messiah-Santa Claus has suffered the hallucination that he himself is his own Santa Claus, and hence he now worships the Nordic Race, that King of the North Pole who comes with gifts to all the world.

Bring a white-robed messenger at midnight to the house of a Senegambian, and he thinks it is the devil come to annoy him—he is apt to go through the window. He acts so because it is his tribal nature. The Nordic thinks that such a visitor, clad in white wool, is Santa Claus come to reward him with presents. He acts differently from the black man because he is of a different tribe.

If you annoy a mule, it kicks; if you annoy a cat, it scratches; if you annoy a dog, it bites. Three different reactions in one mood. But the one mood was in three different tribes. Please a mule and he brays, please a cat, and he purrs; please a dog and he wags his tail. The different ways of reacting to the same mood again proves that the different actions we see in the world of men are due to differences in tribal nature. You cannot teach a mule to purr when he is pleased, nor a cat to wag his tail. You can make a cat happy with fresh fish, but not a dog; you can make a dog happy with carrion, but not a cat. And you cannot please a mule with either.

You can tickle a Turk by telling him there is no Santa Claus. Tell the same thing to a Nordic and you drive him frantic.

There is a rat in Arizona called the trade rat. If it comes in the night and steals peanuts, it will leave in their place some pebbles of the same general size and shape; if it steals a square piece of cheese, it will trade in return a square piece of clay. It never takes anything without trading something for it. It is in the tribal nature of that breed of rats. But why? A trait of nature such as that is useless and ridiculous. We laugh at it. But man's habit of giving a ceremonial to God in return for what man takes from God is as useless and ridiculous in the eyes of Reason as the rat's giving pebbles for peanuts. But it is in the Nordic's nature to give buncombe to God. You cannot argue him out of it; you must kill him and replace him with a different race of men whose nature lacks this trick of trading with God. The Turks, for instance, do not trade with Allah, feeling that it would be useless. To get rid of trading by rats in Arizona it would be necessary to exterminate that breed of rats and replace them with some other kind of rats that do not trade.

Those rats have been trading for ten million years and got no good out of it. The belief that a messiah will come and by magic turn his misery into bliss and his world into a paradise is a trait that both Jews and Nordic have been exhibiting for thousands of years and it never did them any good.

By means of "revivals" the pious tribesman can still work himself into a joyous mood in which the sense of well-being is so ecstatic that he shouts: "The Jubilee has come!"

But any fellow can produce the same mood by drinking a bottle of whiskey.

So we see that our tribal moods, though inexplicable, are under chemical control. In ceremonial hysterics the body gradually creates the chemical; in the other case the chemical is distilled by a moonshiner and poured into the body.

The thinking man is largely non-tribal and cannot induce "the Glory" by tribal orgies; hence he keeps a liquor cellar even though it is against the tribal law. For man is determined to have this feeling of Glory, and he will have it at all costs. It is a manifestation of the Absolute. And any law against the Glory is against God and unenforcible.

For tribal nature is God, and any way to alter tribal nature is unthinkable. There is no power among men but tribal nature. And tribal nature cannot be harassed by legislation and induced to destroy tribal nature. It has the will to persist forever and not the will to kill itself.

Man's tribal nature can destroy the man, but the man cannot destroy his tribal nature. The Aztecs who welcomed Cortez because their tribal nature made them believe he was a Santa Claus were thus killed by their own folly, but the surviving descendants of them still believe in Santa Claus.

33

The Garden of Eden

S. P. Dinsmoor

Born in 1843 near Coolville, Ohio, Samuel Perry Dinsmoor served in the Union Army during the Civil War, seeing action by his own account in some eighteen battles, and witnessing Lee's surrender. He moved to Illinois in 1866 and taught school for five terms. In 1870, Dinsmoor got married on horseback and moved to Lucas, Kansas, in 1888, where he was a farmer. A few miles north of present-day Interstate 70, northeast of the town of Russell, Lucas is, perhaps only by coincidence, 22 miles from Paradise, and about 11 miles from Hell Creek.

In 1907, Dinsmoor began building his Cabin Home, using native limestone cut and fitted like logs, and consisting of eleven rooms, bath, two closets, and a cool cave for storage. Then he began constructing a series of concrete sculptures in the yard, making it, he said, "the most unique home, for living or dead, on earth." On the west side, the sculptures depict Dinsmoor's version of the Mosaic story of the Garden, including God, Adam and Eve, the Devil, Cain and Abel, and so on, all centered around themes of the temptation and expulsion from the Garden. Along the north side are sculptures from the modern period of history, including a Trust Monster and a series depicting a Darwinian Chain of Being. Other structures include a Goddess of Liberty Tree, Labor Crucified, and a Mausoleum, in which Dinsmoor was buried after his death in 1932. By 1927, he had used about 2,273 sacks of cement, or over 113 tons.

Because of Dinsmoor's genius for publicity, the Garden of Eden was visited by thousands, even becoming the subject of a series of theater slides and a short film, shown nationwide. Newspapers and magazines did feature stories. Dinsmoor himself published a *Pictorial History of the Cabin Home in Garden of Eden* in 1927, here excerpted as an explanatory text for the sculptures and other features of the Garden. More recently, the Garden has been included in surveys and studies of American folk art.

More than a mere tourist attraction, a curious remnant of eccentricity, or a bizarre artifact of popular culture, S. P. Dinsmoor's Garden of Eden is a monument to nineteenth-century Freethought, expressing many themes common to its "Golden Age," and especially demonstrating Freethought's connections to the Populist movement which flourished during the same time, peaking in the 1890s. As one local observer, O. D. Hoopes, has written, the fact that Dinsmoor "was another of those ahead of his time in many of his philosophic thoughts and opinions is evident in the current revolutionary trends in many religious bodies toward the adoption of a more liberal approach to biblical interpretation and doctrine. And, that he had the courage of his convictions at a time when such liberalization was highly unpopular amidst an orthodox majority, is evident in what he dared to lay out for all to see."

During the Populist period, speculation about the ancient past flourished, as evidenced by Ignatius Donnelly's books on the legend of Atlantis, and the Nordic creation myth of Ragnarok. Dinsmoor's sculptures and his little book about them are similar attempts to rethink some of the core myths of Western civilization, using only his common sense, and particularly, a wry sense of humor as well. Like other freethinkers, Dinsmoor prided himself on having arrived at his own interpretation, through his own imagination, which, democratically, was as good as anyone else's. His grotesque and disturbing image of the Trust Monster seizing the world was a common motif in the speeches and cartoons of the Populist newspapers. Kansas's own Mary Elizabeth Lease cried out that "farmers should raise less corn and more hell," and that "the vampire of monopoly fattens on the blood of the people!" Both Dinsmoor and Watson Heston depicted Labor as Crucified.

After decades of neglect, the Garden was restored by concerned townspeople, and listed on the National Register of Historic Places in 1977. In 1988, the site was purchased by a group of area artists who plan to maintain it properly, and to keep it open to the thousands of visitors who still make their way to Lucas every year.

ENTRANCE

"This is my sign—'GARDEN OF EDEN'—I hear so many, as they go by, sing out, 'What is this?' so I put this sign up. Now they can read it, stop or go on, just as they please. . . . This is the tree of life. The angel is guarding the apples so we can't live forever. That is tough, but it is according to Moses, and when I put the braces across to the devil's elbow and tree, I noticed he had his fork poised on a little kid. He is always after the kids. I thought if it was my God he would throw up his hand and save the kid. My God would not let him get all the kids, but Moses did not give God credit for any kindness toward the human family, so I don't give him credit for that hand. That is my idea of God, but all the rest is Moses. . . . The devil was in the Garden of Eden. He is in the background here. He has got glass back of his eyes, ears, nose and mouth, a bulb inside, and at night, when he is lit up, he looks like the devil, and the darker the night the more like the devil he looks. Here are the storks. Moses never said a word about them. He just wrote up enough to bring down the fall of man. All the preachers talk about is the original sin. There must have been many things in the Garden of Eden that Moses didn't mention. I have substituted some things that I know were there. The storks were there, because the kids were there: Cain and Abel. The storks always bring the kids. Nowadays they bring them in baskets in their mouths, but the Bible says, 'There was darkness on the face of the earth,' and these storks had to have lights in their mouths to see which way to go, so they carried the babies under their wings. There are three little faces sticking out. There is a hole under the other wing where this little kid, on the limb, has dropped out. . . .

Here is the eye and the hand looking and pointing towards Cain and wife on the next tree. These are the only things that I know of that we have to represent Deity. The heathen beat us on ideals. They have got more of a variety and better lookers, they worship their ideals just as we do the All-Seeing Eye. They reverence God through their ideals; we take off our hats to the All-Seeing Eye. What is the difference between us and other heathens? Look at them over in Europe. More barbarous than any heathen we ever heard of. Say, do you know what I think about things? I believe one man on this earth is just as good as another, and sometimes a darned sight better. They are as good as they act. . . . When I was building this they accused me of being bughouse on religion. I am bughouse good and proper, but not on religion, perpetual motion or any other fool thing that I cannot find out one thing about."

Photo by Fred Whitehead

THE CHAIN OF BEING (detail)

"The dog is after the fox, fox after the bird, bird has its mouth open after a little worm eating a leaf. This shows how one animal is after another down to the leaf.

Now this side is modern civilization as I see it. If it is not right I am to blame, but if the Garden of Eden is not right Moses is to blame. He wrote it up and I built it."

Photo by Verle Muhrer

THE TRUST MONSTER

". . . A claw has the kid, another bonds, another sack of interest. Another claw has the North Pole. Cook and Peary discovered it and they are playing it to us in the picture shows. Another claw is coming over the globe after the Panama Canal. Here is North and South America and Panama Canal cut through, they haven't got it but are after it and probably will get it. Another claw is coming around that limb after more chartered rights and on that sign board are the things that we have chartered away. Money, transportation, manufacturing, coal, oil, land, and lumber, we have chartered away, which has gone to the trusts. The trusts stand on chartered rights. Take away the chartered rights of any trusts or monopoly on earth and it would melt like a snowball below. But we are granting more chartered rights, creating more monopolies and then we are whining over the trusts. Aren't we a fool set of voters? They are protected by the Star Spangled Banner. That flag protects capital today better than it protects humanity. It drafted the boys but asked the money to volunteer. See the difference?"

By permission of the Kansas State Historical Society, Topeka

GODDESS OF LIBERTY TREE

"Here is the next tree bringing down civilization as I think it should be. There is the Goddess of Liberty with one foot on the trusts and a spear in her hand going through the head of the trusts. The trusts' claws are getting nothing. Down below is a man and woman with a crosscut saw marked ballot, sawing off the chartered rights limb that the trust stands on. That shows how we can get away with the trusts and if we don't get away with them with the ballot, they will be shot away with the bullet, as they were in Russia. They are getting too big. They have got all our sugar. Under this tree is a strawberry bed and I have stubs going up joining the tree above, to set out vines that will crawl around, without getting on my strawberry bed. Say! that tree will be a beauty. I want to see it in about ten or fifteen years from now. I may be in the Mausoleum. If I am, some dark night I will slip out and take a look at it, or, some other people will see it which will be just the same."

By permission of the Kansas State Historical Society, Topeka

LABOR CRUCIFIED

"This is my coal house and ash pit, with Labor crucified above. I believe Labor has been crucified between a thousand grafters ever since Labor begun, but I could not put them all up, so I have put up the leaders—Lawyer, Doctor, Preacher, and Banker. I do not say they are all grafters, but I do say they are the leaders of all who eat cake by the sweat of the other fellow's face. The Lawyer interprets the law. The Doctor has his knife and saw ready to carve up the bones. The Preacher is saying to this poor fellow crucified, "Never mind your suffering here on earth, my friend, never mind your suffering here, secure home in heaven for A-l-l E-t-e-r-n-i-t-y and you'll be all right." This is the stuff he is giving Labor for his cake. He knows nothing about Eternity and that he does know if he knows anything. What fools we be to sweat to give the other fellow cake. The Banker has the money, takes the interest, and breaks up more people than any other class."

By permission of the Kansas State Historical Society, Topeka

MAUSOLEUM

"This is my stone log cabin mausoleum. It stands on a cement foundation six feet in the ground and fourteen feet square, the second, nine feet square and the third, four feet. At each corner is a cement tree, or post, faced with native stone, from eighteen to twenty-one feet long. On the top of these is a short flag staff on which is a cement flag 4½ × 7½ feet, balanced with a cement bird, ball-bearing, over forty feet above ground. Inside is a room 7 × 10. Two feet above the floor is a niche in the wall that goes in two and one-half feet, three feet high, in which is my coffin and jug with a plate glass that covers the entire front as it will be when I am in the coffin. Beneath where I will be is the body of my wife, in a steel vault, entirely cemented over on all sides. Her tombstone is on the right, my tombstone is situated at the left. I have a will that none except my widow, my descendants, their husbands and wives, shall go in to see me for less than $1.00. That will pay someone to look after the place, and I promise everyone that comes in to see me (they can look through the plate glass and glass on the lid of my coffin and see my face) that if I see them dropping a dollar in the hands of the flunky, and I see the dollar, I will give them a smile."

34

Folk Humor

Anonymous

Throughout their history, the American people have had a rich heritage of humor, often of the most robust and unruly kind. That this is so may be due to the foundation of the country through the process of a political revolution, with corresponding cultural ferment. We have always enjoyed mocking the pretensions of social elites, and those who consider themselves intellectual superiors of any sort. And Sigmund Freud shrewdly observed that it is not only in dreams, but in wit and humor, that our subterranean fears and resentments find expression. Thus, while we may now be said to be a "religious" people, preachers and churches come in for a great deal of fun in our culture. Of other selections in this volume, there are definite aspects of folk humor in authors like Jack Conroy, Mark Twain, C. L. Edson, and Vance Randolph.

Joke books were a popular form of literature in the nineteenth century, not only general collections but ethnic jokes as well. E. Haldeman-Julius's Little Blue Books included many such titles. The collections of a now-unknown German-American rataionalist in Milwaukee formed the basis for an original volume of freethought humor published by the *American Rationalist* magazine, from which these examples are taken. In addition, readers of the magazine responded to a call for contributions of jokes. Some further material has been drawn from a sequel volume, published more recently.

An elderly cowboy who believed in reincarnation made arrangements to meet a friend at a certain time and place after his death. In due course he died, and the friend kept the appointment. Sure enough, he made contact with the departed one. "You all right, Hank?" he asked. "How's things where you are at?"

"Fine, Buck," came the answer. "The sun is shining brightly. Flowers are in bloom. I'm in a pasture with rich green grass, and yonder by the pond are ten beautiful females with no clothes on."

"Gosh, Hank, I never knowed Heaven was like that."

"Heaven? I ain't in Heaven, Buck. I'm a bull in with the milk cows."

Sam Houston, the lusty Texas hero, at the insistence of his third wife, joined the Baptist Church. After Houston had been immersed, the preacher said, "Your sins are now all washed away." To which Sam replied, "God help the fish."

Northerner (to Kentuckian)—"Is it true that Kentuckians are very bibulous?"

Kentuckian:—"No, suh. Ah don't reckon they're more than a dozen Bibles in the whole state."

The only Protestant church in a Texas town had a member who died while the minister was out of town. The Baptists asked the local priest if he would conduct the burial services as the minister would not return in time. The priest didn't know what the rules were on this occasion and wired his bishop if he could bury the Baptist. The return wire from the bishop read: "Bury all the Baptists you can."

"Had a hard day today," said the backwoods preacher as he sat down to his dinner. "Hadda baptize four adults and and six adulteresses."

"I got a five dollar sermon, a two dollar sermon, an' a one dollar sermon. An' I wants this here audience to take up a collection," said the traveling minister, "so as to determine which one they kin afford to hear."

From *Heavenly Humor* (St. Louis Mo.: Rationalist Association, 1958), and *Heavenly Humor II: The Speaker's Guide Against Religion* (St. Louis, Mo.: Rationalist Association, Inc., n.d.). Reprinted by permission of the Rationalist Association, P.O. Box 984, St. Louis, Mo. 63188.

An active old man had taken over a vacant lot covered with weeds, tin cans, and rubbish. After months of hard work he made a garden spot of it. His preacher, looking over the fence, was very much impressed.

"James," said the minister, "the Lord and you certainly have done a wonderful job here."

"Yes, suh," said James, "yes, suh." Then with a grin, "But you shoulda seen the place when the Lawd was takin' care of it all by Hisself."

At the close of service the minister stood at the door greeting the people as they left, when a rough-looking stranger came by and said, "Parson, that was the best damn sermon I ever heard." The minister thanked him, but the character went on, "I've heard a lot of sermons, but that was the best yet, by a damn sight." At this the minister was moved to remark, "You know, we don't talk that way in church." The character's enthusiasm was not dampened even with the critical eyes of other church people leaving. "I liked your sermon so damn well," he said, "I put a check for $1,000 in the collection plate." The minister got into the spirit of the thing and said, "The hell you did!"

During a revival in a small town church, we're told, a woman seated in the balcony became so wrought up that she leaned out too far and fell over the railing. Fortunately, however, the hem of her dress caught fast on a large chandelier and there she was—suspended in mid-air. The minister took in the situation at a glance and cried out to the congregation: "Any man who dares to look will be stricken blind!" There was silence for several moments; then a man sitting in the center exclaimed to the man sitting next to him: "I'm going to chance one eye!"

A woman near Reeds Springs, Missouri, was having a difficult time in giving birth to her first child. Her husband was a devout Holy Roller, and had a bunch of backwoods preachers in the house, all praying as loud as they could. The local doctor offered to attend the woman free of charge, but the Holy Rollers refused his services, shouting that Gawd Almighty was their physician! "Well, I reckon God's all right in his place," said the doctor, "but he ain't worth a damn in confinement cases."

Swearing is frowned upon by good Mormons. This story concerns a farmer, dressed for church, who found that the hired man hadn't milked the cow. Exasperated, he sat down and went to work. As the bucket brimmed with warm milk, the cow kicked it into his lap.

The apoplectic farmer began slowly, his voice rising in volume and tempo: "If I weren't a good Mormon . . . if I weren't a bishop in the church . . . if I weren't a man of righteousness . . . If I didn't believe that swearing was against God's word . . . I'd sure as hell break your goddamned neck!"

At a Mormon wedding in the days of polygamy, the preacher was a bit hard of hearing and had some difficulty in getting the proper responses.

"Do you take these women to be your lawfully wedded wives?"

"I do," replied the groom.

"Do you take this man to be your lawfully wedded husband?" he asked the women. There was a faint chorus of "I do."

The minister glared. "Some of you girls in the back row will have to speak louder if you want to get in on this."

In the backwoods a stranger talked to a native mentioning Roosevelt. "Never heard of him," said the native. The stranger asked about Lincoln and Washington only to get the same reply. Impatiently he asked: "But you must have heard about God." A short pause and a scratch behind the ear: "It sounds familiar. Is his last name Damn?"

A cowboy who had passed away arrived in his eternal home and said, "Gosh, I didn't think heaven would be so much like Texas."

"Son," said a sepulchral voice, "this ain't heaven."

An old rancher dies after a long life full of gambling, women, and booze, and goes to hell. He finds himself in the section reserved for ranchers, next to two already there, the three of them standing in cowshit right up to their chins.

"Oh, this is pretty terrible!" the newcomer exclaims.

"This isn't the worst," says one of the others.

"What could be worse than this?"

"When the banker comes by in his speedboat."

Part Four

The Contemporary Frontier

35

Slim in Hell

Sterling Brown

The dean of African-American poets, Sterling Brown has spent most of his life in Washington, D.C., where he was born in 1901. After graduating with honors from Williams College in 1921, Brown received his M.A. from Harvard in 1923. He enjoyed a long and distinguished career at Howard University, although he also taught for two years at Lincoln University in Jefferson City, Missouri, and at Fisk University in Nashville. In addition to poetry, Brown has published literary criticism, and he served as an editor on the Federal Writers Project in the 1930s. It is remarkable that, considering his elite background, Brown evolved such a terse and earthy poetic style, as exemplified in his folkloric "Slim Greer" poems. "Slim in Hell" was first published by B. A. Botkin in *Folk-Say IV,* issued by the Oklahoma Folklore Society in 1932.

I

Slim Greer went to heaven;
   St. Peter said, "Slim,
You been a right good boy."
   An' he winked at him.

        "You been a travelin' rascal
           In yo' day.
        You kin roam once mo';
           Den you come to stay.

"Put dese wings on yo' shoulders,
   An' save yo' feet."
Slim grin, and he speak up,
   "Thankye, Pete."

        Den Peter say, "Go
           To Hell an' see,
        All dat is doing, and
           Report to me."

"Be sure to remember
   How everything go."
Slim say, "I be seein' yuh
   On de late watch, bo."

        Slim got to cavortin'
           Swell as you choose,
        Like Lindy in de Spirit
           Of St. Louis Blues.

He flew an' he flew,
   Till at last he hit
A hangar wid de sign readin'
   DIS IS IT.

        Den he parked his wings,
           An' strolled aroun',
        Gittin' used to his feet
           On de solid ground.

II

Big bloodhound came aroarin'
    Like Niagry Falls,
Sicked on by white devils
    In overhalls.

Now Slim warn't scared,
    Cross my heart, it's a fac',
An de dog went on a bayin'
    Some po' devils' track.

        Den Slim saw a mansion
            An' walked right in;
        De Devil looked up
            Wid a sickly grin.

"Suttinly didn't look
    Fo' you, Mr. Greer,
How it happen you comes
    To visit here?"

        Slim say—"Oh, jes' thought
            I'd drop by a spell."
        "Feel at home, seh, an' here's
            De keys to hell."

Den he took Slim around
    An' showed him people
Rasin' hell as high as
    De First Church Steeple.

        Lots of folks fightin'
            At de roulette wheel,
        Like old Rampart Street,
            Or leastwise Beale.

Showed him bawdy houses
    An' cabarets,
Slim thought of New Orleans
    An' Memphis days.

Each devil was busy
Wid a devilish broad,
An' Slim cried, "Lawdy,
Lawd, Lawd, Lawd."

Took him in a room
Where Slim see
De preacher wid a brownskin
On each knee.

Showed him giant stills,
Going everywhere,
Wid a passel of devils
Stretched dead drunk there.

Den he took him to de furnace
Dat some devils was firing,
Hot as hell, an' Slim start
A mean presspirin'.

White devils wid pitchforks
Threw black devils on,
Slim thought he'd better
Be gittin' along.

An' he say—"Dis makes
Me think of home—
Vicksburg, Little Rock, Jackson,
Waco and Rome."

Den de devil gave Slim
De big Ha-Ha;
An' turned into a cracker,
Wid a sheriff's star.

Slim ran fo' his wings,
Lit out from de groun'
Hauled it back to St. Peter,
Safety boun'.

III

St. Peter said, "Well,
    You got back quick.
How's de devil? An' what's
    His latest trick?"

An' Slim say, "Peter,
    I really cain't tell,
De place was Dixie
    That I took for hell."

Then Peter say, "You must
    Be crazy, I vow,
Where'n hell dja think Hell *was*,
    Anyhow?

"Git on back to de yearth,
    Cause I got de fear,
You'se a leetle too dumb,
    Fo' to stay up here. . . ."

36

"I Hadn't Seen Jesus"

Langston Hughes

One of the most prolific African-American writers of the twentieth century, Langston Hughes was born in Joplin, Missouri, in 1902, and spent much of his early childhood living with his maternal grandmother, Mary Langston, in Lawrence, Kansas. Young Langston could boast a proud if impoverished African-American abolitionist tradition in a frontier state. Lewis Sheridan Leary, his grandmother's first husband, had been one of John Brown's men killed at Harper's Ferry; she long preserved his blood-stained shawl with which she would cover Langston as he slept. Mary's second husband, Charles Langston, had recruited black soldiers for the Union Army in the Civil War.

After studies at Columbia University and periods of work and travel abroad, Hughes found a position as a busboy at a posh Washington, D.C., hotel, where Vachel Lindsay praised his poetry and brought him to public attention. Thereafter, Hughes became a major figure in the Harlem Renaissance, and his career as a writer flourished. He authored many volumes of poetry, prose, anthologies, and folklore collections. The excerpt from his autobiography, *The Big Sea*, which is printed here, describes a childhood religious experience in a small Lawrence church. Shortly before his death in 1967, Hughes instructed in his will that his funeral should be held in a Harlem funeral home with jazz accompaniment, rather than in a church with solemn liturgical music.

SALVATION

I was saved from sin when I was going on thirteen. But not really saved. It happened like this. There was a big revival at my Auntie Reed's church. Every night for weeks there had been much preaching, singing, praying, and shouting, and some very hardened sinners had been brought to Christ, and the membership of the church had grown by leaps and bounds. Then just before the revival ended, they held a special meeting for children, "to bring the young lambs to the fold." My aunt spoke of it for days ahead. That night I was escorted to the front row and placed on the mourners' bench with all the other young sinners, who had not yet been brought to Jesus.

My aunt told me that when you were saved you saw a light, and something happened to you inside! And Jesus came into your life! And God was with you from then on! She said you could see and hear and feel Jesus in your soul. I believed her. I had heard a great many old people say the same thing and it seemed to me they ought to know. So I sat there calmly in the hot, crowded church, waiting for Jesus to come to me.

The preacher preached a wonderful rhythmical sermon, all moans and shouts and lonely cries and dire pictures of hell, and then he sang a song about the ninety and nine safe in the fold, but one little lamb was left out in the cold. Then he said: "Won't you come? Won't you come to Jesus? Young lambs, won't you come?" And he held out his arms to all us young sinners there on the mourners' bench. And the little girls cried. And some of them jumped up and went to Jesus right away. But most of us just sat there.

A great many old people came and knelt around us and prayed, old women with jet-black faces and braided hair, old men with work-gnarled hands. And the church sang a song about the lower lights are burning, some poor sinners to be saved. And the whole building rocked with prayer and song.

Still I kept waiting to *see* Jesus.

Finally all the young people had gone to the altar and were saved, but one boy and me. He was a rounder's son named Westley. Westley and I were surrounded by sisters and deacons praying. It was very hot in the church, and getting late now. Finally Westley said to me in a whisper: "God damn! I'm tired o' sitting here. Let's get up and be saved." So he got up and was saved.

Then I was left alone on the mourners' bench. My aunt came and knelt at my knees and cried, while prayers and songs swirled all around me in the little church. The whole congregation prayed for me alone, in a mighty wail of moans and voices. And I kept waiting serenely for Jesus, waiting, waiting—but he didn't come. I wanted to see him, but nothing happened to me. Nothing! I wanted something to happen to me, but nothing happened.

I heard the songs and the minister saying: "Why don't you come? My dear child, why don't you come to Jesus? Jesus is waiting for you. He wants you. Why don't you come? Sister Reed, what is this child's name?"

"Langston," my aunt sobbed.

"Langston, why don't you come? Why don't you come and be saved? Oh, Lamb of God! Why don't you come?"

Now it was really getting late. I began to be ashamed of myself, holding everything up so long. I began to wonder what God thought about Westley, who certainly hadn't seen Jesus either, but who was now sitting proudly on the platform, swinging his knickerbockered legs and grinning down at me, surrounded by deacons and old women on their knees praying. God had not struck Westley dead for taking his name in vain or for lying in the temple. So I decided that maybe to save further trouble, I'd better lie, too, and say that Jesus had come, and get up and be saved.

So I got up.

Suddenly the whole room broke into a sea of shouting, as they saw me rise. Waves of rejoicing swept the place. Women leaped in the air. My aunt threw her arms around me. The minister took me by the hand and led me to the platform.

When things quieted down, in a hushed silence, punctuated by a few ecstatic "Amens," all the new young lambs were blessed in the name of God. Then joyous singing filled the room.

That night, for the last time in my life but one—for I was a big boy twelve years old—I cried. I cried, in bed alone, and couldn't stop. I buried my head under the quilts, but my aunt heard me. She woke up and told my uncle I was crying because the Holy Ghost had come into my life, and because I had seen Jesus. But I was really crying because I couldn't bear to tell her that I had lied, that I had deceived everybody in the church, that I hadn't seen Jesus, and that now I didn't believe there was a Jesus any more, since he didn't come to help me.

WHO BUT THE LORD

I looked and I saw
That man they call the Law.
He was coming
Down the street at me!
I had visions in my head
Of being laid out cold and dead,
Or else murdered
By the third degree.

I said, O Lord, if you can,
Save me from that man!
Don't let him make a pulp out of me!
But the Lord he was not quick.
The Law raised up his stick
And beat the living hell
Out of me!

Now I do not understand
Why God don't protect a man
From police brutality.
Being poor and black,
I've no weapon to strike back
So who but the Lord
Can protect me?

We'll see.

37

Poems

H. H. Lewis

H. H. Lewis first saw the light of day on a farm near Cape Girardeau, Missouri, in 1901. A shy and awkward child, he spent most of his life on the same farm. However, by the late 1920s, his poetry attracted the notice of Mike Gold at *The New Masses* for its rough yet authentic cadences and pungent scenes of rural poverty. Gold had risen to prominence for seeking out and encouraging young workers to write truthfully and with pride of their own experiences in shops and slums; Gold also wrote about the theory of "proletarian literature." Throughout the 1930s, Lewis drew praise from critics such as Jack Conroy and William Carlos Williams, and published in the little magazines of the time, becoming known as "The Plowboy Poet of the Gumbo," and "The Mayakovsky of Missouri." He published four small books of poetry: *Red Renaissance* (1930), *Thinking of Russia* (1932), *Salvation* (1934), and *Road to Utterly* (1935). Lewis's vivid autobiographical prose appeared in Mencken's *American Mercury*. However, in 1942 Lewis ceased to publish and, according to ex-coal miner and poet Ed Falkowski, he "dropped out of sight like a ten-pound rock in a lake." He was rediscovered by historian Harold Dellinger in 1976, living quietly near his ancestral farm. In later life, he became a supporter of the Worldwide Church of God, though apparently a contentious one. Lewis died in 1985. Mike Gold once prophesied: "Perhaps on his birthday each year, the cows on all the collective farms will be hung with garlands and the young farmer poets will remember their mudstained Grandaddy Lewis in solemn and heroic verse."

MIDNIGHT MISSION

Those big fat cooties crawl to hair
    On the necks of starving men,
As tumble-bugs ooze up to air
    And then ooze down again.
It's slop-time, and the hoboes grunt
    Grace in that lousy den.

That's him! that's Brother Tom himself
    With cold, unbrotherly eyes,
A churchman keen for charity-pelf
    To run his enterprise;
He looms above the droning mob
    And prays in humble guise.

In the first room's fetid lack of space
    More bellies gnaw for rot;
Lectured by converts of the place,
    The scab, the pimp, the sot.
And more yet push to get inside—
    A starved, a vulturous lot.

Upstairs they truly "pound their ears,"
    Each to each on his side,
Cramped in, sardined, for it appears
    God has made the bums too wide.
Then in the morning, like as not,
    Some old derelict has died.

The Midnight Mission—how I know
    and painfully must tell;
Down where the jobless workers go
    I knew that social hell:
For see—the lice, abhorrent lice
    That faith cannot repel!

"Midnight Mission," from *New Masses,* December 1928. By permission of Catharine Bock.

What is the LOUSE I'm seeing here
    Upon the social frame?
The lie that Jee-sus dear, oh dear,
    Makes penury not a shame—
The lie that penury must be . . .
    Religion, that's its name!

LIBERAL

While social tremblors rock the scene
And sift us, man from man,
He rides the bounding fence between
—As only a eunuch can.

"Liberal," from *Writers in Revolt: The Anvil Anthology,* Jack Conroy and Curt Johnson, eds. (New York: Lawrence Hill and Company, 1973). Reprinted by permission of Douglas Wixson, literary executor Conroy Estate.

38

Reincarnation

Wallace D. McRae

A third-generation livestock rancher on Rosebud Creek in Montana, Wallace McRae was born in 1936, and educated in the public schools of Colstrip and at Montana State University from which he received a B.S. degree in Zoology. Though "Reincarnation" is his most widely known poem, McRae has written several books of poems, including *Up North Is Down the Crick* (1985), *It's Just Grass and Water* (1986), and *Things of Intrinsic Worth* (1989). These books reflect McRae's deep-running love of the West and her culture, as well as a rough-hewn philosophy of life and a commitment to the defense of the environment, which is currently threatened by mining. McRae is a past chairman of the Northern Plains Resource Council, a distinguished lecturer at the University of Montana, and a leader in community theater in Montana. A participant in the remarkable grassroots revival of Cowboy Poetry, McRae was featured, along with others, in a recent PBS television documentary on this subject.

"What does reincarnation mean?"
A cowpoke ast his friend.
His pal replied, "It happens when

From Wallace McRae, *It's Just Grass and Water: Poems* (Spokane, Wash.: The Oxalis Group, 1986). Reprinted by permission of the author, Box 2055, Forsyth, Mont. 59327.

Yer life has reached its end.
They comb yer hair, and warsh yer neck,
And clean yer fingernails,
And lay you in a padded box
Away from life's travails.

"The box and you goes in a hole,
That's been dug into the ground.
Reincarnation starts in when
Yore planted 'neath a mound.
Them clods melt down, just like yer box,
And you who is inside.
And then yore just beginnin' on
Yer transformation ride.

"In a while the grass'll grow
Upon yer rendered mound.
Till some day on yer moldered grave
A lonely flower is found.
And say a hoss should wander by
And graze upon this flower
That once wuz you, but now's become
Yer vegetative bower.

"The posey that the hoss done ate
Up, with his other feed,
Makes bone, and fat, and muscle
Essential to the steed.
But some is left that he can't use
And so it passes through,
And finally lays upon the ground.
This thing, that once wuz you.

"Then say, by chance, I wanders by
And sees this on the ground,
And I ponders, and I wonders at,
This object that I found.
I thinks of reincarnation,
Of life, and death, and such,
And come away concludin': Slim,
You ain't changed, all that much."

39

Poems

Thomas McGrath

Born on a farm near Sheldon, North Dakota, in 1916, Tom McGrath's early experiences gave him a frame of reference to the frontier and the West which remained constant in his literary work. An omnivorous reader from youth, he excelled academically at the University of North Dakota, receiving a Rhodes scholarship. McGrath's father was familiar with the Industrial Workers of the World, if not a member, and the beating of an I.W.W. organizer named Cal on his uncle's farm was later retold as an important section of McGrath's long poem, *Letter to an Imaginary Friend*. In a career spanning fifty years, McGrath published several books of poetry, two novels, children's books, and film scripts. In 1986 there was a public celebration of his life and work in Minneapolis, and his writing has been translated into several languages. He died in 1990.

THE HEROES OF CHILDHOOD

The heroes of childhood were simple and austere,
And their pearl-handled six-guns never missed fire.
They filled all their straights, were lucky at dice,
In a town full of badmen they never lost face.
When they looked under beds there was nobody there.

We saluted the outlaw whose heart was pure
When he stuck up the stage or the mail car—
Big Bill Haywood or Two Gun Marx,
Who stood against the bankers and all their works—
They robbed the rich and gave to the poor.

But we in our time are not so sure:
When the posse catches us our guns hang fire,
And strung up from the wagon-tongues of long reflection
Our hearts are left hanging by the contradiction
Which history imposes on our actions here.

Perhaps we were mistaken, it has been so long,
In the fierce purpose of these Dead Eye Dans?
Did they too wake at night, in a high fever,
And wonder when direction would be clear if ever?
—For the saint is the man most likely to do wrong.

In any case we later ones can only hope
For the positive landmark on the distant slope.
Moving through this dead world's Indian Nation
The heart must build its own direction—
Which only in the future has a permanent shape.

From *Selected Poems: 1938–1988* (Port Townsend, Wash.: Copper Canyon Press, 1988). Reprinted by permission of Thomas S. McGrath, son of Thomas M. McGrath (deceased September 20, 1990).

VISION OF THREE ANGELS
VIEWING THE PROGRESS OF SOCIALISM

And the first with his hands folded and a money belt for a truss
Said looking into the Commune: Well I will be damned and buggered,
Having been a banker in real life, to see how those burrowing beggars
Live without mortgages or rents and with no help from us.

And the second who had been a soldier in civilian life said: Jesus
Christ they'll never believe me when I tell the boys
    in the squad-room
That no one down there says sir, and they won't believe what's harder,
That even bughouse nuts don't want to be Julius Caesar.

And the third with the teamster's cap and callouses on his wing
Said I fell away from the flesh and into the hands of heaven
But the working stiffs down there are finally getting even
So I'll stick around until Judgment. Heaven is a sometime thing.

THE USE OF BOOKS

What's there to praise.
In that vast library of long gone days
Bound in the failed and fading leather
Of ancient weather?

To free what's trapped or bound
Is my whole law and ground:
Since it's myself I find
Out on the rough roads traveling blind.

Yet, for another's use,
I bind what I let loose
So others may make free
Of those lost finds no longer use to me.

Bibliography

I. INTRODUCTION

General

Botkin, B. A., ed. *A Treasury of Western Folklore.* New York: Crown, 1951.

Brown, Marshall G., and Gordon Stein. *Freethought in the United States: A Descriptive Bibliography.* Westport, Conn.: Greenwood Press, 1978.

Dunham, Barrows. *Heroes and Heretics: A Political History of Western Thought.* New York: Knopf, 1964.

Egbert, Donald Drew, and Stow Persons, eds. *Socialism and American Life.* 2 vols. Princeton: Princeton University Press, 1952.

Fiske, John. "The Origins of Liberal Thought in America." Vol. 10 of *Miscellaneous Writings.* Boston: Houghton Mifflin, 1902.

Foster, William Z. *Outline Political History of the Americas.* New York: International, 1951.

Heilbroner, Robert L. *The Worldly Philosophers.* 6th ed. New York: Simon & Schuster, 1986.

Nemanic, Gerald, ed. *A Bibliographical Guide to Midwestern Literature.* Iowa City: University of Iowa Press, 1981.

Seldes, Gilbert. *The Stammering Century.* 1928. Reprint. New York: Harper, 1965.

Smith, Homer W. *Man and His Gods.* 1952. Reprint. New York: Grosset & Dunlap, 1956.

Stein, Gordon. *God Pro and Con: A Bibliography of Atheism*. New York: Garland, 1990.

———, ed. *An Anthology of Atheism and Rationalism*. Buffalo, N.Y.: Prometheus Books, 1980.

———,ed. *The Encyclopedia of Unbelief*. 2 vols. Buffalo, N.Y.: Prometheus Books, 1985.

———, ed. *A Second Anthology of Atheism and Rationalism*. Buffalo, N.Y.: Prometheus Books, 1987.

Thoreau, Henry David. "A Plea for Captain John Brown." In *Selected Works*, edited by Walter Harding. Boston: Houghton Mifflin, 1975.

Turner, James. *Without God, Without Creed: The Origins of Unbelief in America*. Baltimore, Md.: Johns Hopkins University Press, 1985.

Vernon, Thomas S. *Great Infidels*. Fayetteville, Ark.: M & M Press, 1989.

Definitions

Babcock, C. Merton. *The American Frontier: A Social and Literary Record*. New York: Holt, 1965.

Cockcroft, James P. *Intellectual Precursors of the Mexican Revolution 1900–1913*. 1968. Reprint. Austin: University of Texas Press, 1976.

Gomez-Quiñones, Juan. *Sembradores Ricardo Flores Magon y el Partido Liberal Mexicano: A Eulogy and Critique*. Rev. ed. Monograph No. 5, Chicano Studies Center Publications. Los Angeles: University of California, 1977.

Hodges, Donald C. *Intellectual Foundations of the Nicaraguan Revolution*. Austin: University of Texas Press, 1986.

Klose, Nelson. *A Concise Study Guide to the Frontier*. Lincoln: University of Nebraska Press, 1964.

Putnam, Samuel Porter. *Four Hundred Years of Freethought*. New York: Truth Seeker, 1894.

Turner, Frederick Jackson. *The Frontier in American History*. New York: Holt, 1950.

Webb, Walter Prescott. *The Great Frontier*. 1952. Reprint. Lincoln: University of Nebraska Press, 1986.

The Early Frontier

Aptheker, Herbert. *Abolitionism: A Revolutionary Movement*. Boston: Twayne, 1989.

Cobb, Sanford H. *The Rise of Religious Liberty in America*. 1902. Reprint. New York: Cooper Square, 1968.

Cooper, Berenice. *"Die freie Gemeinde*: Freethinkers on the Frontier." *Minnesota History* 41 (Summer 1968): 53–60.

———. "Die Freie Gemeinden in Wisconsin." *Transactions of the Wisconsin Academy of Sciences* 53 (1964): 53–65.

Curti, Merle. *The Growth of American Thought*. 2d ed. New York: Harper, 1951.

Doepke, Dale K. *"The Western Examiner*: A Chronicle of Atheism in the West." *Bulletin of the Missouri Historical Society* 30 (1973): 29–43.

Hall, David, ed. *The Antinomian Controversy, 1636–1638: A Documentary History*. Middletown, Conn.: Wesleyan University Press, 1968.

Marx, Karl, and Frederick Engels. *The Civil War in the United States*. 3rd ed. New York: Citadel, 1961.

Phares, Ross. *Bible in Pocket, Gun in Hand: The Story of Frontier Religion*. 1962. Reprint. Lincoln: University of Nebraska Press, 1971.

Post, Albert. *Popular Freethought in America, 1825–1850*. New York: Columbia University Press, 1943.

Tyler, Alice Felt. *Freedom's Ferment: Phases of American Social History from the Colonial Period to the Outbreak of the Civil War*. 1944. Reprint. New York: Harper, 1962.

Vanderwerth, W. C., ed. *Indian Oratory: Famous Speeches by Noted Indian Chieftains*. 1971. Reprint. New York: Ballantine, 1972.

Wittke, Carl. *Refugees of Revolution: The German Forty-Eighters in America*. Philadelphia: University of Pennsylvania Press, 1952.

Wood, Forrest G. *The Arrogance of Faith: Christianity and Race in America from the Colonial Era to the Twentieth Century*. New York: Knopf, 1990.

The WPA Guide to 1930s Missouri. Work Projects Administration. 1941. Reprint. Lawrence: University Press of Kansas, 1986.

The Golden Age of Freethought

Cargill, Oscar, ed. *The Social Revolt: American Literature from 1888 to 1914*. New York: Macmillan, 1933.

Garver, Bruce. "Czech-American Freethinkers on the Great Plains, 1871–1914." In *Ethnicity on the Great Plains*, edited by Frederick C. Luebke. Lincoln: University of Nebraska Press, 1980.

Gaylor, Anne Nicol. "Freethought Trunks and Traveling Bags." *Freethought Today*, June/July 1990.

Goodwyn, Lawrence. *The Populist Moment: A Short History of the Agrarian Revolt in America*. Oxford: Oxford University Press, 1978.

Holbrook, Stewart H. *Dreamers of the American Dream*. Garden City, N.Y.: Doubleday, 1957.

Jordan, Terry G. "A Religious Geography of the Hill Country Germans of Texas." In *Ethnicity on the Great Plains*, edited by Frederick C. Luebke. Lincoln: University of Nebraska Press, 1980.

LeSueur, Meridel. *North Star Country*. 1945. Reprint. Lincoln: University of Nebraska Press, 1984.

Lewis, Marvin. "A Free Life in the Mines and on the Range." *Western Humanities Review* 12 (1958): 87–95.

Miller, Howard S. Introduction to "Sowing the Wind," by Kate Austin. In *Haymarket Scrapbook*, edited by Dave Roediger and Franklin Rosemont. Chicago: Charles H. Kerr, 1986.

Noyes, John Humphrey. *History of American Socialisms*. 1870. Reprint. New York: Hillary House, 1961.

Pizer, Donald, ed. *American Thought and Writing: The 1890s*. Boston: Houghton Mifflin, 1972.

Shannon, Fred A. *American Farmers' Movements*. Princeton, N.J.: Van Nostrand, 1957.

Stanton, Elizabeth Cady, et al. *The Original Feminist Attack on the Bible (The Woman's Bible)*. 1895–1898. Reprint. New York: Arno, 1974.

Warren, Sidney. *American Freethought, 1860–1914*. 1943. Reprint. New York: Gordian, 1966.

Weinberg, Arthur, and Lila, eds. *Passport to Utopia: Great Panaceas in American History*. Chicago: Quadrangle, 1968.

Weston, Jack. *The Real American Cowboy*. New York: New Amsterdam, 1985.

The Revolt from the Village

Commager, Henry Steele. *The American Mind: An Interpretation of American Thought and Character Since the 1880s*. New Haven: Yale University Press, 1950.

Hilfer, Anthony C. *The Revolt from the Village, 1915–1930*. Chapel Hill: University of North Carolina Press, 1969.

Kramer, Dale. *Chicago Renaissance: The Literary Life in the Midwest 1900–1930*. New York: Appleton-Century, 1966.

LeSueur, Meridel. *Crusaders: The Radical Legacy of Marian and Arthur LeSueur.* 1955. Reprint. St. Paul: Minnesota Historical Society Press, 1984.

———. In "Edward Dahlberg: A Memorial." *Quindaro* 3 (January 1979): 29–37.

Peterson, H. C., and Gilbert C. Fite. *Opponents of War 1917–1918.* 1957. Reprint. Seattle: University of Washington Press, 1968.

Veblen, Thorstein. *The Portable Veblen.* Edited by Max Lerner. New York: Viking, 1958.

Yatron, Michael. *America's Literary Revolt.* New York: Philosophical Library, 1959.

The Contemporary Frontier

Day, Robert. *The Last Cattle Drive.* 1977. Reprint. Lawrence: University Press of Kansas, 1983.

Goldman, Ari L. "Portrait of Religion in U.S. Holds Dozens of Surprises." *New York Times,* April 10, 1991.

Malone, Michael P., and Richard W. Etulian. *The American West: A Twentieth-Century History.* Lincoln: University of Nebraska Press, 1989.

New Interpretations of American History

Barrow, Logie. *Independent Spirits: Spiritualism and English Plebeians, 1850–1910.* London and New York: Routledge & Kegan Paul, 1986.

Bering-Jensen, Helle. "Life in the Old West Is Getting a New Look." *Insight,* February 4, 1991.

Braude, Ann. *Radical Spirits: Spiritualism and Women's Rights in Nineteenth-Century America.* Boston: Beacon, 1989.

Bredahl, A. Carl, Jr. *New Ground: Western American Narrative and the Literary Canon.* Chapel Hill: University of North Carolina Press, 1989.

Burnes, Brian. "A New Look at the Old West." *Kansas City Star,* December 4, 1990.

DuBois, W. E. B. *Black Reconstruction in America.* 1935. Reprint. New York: Atheneum, 1979.

Foner, Eric. *Nothing But Freedom: Emancipation and Its Legacy.* Baton Rouge: Louisiana State University Press, 1983.

———. *A Short History of Reconstruction 1863–1877.* New York: Harper, 1990.

Foner, Eric, and Jon Wiener. "Fighting for the West." *The Nation*, July 29, 1991.

Fram, Alan. "Washington Disputes How the West Was Won." *Kansas City Star*, June 10, 1991.

Gramsci, Antonio. *The Modern Prince and Other Writings*. New York: International, 1967.

Huckshorn, Kristin. "A Roundup of Revisionist Art." *Chicago Tribune*, May 24, 1991.

Jennings, Francis. *The Invasion of America: Indians, Colonialism, and the Cant of Conquest*. 1975. Reprint. New York: Norton, 1976.

Kilian, Michael. "Exhibit Shoots Halos off Western Heroes." *Kansas City Star*, June 16, 1991.

Limerick, Patricia Nelson. *The Legacy of Conquest: The Unbroken Past of the American West*. New York: Norton, 1988.

McMurtry, Larry. "How the West Was Won or Lost." *New Republic*, October 22, 1990.

Slotkin, Richard. *The Fatal Environment: The Myth of the Frontier in the Age of Industrialization, 1800-1890*. 1985. Reprint. Middletown, Conn.: Wesleyan University Press, 1986.

Smith, Page. *Killing the Spirit: Higher Education in America*. New York: Penguin, 1991.

Thomas, Evan. "Time to Circle the Wagons: A Senator Attacks the Smithsonian's 'Politics.' " *Newsweek*, May 27, 1991.

Truettner, William H., ed. *The West as America: Reinterpreting Images of the Frontier, 1820-1920*. Washington, D.C.: Smithsonian Institution Press, 1991.

Wallace, Anthony F. C. *Rockdale: The Growth of an American Village in the Early Industrial Revolution*. New York: Norton, 1980.

Weatherford, Jack. *Indian Givers: How the Indians of the Americas Transformed the World*. New York: Fawcett Columbine, 1990.

Williamson, Chilton, Jr. "Space Art." *Chronicles* (February 1990):30-31.

Worster, Donald. *Rivers of Empire: Water, Aridity, and the Growth of the American West*. New York: Pantheon, 1985.

II. SELECTIONS

Red Jacket

Warner, Robert A. "Red Jacket." *Dictionary of American Biography.* New York: Scribner's, 1935.

Robert Owen

Bestor, Arthur. *Backwoods Utopias: The Sectarian Origins and the Owenite Phase of Communitarian Socialism in America, 1663–1829.* 2d ed. Philadelphia: University of Pennsylvania Press, 1970.

Carmony, Donald F., and Josephine M. Elliott. "New Harmony, Indiana: Robert Owen's Seedbed for Utopia." *Indiana Magazine of History* 76 (1980) 1: 161–261.

Lockwood, George B. *The New Harmony Movement.* New York: Appleton, 1905.

Morton, A. L. *The Life and Ideas of Robert Owen.* 2d ed. New York: International, 1978.

Pitzer, Donald E. "The Original Boatload of Knowledge Down the Ohio River: William Maclure's and Robert Owen's Transfer of Science and Education to the Midwest, 1825–1826." Reprint from *Ohio Journal of Science* 89 (December 1989).

———, ed. *Robert Owen's American Legacy: Proceedings of the Robert Owen Bicentennial Conference.* Indianapolis: Indiana Historical Society, 1972.

Wilson, William E. *The Angel and the Serpent: The Story of New Harmony.* Bloomington: Indiana University Press, 1964.

Jack Conroy

Conroy, Jack. *The Disinherited.* Introduction by Douglas Wixson. 1933. Reprint. Columbia: University of Missouri Press, 1991.

———. *The Weed King and Other Stories.* Edited by Douglas C. Wixson. Westport, Conn.: Lawrence Hill, 1985.

Friedrich Münch

Bek, William G. *The German Settlement Society of Philadelphia and Its Colony Hermann, Missouri.* Reprint. American Press, 1984.

Muehl, Siegmar. "Eduard Mühl: 1800–1854, Missouri Editor, Free-

Thinker and Fighter for Human Rights." *Missouri Historical Review* 81 (1986): 18–36.

Muehl, Siegmar. "Hermann's 'Free Men': 1850s German-American Religious Rationalism." *Missouri Historical Review* 85 (1991): 361–80.

Muehl, Siegmar, and Lois B. *Hermann, Missouri 1852 News and Voices.* Iowa City: S. and L. Muehl, 1987.

Münch, Frederick. *School for American Grape Culture.* St. Louis, Mo.: Conrad Witter, 1865.

Petermann, Gerd Alfred. "Friends of Light (*Lichtfreunde*): Friedrich Münch, Paul Follenius, and the Rise of German-American Rationalism on the Missouri Frontier." *Yearbook of German-American Studies* 23 (1988): 119–39.

Rowan, Steven, and James Neal Primm, eds. *Germans for a Free Missouri: Trnaslations from the St. Louis Radical Press, 1857–1862.* Columbia: University of Missouri Press, 1983.

Tolzman, Don Heinrich. "The St. Louis Free Congregation Library: A Study of German-American Reading Interests." *Missouri Historical Review* 70 (1975–76): 142–61.

Denton J. Snider

Forbes, Cleon. "The St. Louis School of Thought." 5 Parts. *Missouri Historical Review* 25–26 (1930–31).

Leighton, Denys P. "William Torrey Harris, 'The St. Louis Hegelians,' and the Meaning of the Civil War." *Gateway Heritage* 10, no. 2 (Fall 1989): 32–45.

Perry, Charles M., ed. *The St. Louis Movement in Philosophy: Some Source Material.* Norman: University of Oklahoma Press, 1930.

Pochmann, Henry A. *New England Transcendentalism and St. Louis Hegelianism.* Philadelphia: Carl Schurz Memorial Foundation, 1948.

Snider, Denton J. *The American Ten Years' War 1855–1865.* St. Louis, Mo.: Sigma, 1906.

———. *The St. Louis Movement.* St. Louis, Mo.: Sigma, 1920.

Oliver Wendell Holmes

Clark, Harry Hayden. "Dr. Holmes: A Re-interpretation." *New England Quarterly* 12, no. 1 (March 1939): 19–34.

Holmes, Oliver Wendell. *The Autocrat's Miscellanies.* Edited by Albert Mordell. New York: Twayne, 1959.

Kreymborg, Alfred. "Dr. Holmes and the New England Decline." In *Our Singing Strength: An Outline of American Poetry.* New York: Tudor, 1934.

Anonymous

Cannon, Hal, ed. *Cowboy Poetry: A Gathering.* Layton, Utah: Gibbs M. Smith, 1985.

Robert M. Wright

Miller, Nyle H., and Joseph W. Snell. "Some Notes on Kansas Cowtown Police Officers and Gun Fighters: Mather, Dave." *Kansas Historical Quarterly* 27 (1961): 544–62.

Rickards, Colin. *Mysterious Dave Mather.* Santa Fe, N.M.: Press of the Territorian, 1968.

Wright, Robert M. "Personal Reminiscences of Frontier Life in Southwest Kansas." *Kansas Historical Collections* 7 (1901–1902): 47–83.

Robert G. Ingersoll

Plummer, Mark A. *Robert G. Ingersoll: Peoria's Pagan Politician.* Western Illinois Monograph Series, No. 4. Macomb: Western Illinois University, 1984.

Smith, Frank. *Robert G. Ingersoll: A Life.* Buffalo, N.Y.: Prometheus Books, 1990.

Lois Waisbrooker

Sears, Hal. *The Sex Radicals: Free Love in High Victorian America.* Lawrence: Regents Press of Kansas, 1977.

Waisbrooker, Lois. *A Sex Revolution.* With an Introduction by Pam McAllister. Philadelphia: New Society, 1985.

Watson Heston

"Death of Watson Heston." *The Truth Seeker,* March 4, 1905.

Heston, Watson. *The Bible Comically Illustrated.* New York: Truth Seeker, 1892.

———. *The Freethinker's Pictorial Text-Book.* 2 vols. New York: Truth Seeker, 1890–1898.

George Henry Walser

Grant, H. Roger. "Freethinkers and Spiritualists: A Missouri Case Study." *Bulletin of the Missouri Historical Society* 27 (1971): 259–71.

Natta, Larry. "No Priest, No Preacher, No Church, God, Saloon or Hell: The Strange Story of Liberal, MO." *Kansas City Star Magazine,* October 16, 1977.

"A Unique Community Experiment." *Missouri Historical Review* 13 (1937): 295–301.

William Cowper Brann

Carver, Charles. *Brann and the Iconoclast.* Austin, Tex.: University of Texas Press, 1957.

Gunn, John W. *Brann: Smasher of Shams.* Ten Cent Pocket Series, No. 33. Girard, Kans.: Haldeman-Julius, n.d.

Moses Harman

McCormick, John Steele. "Moses Harman: Forerunner of Women's Liberation." *American Rationalist* (September–October 1972): 3–5.

Etta Semple

Fisher, James J. "Iconoclast Outraged Kansas." *Kansas City Times,* July 10, 1987.

Lambertson, John Mark. "Atheist's Samaritan Bent Won Over Ottawa" and "An Ottawa Pioneer With A Touch of Infamy." *Ottawa Herald,* September 26 and 27, 1987.

Mark Twain

Twain, Mark. *Selected Writings of an American Skeptic.* Edited by Victor Doyno. Buffalo, N.Y.: Prometheus Books, 1983.

Clarence Darrow

Darrow, Clarence. *The Story of My Life.* New York: Scribner's, 1932.

Darrow, Clarence, and Wallace Rice, eds. *Infidels and Heretics: An Agnostic's Anthology.* Boston: Stratford, 1929.

Theodore Dreiser

Lingeman, Richard. *Theodore Dreiser: An American Journey 1908–1945.* New York: Putnam, 1990.
———. *Theodore Dreiser: At the Gates of the City 1871–1907.* New York: Putnam, 1986.
Swanberg, W. A. *Dreiser.* New York: Scribner's, 1965.

Wilbur D. Nesbit

Coyle, William, ed. *Ohio Authors and Their Books.* Cleveland, Ohio: World, 1962.

Robert Service

Klinck, Carl F. *Robert Service: A Biography.* New York: Dodd, Mead, 1976.

Vachel Lindsay

Massa, Ann. *Vachel Lindsay: Fieldworker for the American Dream.* Bloomington: Indiana University Press, 1970.
Masters, Edgar Lee. *Vachel Lindsay.* New York: Scribner, 1935.

Carl Sandburg

Allen, Gay Wilson. *Carl Sandburg.* Minneapolis: University of Minnesota Press, 1972.
Callahan, North. *Carl Sandburg: Lincoln of Our Literature.* New York: New York University Press, 1970.
Niven, Penelope. *Carl Sandburg: A Biography.* New York: Scribner's, 1991.
Sandburg, Carl. *Always the Young Strangers.* New York: Harcourt Brace, 1953.
———. *Ever the Winds of Chance.* Urbana: University of Illinois Press, 1983.

Industrial Workers of the World

Dubovsky, Melvyn. *We Shall Be All: A History of the Industrial Workers of the World.* Chicago: Quadrangle, 1969.

Kornbluh, Joyce, ed. *Rebel Voices: An I.W.W. Anthology.* 2d ed. Chicago: Charles H. Kerr, 1988.

Smith, Gibbs M. *Joe Hill.* Salt Lake City, Utah: Peregrine Smith, 1984.

Thompson, Fred, and Patrick Murfin. *The I.W.W.: Its First Seventy Years (1905–1975).* Chicago: Industrial Workers of the World, 1976.

Vance Randolph

Cochran, Robert. *Vance Randolph: An Ozark Life.* Urbana: University of Illinois Press, 1985.

Cochran, Robert, and Michael Luster. *For Love and For Money: The Writings of Vance Randolph; An Annotated Bibliography.* Arkansas College Folklore Monograph Series, No. 2, 1979.

Randolph, Vance. "Naked in the Ozarks." In *Folklore of the Great West,* edited by John Greenway. Palo Alto, Calif.: American West, 1969.

———. *Pissing in the Snow and Other Ozark Folktales.* 1976. Reprint. New York: Avon, 1977.

Sinclair Lewis

Schorer, Mark. *Sinclair Lewis: An American Life.* New York: McGraw-Hill, 1961.

Emanuel Haldeman-Julius

Graham, John, ed. *"Yours for the Revolution": The Appeal to Reason, 1895–1922.* Lincoln: University of Nebraska Press, 1990.

Haldeman-Julius, E. *My First 25 Years.* Girard, Kans.: Haldeman-Julius, 1949.

———. *My Second 25 Years.* Girard, Kans.: Haldeman-Julius, 1949.

Haldeman-Julius, Sue. "An Intimate Look at Haldeman-Julius." *The Little Balkans Review* 2, no. 2 (Winter 1981–82): 1–19.

Mordell, Albert. *My Relations with Theodore Dreiser. Haldeman-Julius as a Writer on Freethought. Some Reflections on Freethought: And Haldeman-Julius Publications in Freethought.* Girard, Kans.: Haldeman-Julius, 1951.

———. *Sham-Smashers at Work: A Study of the Aims and Methods of Haldeman-Julius' Monthly and the Debunker.* Girard, Kans.: Haldeman-Julius, 1950.

Popper, Joe. "J. A. & the Radical Rag." *Kansas City Star Magazine,* April 17, 1988.

Saricks, Ambrose. "Emanuel Haldeman-Julius." In *The Kansas Arts Reader,* edited by Jonathan Wesley Bell. Lawrence: Independent Study, University of Kansas, 1976.

Scott, Mark. "The Little Blue Books in the War on Bigotry and Bunk." *Kansas History* 1 (1978): 155–76.

Shore, Elliott. *Talkin' Socialism: J. A. Wayland and the Role of the Press in American Radicalism, 1890–1912.* Lawrence: University Press of Kansas, 1988.

Whitehead, Fred. "Kansas Celebration Honors Socialist Creator of Little Blue Books." *People's Daily World,* August 23, 1989.

Charles L. Edson

Anonymous [C. L. Edson]. *"The Great American Ass."* New York: Brentano's, 1926.

Gusewelle, C. W. "Leaving a Legacy of Verses, a Poet Looks Back Over His Years." *Kansas City Star,* March 10, 1963.

Leland, Lorrin. "Three Poets." In *The Kansas Arts Reader,* edited by Jonathan Wesley Bell. Lawrence: Independent Study, University of Kansas, 1976.

S. P. Dinsmoor

Dinsmoor, S. P. *Pictorial History of the Cabin Home in Garden of Eden.* Lucas, Kans., 1927.

Hoopes, O. D. *"This Is My Sign—'Garden of Eden.' "* Rev. ed. Lucas, Kans.: Lucas Publishing Co., 1981.

Langston Hughes

Berry, Faith. *Langston Hughes: Before and Beyond Harlem.* Westport, Conn.: Lawrence Hill, 1983.

Rampersand, Arnold. *The Life of Langston Hughes.* 2 vols. New York: Oxford University Press, 1986–1988.

H. H. Lewis

Dellinger, Harold. "Pegasus of the Plow." *Foolkiller* 3, no. 1 (Fall 1976).

Williams, William Carlos. "An American Poet." In *New Masses:*

An Anthology of the Rebel Thirties. Edited by Joseph North. New York: International, 1972.

Wallace McRae

Cannon, Hal, ed. *Cowboy Poetry: A Gathering.* Layton, Utah: Gibbs M. Smith, 1985.
———, ed. *New Cowboy Poetry: A Contemporary Gathering.* Layton, Utah: Gibbs M. Smith, 1990.
"Cowboy Poets." Television documentary. Directed by Kim Shelton. Public Broadcasting Service, 1989.
McRae, Wallace. *Things of Intrinsic Worth.* Bozeman, Mont.: Outlaw Books, 1989.
———. *Up North Is Down the Crick.* Bozeman, Mont.: Outlaw Books, 1985.

Thomas McGrath

Gibbons, Reginald, and Terrence des Pres, eds. *Thomas McGrath: Life and the Poem.* Urbana: University of Illinois Press, 1991.
McGrath, Thomas. *Letter to an Imaginary Friend Parts I and II.* Chicago: Swallow, 1970.
———. *Letter to an Imaginary Friend Parts Three & Four.* Port Townsend, Wash.: Copper Canyon, 1985.
Stern, Frederick C., ed. *The Revolutionary Poet in the United States: The Poetry of Thomas McGrath.* Columbia: University of Missouri Press, 1988.
Whitehead, Fred, ed. *The Dream Champ: Thomas McGrath.* Festschrift, *North Dakota Quarterly* 50, no.4 (Fall 1982).